THOR
BALLISTIC
MISSILE

THOR BALLISTIC MISSILE

THE UNITED STATES AND THE UNITED KINGDOM IN PARTNERSHIP

JOHN BOYES

FONTHILL

Mulier qui amo—

and to all those who served, willingly or unwillingly, in support of Thor.

Fonthill Media Limited
Fonthill Media LLC
www.fonthillmedia.com
office@fonthillmedia.com

First published in the United Kingdom
and the United States of America 2015

British Library Cataloguing in Publication Data:
A catalogue record for this book is available from the British Library

Copyright © John Boyes 2015

ISBN 978-1-78155-481-4

Typeset in 10pt on 13pt Minion Pro
Printed and bound by CPI Group (UK) Ltd, Croydon, CR0 4YY

CONTENTS

Acknowledgements   7
Foreword   8
Glossary   10
Introduction   12

1   From Second World War to Cold War   13
2   Thor—The Early Days   20
3   Failures and Successes   28
4   A British IRBM?   33
5   The Thor Agreement—Substance and Interpretation   49
6   Opening for Business   73
7   Vandenberg Air Force Base—The Western Test Range   84
8   RAF Training Begins   95
9   RAF Launches   106
10   Combat Training Launches   117
11   UK Bases   134
12   Logistics   145
13   What Happened to the RAF's Thors?   152

Epilogue   160
Appendix 1: Memories of Project Fishbowl—Jay Simmons   164
Appendix 2: The Epistle of St Bernadino   166
Appendix 3: RAF Thor Launches at Vandenberg AFB   167
Appendix 4: Thor Bases and Squadrons   170
Appendix 5: Markings   171
Appendix 6: Thor Programme Major Contractors   172
Appendix 7   173
Appendix 8   174
Endnotes   187
Bibliography   201
Index   204

Launch Key:
LE 40.RAF BREIGHTON

Acknowledgements

I am as always indebted to a large number of people who helped with their contributions to this volume. They are identified in both the text and the endnotes. However, extra mention must be made of some others without whose help the writing of this book would have been more difficult. My thanks to Vernita Laws and Fran Thomas for the invitation to attend the 'Project Emily 50th Reunion' in Costa Mesa where many of the Douglas veterans willingly shared their memories. Maurice Botley, who also attended the reunion and joined the visit to Vandenberg. With regards to the latter, to Dick Parker and Jay Simmons for facilitating the visit, and to Group Captain Peter Finlayson and Colonel John Watters for their memories of their time at Vandenberg. To Squadron Leader Bob Broad for his memories of Ops BM. He has the possibly unique distinction of seeing three missile launches and one landing, when he witnessed a V-2's wartime arrival at Hatfield Heath. I am also grateful to Larry Kasulka, who provided much useful information along with photographs, and to Jeff Jefford, a source of 'everything RAF' who is always at hand to answer questions, however obscure, and never fails to find an answer. To Paul Bellamy, Stephen Cooke, and Dale McCann for their untiring and informed interest in Thor—particularly with respect to the former RAF Harrington. And to the late Rowland Hall, who provided a fascinating insight into the drawing of plans for the Thor bases, as well as being the custodian of the knowledge of the reason for the name 'Project Emily'. John Primm for his helpful guidance. I am appreciative of English Heritage's interest in the Cold War, which manifested itself in the assistance of Wayne Cocroft. Both John Burt and Richard Pratt helped me to understand the sheer complexity of the engineering side of things. My thanks also to Peter Elliott and the staff of the RAF Museum for their help. Brian Finch provided the drawing of the RAF Launch Emplacement. I am particularly grateful to Mark Burgess of Acute Concepts for his patience and interest in using his graphic skills to complete the illustrations and plans, much of it with very little information available. And to my wife Sylvia, who now knows more about ballistic missiles than she ever thought necessary. As always, responsibility for errors, omissions, or inaccuracies, whether of interpretation or fact, is entirely mine.

John Boyes
West Wickham, March 2015
Thor64irbm@aol.com

Foreword

My time as a Flight Cadet at the RAF College Cranwell coincided exactly with the deployment of sixty Thor Intermediate Range Ballistic Missiles (IRBMs) in East Anglia and Yorkshire. Other than the occasional overflight of the twenty sites in my Jet Provost (probably by mistake), they made little impression on me until the day my very depressed ex-Hunter pilot flying instructor announced that he had been posted to command one of the sites. He protested so vehemently that his posting was changed to that of learning to be an instructor on helicopters. Shortly after beginning the flying phase on the course, he was killed in an accident. From that moment, I remained largely uninterested and ignorant of the RAF's Thor IRBMs until our author, my RAF Historical Society committee colleague John Boyes, published his first volume, *Project Emily: Thor IRBM and the RAF*, in 2008.

When it was published, several US and British veterans contacted John Boyes, including the civil servant who had drawn up the initial plans, and the now ninety-eight-year-old USAF colonel who had been in charge of the training of the RAF Thor crews at Vandenberg AFB in California. When the author visited Vandenberg for the 50th reunion of those former employees of the Douglas Aircraft Company who had worked on the project, built the missile, trained the crews, and brought it to the United Kingdom, he decided that there was enough meat in the subject for a follow-up volume to be written. Inevitably there is some duplication with Volume 1, but not much. What there is, in addition to the substantial text, is a generous selection of previously unseen photographs and especially drawn plans of all the UK's Thor bases, which will appeal to those who served there in particular. Names such as RAF Shepherds Grove, now long forgotten; RAF Ludford Magna (home in the Second World War to No. 101 Squadron, whose aircrew in their Lancasters flew more raids than any other Bomber Command squadron losing 1,176 lives in the process); and RAF Polebrook (where the first B-17s of the US Army Air Corps were stationed from the summer or 1942).

John Boyes has been fascinated by the Thor story since he was a schoolboy, and finding that nobody else had recorded its genesis and subsequent history decided to do it himself. I spent most of my flying career on the Vulcan: for two tours, much of the time holding nuclear alert, just up the road from a Thor site. The book is a great compliment to those who, no doubt having to overcome their initial reluctance, and unlike my flying instructor, had to be stuck way out in the sticks with a strange inanimate flying machine with a temper of its own. And that is before they had to worry about what the missile could do. But doubtless like my young Vulcan crew, they took comfort from the fact that, so long as they did their job properly, there would be no need for them to do their job....

Air Vice-Marshal Nigel Baldwin CB CBE
Chairman, Royal Air Force Historical Society

Glossary

AAF	Army Air Force (US)
ABMA	Army Ballistic Missile Agency
AD	Air Division (USAF)
AFB	Air Force Base
AFMTC	Air Force Missile Test Center (Patrick AFB)
AMFEA	Air Materiel Force European Area
APU	Auxiliary Power Unit
ARDC	Air Research and Development Command
ASAT	Anti-Satellite
AVM	Air Vice-Marshal
AWRE	Atomic Weapons Research Establishment
BAFS	British Joint Services Mission (Air Force Section)
BCMC	Bomber Command Modification Centre
BJSM	British Joint Services Mission (in Washington)
BMD	Ballistic Missile Division
BSD	Ballistic Systems Division
CEA	Control Electronic Assembly
CEP	Circular Error Probable
CND	Campaign for Nuclear Disarmament
CPA	Critical Path Analysis
CTC	Combat Training Capability
CTL	Combat Training Launch
DAC	Douglas Aircraft Company
DCAS	Deputy Chief of the Air Staff
DM	Douglas Model (as in DM-18)
DSACEUR	Deputy Supreme Allied Commander Europe
EDPF	Electronic Data Processing Flight
ETR	Eastern Test Range (Cape Canaveral Air Force Station)
FBM	Fleet Ballistic Missile
GN2	Gaseous Nitrogen
GSE	Ground Support Equipment
ICBM	Intercontinental Ballistic Missile
IOC	Initial Operational Configuration

IRBM	Intermediate Range Ballistic Missile
IWST	Integrated Weapons System Training
LASL	Los Alamos Scientific Laboratory
LE	Launch Emplacement
LOX	Liquid Oxygen
MATS	Military Air Transport Service
MD	Missile Division
MILS	Missile Impact Location System
MOCP	Missile Out of Commission awaiting Parts
MOSD	Missile and Ordnance Systems Division (of GE)
MRAF	Marshal of the Royal Air Force
MRBM	Medium Range Ballistic Missile
M/Sig	Master Signaller
MWDP	Mutual Weapons Development Program
NSC	National Security Council
ODM-SAC	Office of Defense Management – Scientific Advisory Committee
ORBAT	Order of Battle
PERT	Performance Evaluation and Review Technique
PMR	Pacific Missile Range
RIM	Receipt, Inspection and Maintenance (Building)
RSO	Range Safety Officer
RV	Re-entry Vehicle
SAC	Strategic Air Command
SACEUR	Supreme Allied Commander Europe
SBAMA	San Bernardino Air Materiel Area
SecAF	US Secretary of the Air Force
SecDef	Secretary of Defense
SHAPE	Supreme Headquarters Allied Powers Europe
SM	Strategic Missile (as in SM-75)
SOS(A)	Secretary of State Air
SrA	Senior Airman (E-4)
SSM	Surface to surface missile
TAC	Tactical Air Command
TBM	Tactical Ballistic Missile
TEL	Transporter Erector Launcher
USAF	United States Air Force
USAAF	United States Army Air Force
WADC	Wright Air Development Center
WDD	Western Development Division
WSECL	Weapons System Equipment Components List
WSSL	Weapons System Stock List
WTR	Western Test Range (Vandenberg AFB)

Introduction

On 24 December 1955, just as a group of Douglas Aircraft Company (DAC) engineers were enjoying a pre-Christmas celebration before going home to their families, word came from the US Air Force's (USAF) Western Development Division (WDD) to Donald W. Douglas Jr, President of DAC, of the award of an important contract. Douglas had been one of three aircraft manufacturers who had tendered for the Air Force's requirement for an Intermediate Range Ballistic Missile (IRBM) capable of travelling 1,500 nm. The other two were the Lockheed Corporation and North American Aviation.[1] Douglas already had a background of missile experience which dated back to 1941 and therefore considered themselves to be a serious contender for the missile contract. Accordingly, on 28 December the contract for Weapon System 315A (WS-315A)[2] was formally signed in the WDD offices.[3] The missile itself was designated SM-75. Douglas Jr signed on behalf of DAC while Lieutenant-Colonel W. D. Smith from Air Materiel Command signed on behalf of the Air Force. Douglas had Joe Rowland, Director of Public Relations for the Glenn L. Martin Company, to thank for the name of their proposed missile. They had not initially given their missile a name as a result of a misunderstanding. Rowland had been given the task of suggesting names for Martin's ICBM proposal and from his list of suggestions the name 'Titan' was selected, with 'Thor' as a back-up. When Titan was selected for the ICBM, Rowland suggested to Douglas that he may like to adopt 'Thor' for DAC's IRBM. Douglas agreed and proposed the name to the Air Research and Development Command (ARDC), who confirmed the choice. Thus was Thor born.[4]

From Second World War to Cold War

On 8 May 1945 the European chapter of the Second World War formally came to a close. Allies held together by a common cause in fighting Nazi Germany now took stock and had to reappraise their relationships. Significant changes were afoot. Great Britain, brought to near national bankruptcy by the war, also had to contend with the dismantling of its Empire but still sought to sit at the top table of international influence. To the surprise of many, Britain's wartime leader, Winston Churchill, had lost the general election held in July 1945 in favour of the Labour Party under the leadership of the wartime Deputy Prime Minister, Clement Attlee. The Soviet Union had suffered the monumental loss of nearly 14 per cent of its population, more than half of which had been civilian casualties. And the United States, still occupied in its war against Japan, was secretly on the verge of testing a new type of weapon: one which would eclipse all the other assembled ordnance of the war. On 16 July at a remote desert location in New Mexico, the first atomic weapon was tested by a US Army project team. It was spherical in design but although just compact enough to be carried in an aircraft it was not yet an operational weapon. It contained 5,000 lb of High Explosive (HE), 14 lb of plutonium, and produced an explosion equivalent to about 18 kilotons (kts) of TNT. This event inaugurated the atomic age and was to shape the post-war world. Two demonstrations of the power of the atom bomb took place over Hiroshima on 6 August 1945 and Nagasaki three days later. These forced the Japanese to surrender on 15 August. During the Potsdam Conference, when the leaders of the Allied Powers sought to determine the nature of post-war Europe, US President Harry S. Truman had felt it incumbent on him to tell the Soviet Union's Josef Stalin that the US possessed a new weapon of 'unusual destructive force'. This he did on 24 July. Stalin, inscrutable as ever, showed little emotion, which was interpreted by observers as Stalin not understanding the full significance of the statement. In fact, the information came as no surprise to him: he already knew, thanks to information passed covertly to the Soviets from Los Alamos (where the US bomb was created), that a test of a plutonium bomb was imminent. After two bombs of differing designs were dropped on Japan, it was quite clear that the Soviet Union had no option but to develop its own atomic bomb; there was no conventional weapon that could in any way counter the power of the atom, and it was not prepared to let America use its strategic advantage to dominate the post-war world. Once the niceties of the military alliance dwindled in the aftermath of the conflict and the former allies rearranged—or were forced to rearrange—their allegiances, the US was quick to close atomic ranks against Great Britain and Canada, even though the role played by their scientists had not been insignificant in the development of the bomb.[1] Despite the powerful military advantage that the US now possessed, Stalin was nonetheless willing to test the Western Allies' resolve: he did so by flexing his muscles over Berlin, in the hope that the allies would back down and allow the Soviet Sector to supply food and fuel to the Allied Sectors, thereby effectively controlling the whole city. But in a remarkable exercise in integrated logistic support, the Berlin Airlift underscored allied determination not to knuckle under to the Soviet threats and forced Stalin to back down. Clearly, the Soviet Union could not tolerate such continued embarrassment by the West.

Once hostilities with Japan were concluded, it was time for a complete review of US military doctrine as it now faced a new and capable enemy in the form of the Soviet Union. Strategic air power had established itself as a powerful force in its own right and the formation of a separate US Air Force on 18 September 1947 created a new service which had to quickly define its role. General Henry H. 'Hap' Arnold, Commander of the AAF with the assistance of his scientific adviser Theodore von Kármán had already created a study, 'Towards New Horizons', which set out a path for the development of technologies resulting from the Second World War, and this, not surprisingly, included a framework for the development of long-range missiles. Arnold had been impressed by the German V-2 missile, both as a weapon and the influence it had had on the war planners. However, the late 1940s were a time of fiscal belt-tightening; this and a range of higher military priorities set out by a still largely conservative military hierarchy resulted in the missile programme, still perceived by many as an extension to the artillery, being largely set aside. Doctrinally, the USAF was to plan development of an ICBM as its future main strategic missile asset. In doing so it recognised that the day of the manned bomber would in due course be over, while enemy air defences would become ever more effective. However, there was a lack of actual enthusiasm for moving things forward. Perhaps this was understandable, as the emergence of powerful jet-powered bombers promised—at least provisionally—an effective way of maintaining the supremacy of a long-range bomber force. It also reflected the brand new USAF's interest in not risking the pursuit of unproven technology in its formative years. Significantly, though, Major-General Curtis E. LeMay—who was to transform the USAF's Strategic Air Command (SAC) when he took command in 1948—had presciently already placed a marker in the complex ground of inter-service rivalries when in 1946 he declared the AAF interest in a satellite programme. This set the agenda for the bitter infighting that was to evolve within the US Armed Forces as the significance and potential of missile technology became more fully understood. The AAF had effectively won the first round over Army ground-based forces when Assistant Secretary for War W. Stuart Symington declared on 7 October 1946 that the AAF should pursue research and development projects related to missile programs, although little actually happened as a result. The following years were to see an ever more acrimonious debate over the role and ownership of missile assets.

Although the sizeable reduction in US forces after the war had left the Soviet ground forces with a significant superiority, the communist state lagged behind considerably in air and naval capability. They had neither atomic bombs nor the ability to produce fissionable materials as yet. Ravaged by the occupying Germans their industrial base had suffered accordingly and was estimated to have been reduced to about 15 per cent of that of the United States. Jet engine technology was only to come providently through surprising British generosity. With negligible human assets 'on the ground' in the Soviet Union, US intelligence resources presumed that the Soviets would develop their own atomic bomb, but knew next to nothing about what was or might be happening and had to rely on scientific estimates based on their own experience and the complexity of developing the US bomb. The creation of the bomb had required an enormous investment and an order of similar magnitude would have to be made by the Soviets. They did, however, have one useful advantage—they knew that the technology worked. The US estimates also failed to understand the Soviets' singleness of purpose and predicted the date of a first test in the early to mid-1950s. This was in fact a significant miscalculation.

On 1 September 1949, a USAF Weather Service WB-29A from No. 375 Weather Reconnaissance Squadron on a routine flight from Japan to Alaska picked up radioactive debris in its filters.[2] This was not an unknown scenario as such, as various naturally occurring events could produce radioactive traces and there had been 111 previously recorded incidents. Further flights were made to collect more samples, which were duly analysed, and the conclusion reached that this debris could only have come from a Soviet atomic bomb. As the cloud of radioactivity moved eastwards, the RAF in Gibraltar were alerted and flew sampling missions to 70 degrees north.[3] Some of the administration were reluctant to accept the evidence as *de facto* proof of Soviet atomic capability, still believing that it was impossible that the Soviets could have caught up so quickly. But on 23 September, President Truman's announcement that '[w]e have evidence that within recent weeks an atomic explosion occurred in the USSR' sent shock waves through the Pentagon and the American continent.[4] The whole matter was nonetheless still treated with caution, and Senator Edwin C. Johnson from Colorado, a member of the Congressional Joint Committee on Atomic Energy, was reprimanded by Truman for mentioning in a television interview that the Soviet bomb had contained plutonium.[5] Had the Americans been able to see the Soviet bomb, which they nicknamed 'Joe-1', they would have no doubt expressed surprise at the almost uncanny resemblance to the 'Fat Man' bomb dropped on Nagasaki. Spies within the Manhattan Engineer District—the code name for the US atom bomb project—had apparently for ideological, if often misguided, reasons given information to the Soviets which in the very least had assisted their programme. It is often believed that this was the major factor in the development of Soviet atomic weapons, but in fact the Soviets had already started their own wartime research into nuclear fission in 1942 under Igor Kurchatov but were hampered by paranoid bureaucracy, a lack of uranium, and the technical infrastructure to process the fuel.[6] Failure usually meant transport to the gulags and this in itself made people who dared venture into uncertain areas of research very cautious. To reduce time spent on ultimately unproductive research, Kurchatov actively identified questions for which he sought answers and these were passed on through the espionage network to the Soviet agents. Klaus Fuchs, who had been part of the British 'Tube Alloys' programme before going with other British scientists to Los Alamos, was instrumental in passing on information to US spy Harry Gold. NKVD Chief Lavrenti Beria, who in a bizarre sequence of events that could arguably only happen in a totalitarian state, was later to be responsible for the post-war Soviet atomic bomb programme, and was highly suspicious of the information passed on, believing that it was deliberate disinformation designed to lead the Soviet bomb programme in the wrong direction. He encouraged Stalin to think likewise. This possibly accounted for reluctance on the part of the Soviet hierarchy to divert funds to a project which was largely dependent on theoretical analysis and may not have yielded positive results when the economy was still recovering from the previous war.[7] It was not until 1950 that Fuchs admitted his activities, which led to his arrest, swift trial, and imprisonment for espionage. The trial of the American David Greenglass, a soldier in the US Army, was not so simple. He admitted to passing drawings to the Soviets, but some of his evidence is now considered to have been unsafe. To what extent this espionage actually helped the Soviet programme is still unclear and may never be fully understood, since some of the evidence is still classified in America. At the time, however, blaming significant help with the Soviet bomb on him was a face-saving way of masking greater shortcomings in US intelligence, and also explained away how a largely peasant-based economy—as it was perceived—could catch up with the industrial might of the US in such a short time. As the mutual paranoia of the Cold War set in, the US could not accept nuclear parity with the Soviet Union and took the almost inevitable path towards the development of the fusion bomb. There were eminent scientists who argued against this, including some who had worked on the Manhattan Project; but however altruistic their views may have been, it was unlikely that such moral considerations would be taken into account by the Soviets, who, it was believed, would now move towards development of its own fusion bomb. There was even concern that the Soviets, and possibly the British too, were ahead of the US in its development of a fusion bomb. In light of these concerns, therefore, the US programme to develop the 'super' bomb was inevitable.

By the early 1950s, after the Korean conflict had readdressed US military thinking on the potential for real conflict, the Soviet threat loomed ever larger in many American minds. The continuing inability to obtain real intelligence on Soviet military capability remained a constant problem, but judging from what evidence was available it was reasonable to suppose that Soviet aspirations and capabilities would mirror those of the US, as they had with the atomic bomb, and that they too would be looking at long-range missiles.

The USAF ICBM programme was initiated as the Convair SM-65 in 1953 under contract WS-107A-1.[8] Called 'Atlas', it was proving to be a demanding programme which stretched technological capability at that time to the limit. It was considered that it may take ten years to reach operational status.[9] The US Army, meanwhile, was forging ahead with its own missile programme under the leadership of the German rocket engineer Dr Wernher von Braun, who had been the technical genius behind the German Army's A4 (V-2) missile programme (which had become operational in Western Europe in September 1944). Temperamental and often unreliable in the hands of its launch battalions, the weapon had nonetheless proved to be a thorn in the side of the Allied armies moving eastwards after D-Day. Resources which were sorely needed in support of the advancing Allied armies had to be diverted to counter the V-2s until, as they retreated east, the launch sites were no longer in range of strategic Allied targets. After Hitler's suicide and the end of the European war, von Braun and a number of his fellow scientists had surrendered to the Americans and in due course this group of engineers had been taken to America as part of Operation

Paperclip, where they set about assembling and launching A4s made from parts captured by the Americans in the underground production facility at Nordhausen, in the Harz Mountains.[10] The US Army was not slow in perceiving either what von Braun had achieved or its future significance. After launching a number of A4s from the White Sands Proving Ground in New Mexico, thereby getting valuable experience of handling the weapon, von Braun's team had gone on to develop the 200-nm-range Redstone missile—essentially an improved A4—which would be deployed by the US Army in Europe armed with a W-39 nuclear warhead.[11] The Redstone proved to be a highly successful and reliable missile. In November 1956, Major-General John B. Medaris,[12] Commanding General of the Army Ballistic Missile Agency (ABMA),[13] commented,

> [...] we have challenged the Redstone system to a wide variety of objectives above and beyond those already achieved by the missile as a single weapon system. Every such challenge has been met in superlative fashion, successfully and on time.[14]

This may also be taken as a direct warning to the Air Force of what the Army's plans were. Von Braun's next objective was a 1,500-nm IRBM which would be called 'Jupiter' (SM-78).[15] This was a logical successor to Redstone and would give the Army's artillery units still further reach. The verbal battle that ensued between the Army and the Air Force for control of the IRBM programme was one of the most bitterly fought inter-service rivalries of the post-war years. The Army argued from the start that non-strategic missiles were simply an extension of the artillery's capability. The V-2s had been developed and deployed by the German Army, and before that, in the First World War, the German artillery had fielded the 81-mile-range Krupp Paris Gun (*Paris-Geschütz*). Technological developments to deliver a projectile over every increasing ranges were naturally embraced by the artillery, and the IRBM was merely a further manifestation of this. Von Braun and his team were pre-eminent in their field and had the necessary practical experience. By contrast, the Air Force's role was the projection of force over long ranges. Consequently, the ICBM fell naturally within the Air Force's operational orbit, but there was no way it was going to let the Army take over the medium-range role, for it feared that proven expertise at this range may encourage the Army to seek to project its influence still further. Initially, the Air Force described its early missiles as 'unmanned winged bombers', which in many ways they were.

The Air Force's IRBM programme—distinct from the ICBM programme—can trace its roots to the Matador missile. Essentially an air-breathing cruise missile with its origins going back to 1946, the Martin B-61A Matador was fully operational under Tactical Air Command (TAC) from 1954, but was soon seen as vulnerable to Soviet interception, and the USAF's Wright Air Development Center (WADC) was tasked with recommending its replacement.[16] Their studies determined that while the Matador was capable of further development, the only secure way of developing immunity from interception was a ballistic missile. Accordingly, the USAF Headquarters directed the ARDC to develop an improved low-level Matador, the TM-61B, and also to outline a development plan for a Tactical Ballistic Missile (TBM) by 1 June 1955 with a projected in-service date of 1960. In October 1954,

Lieutenant-General Donald L. Putt, Deputy Chief of Staff for Development and Military Director of the Scientific Advisory Board to the Chief of Staff, USAF, gave instruction to the Commander ARDC, Lieutenant-General Thomas S. Power, to initiate competitive bids for a TBM design.[17] Putt's parameters for the missile were specific: range 800–1,000 nm, with the capacity to stretch this in later development to 1,500 nm; payload 3,000 lb, reducing to 1,500 lb over longer ranges; and a Circular Error Probable (CEP) of 6,000 feet, reducing in time to 1,500 feet. The missile also needed to be air-portable. A General Operational Requirement followed in December which re-stated the in-service date as 1960. By September 1955, the range parameters had been increased to 1,200–1,500 nm from the start. The weapon was now classed as a Medium Range Ballistic Missile (MRBM).

However, what were the Soviets up to and what were their capabilities? In an effort to answer this question, a secret committee was established to consider US vulnerability to Soviet aggression. This committee, the Technological Capabilities Panel of the Office of Defense Management—Scientific Advisory Committee (ODM-SAC) was chaired by Dr James R. Killian Jr, from the Massachusetts Institute of Technology (MIT). Killian was much respected on both sides of the US political spectrum and was later to hold the influential position of President Eisenhower's special adviser on science and technology. The report, 'Meeting the Threat of Surprise Attack', was submitted to Eisenhower on 14 February 1955.[18] It identified four distinct phases: firstly, the existing US position of advantage in terms of air power, yet vulnerability to surprise attack. The second phase anticipated that during the late 1950s the US would have advanced ahead of the Soviet Union to the point where it was better equipped to deal with a surprise attack. Thereafter, in the third phase, Soviet capability would increase until, in the final phase, nuclear parity was reached, whereby an attack by either side would result in mutual destruction. The report recommended that the Air Force programme for the development of an ICBM be treated as a nationally supported effort of the highest priority, that an IRBM with around a 1,500-nm range and a 1 megaton warhead be developed for strategic use, and that both land-basing and ship-basing should be considered.

The second recommendation appeared to exclude the Air Force from an IRBM programme of its own. While the von Neumann 'Teapot' Committee had laid the foundations for the missile programme, it was the NSC's response to Dr Killian's report which gave the three services the necessary confidence to proceed.[19] The recommended IRBM development programme was to emerge as a joint Army–Navy programme for a ground-launched and a seaborne missile based on a common design, which was in essence von Braun's Jupiter proposal. Sensing competition and not wanting to be caught out unprepared, Air Force planners, notwithstanding Killian's recommendations, considered whether or not they themselves should also have an IRBM programme. Influenced by the need for an insurance policy against problems with Atlas, the emergent IRBM proposal did not, however, enjoy total support from within the Air Force hierarchy. Resources, both financial and personnel-related, were constrained and some believed that the Atlas programme, now itself a high priority programme under considerable pressure, would suffer if these resources were diluted across two significant missile programmes, one of which would become essentially obsolete when the ICBM became operational. Atlas was being developed under the control of the Western Development Division (WDD) of the ARDC. This unassumingly named organisation based in an equally unassuming former schoolhouse at Inglewood, a suburb of Los Angeles, was to become the nerve centre of the Air Force's missile programme. Its dynamic head, Major-General Bernard A. 'Bennie' Schriever, was sceptical about taking on another major missile programme, wanting instead to concentrate all his resources on the ICBM project. Schriever was a man of strong convictions and had near total control over the Air Force's missile aspirations. In an earlier Air Force posting, Schriever had dared to confront General Curtis LeMay, now the Commanding Officer of SAC and a man known for his ruthlessness, and had, remarkably, survived the resulting fallout. He had already upset the aero-industry by taking control of the ICBM programme in-house. Traditionally, one contractor would have been given the contract—in this case Convair—and reaped huge profits. Major-General Schriever considered that, while there was considerable aeronautical skill within the industry, there was little or no aero*space* skill—the very heart of this new undertaking. Convair had been given the contract for co-ordinating the whole programme, relying on a number of subcontractors to develop the component parts, so Schriever's approach was novel, but deemed necessary to give momentum to the programme.

There was ever-growing concern about the potential capability of the Soviets, who, intelligence sources believed, were now undertaking their own ICBM programme. Furthermore, from a strategic point of view, the fact that a Soviet IRBM would be capable of reaching targets anywhere in Europe was deeply troubling. If Atlas was further delayed, then it would not be inconceivable for the Soviets to field an IRBM and an ICBM before the Americans, thereby commanding a huge strategic advantage with unpredictable implications for the West. This was not an option. Von Braun's team, meanwhile, were developing their IRBM unencumbered by a parallel missile development programme, and were thus able to concentrate their efforts on one project—albeit for certain modifications which had to be made to the original design concept in order to fit naval requirements. The seaborne missile, for instance, would be launched from tubes and could not, therefore, have stabilising fins. To add further to Air Force concerns, von Braun's track record was impressive: he and his German colleagues had years of collective experience in the field of rockets. By contrast, Major-General Schriever was almost totally dependent on more limited, home-grown expertise. The Army might quickly establish itself as the custodian of the IRBM programme and thereby be encouraged to set its sights higher—towards an Army ICBM.

Notwithstanding Major-General Schriever's reluctance to embrace the IRBM programme, it was clear to Air Force planners that a USAF IRBM programme was essential. On 8 November, Secretary of Defense (SecDef) Charles E. Wilson directed the USAF to embark on its own IRBM programme and also gave the Air Force sole rights to deploying missiles of ranges greater than 200 nm. Even this assurance was a bitter pill to swallow for many in the senior ranks of the Air Force, as they hung on staunchly to the belief in the omnipotence of the manned bomber. But while the Air Force had been given the go-ahead, the Army's IRBM programme had not yet been terminated, and von Braun continued development of Jupiter, still convinced that when a final decision was made, his missile would be the winner.

Thor—The Early Days

Thor was built under the concurrency concept. This was the forerunner of Performance and Review Technique (PERT) and Critical Path Analysis (CPA), both of which later proved essential to the management of the very complex US Polaris Fleet Ballistic Missile (FBM) programme. Concurrency, also known as the 'weapons system concept', was a development of the parallel concept which was adopted for Atlas. It was, however, a high-risk strategy in terms of technology, manpower, and finance, and was ultimately inefficient, yet was seen as the only way of achieving the set target dates. Each operation could be classed as a serial or parallel task, and the progression of serial tasks determined the critical path. The plan was such that missile production, operational deployment, and personnel training were all to be completed concurrently, ideally reaching operational capability at the same time. There would be no prototypes in the conventional sense and, at the request of the Air Force, production tooling was used from the start. The missiles and their supporting equipment would in essence be built as production models from the beginning, although modifications identified from the test programme and even in operational missiles would be incorporated in subsequent production. Colonel John C. Bon Tempo, who was later to head the Air Force team that launched the first Thor from Vandenberg Air Force Base, remembered:

> Engineers were putting their ideas on butcher paper and draping it along the walls in their work area. Technical writers were adjusting their operating and maintenance procedures [which] were in a constant state of change with everyone's ideas being incorporated or eliminated on an hourly basis.[1]

After a visit to the Douglas facility at Santa Monica in the spring of 1959, *Flight*'s correspondent commented,

> [Main] impressions following this tour were the simplicity of the production line, coupled with the comprehensiveness of the system as a whole [...] elaborate facilities and techniques were not required in the construction of the airframe (conventional aircraft-type construction is used in the guidance and centre sections).[2]

Emphasis was also placed on the use of existing components wherever possible, although Thor was deliberately not to be seen as a scaled-down Atlas, in case problems in the Atlas programme were transferred to the smaller missile. It was a challenging task. The time frame was tight, but it did result in one of the quickest projects in Air Force history. The Thor contract appointed DAC as prime contractor for airframe and integration. Normally, one company could expect to be prime contractor for the whole aircraft or missile, but in this case, separate contracts were awarded to the Rocketdyne division of North American Aviation for the rocket engine, AC Spark Plug for the inertial guidance navigation system, Bell Laboratories for the back-up radio guidance system, and General Electric (GE) for the re-entry vehicle. Technical direction was provided by the Ramo-Wooldridge Corporation. This arrangement provided a degree of insurance against component parts of the project experiencing difficulties and also enhanced the concurrency concept—but it was a politically charged chalice from which Douglas was to drink. The development of Jupiter continued, and despite Thor being the 'in-house' Air Force design, there was the possibility that Jupiter might be chosen for the IRBM role, thereby rendering Thor redundant—particularly if it was hit. However, having better funding than the Army gave the Air Force the ability to push the project ahead with gusto. The timeline was, to say the least, ambitious. Initial key dates were set as follows:

R&D Launch	by the end of 1956
Full Range Test Flight	July 1957
IOC[3] Launch	July 1958
Operational Deployment	July 1959[4]

It was a demanding schedule.

Douglas had placed Jack L. Bromberg in charge of the project as weapon systems manager, with Hal M. Thomas as chief project engineer and Robert L. Johnson as chief engineer. Bromberg was well respected by the Air Force for his organisational ability, and this may have been a contributory factor in his selection by DAC. At senior level, design and development was overseen by E. P. Wheaton, vice-president (engineering), missiles and space systems and production and development by Leo A. Carter, vice-president and general manager, both of the Santa Monica Division of DAC.

In terms of design, certain parameters of the missile were reasonably easy to set. There was little choice but to use kerosene and liquid oxygen (LOX) as fuel and oxidant. Range would determine the volume of the fuel and LOX tanks, which would in turn set the broad dimensions of the missile. The Air Force had also determined that the missile would be portable by air and its dimensions would therefore also be constrained by the size of transport aircraft—initially the C-124 Globemaster II, but in January 1959 this was joined by the C-133 Cargomaster, both, fortuitously, Douglas products.[5] The configuration of the missile is shown in the figure on p. 22.

Thor was 64 feet 10 inches long and had a diameter of 8 feet. The basic construction was formed from three aluminium alloy panels, each forming a 120-degree arc with double-plane curvature. The US Chemical Milling Corporation then etched the interior of these panels into a waffle pattern to provide maximum strength to the airframe with minimum weight. This was a relatively novel form of construction at the time and different from the Army's Jupiter,

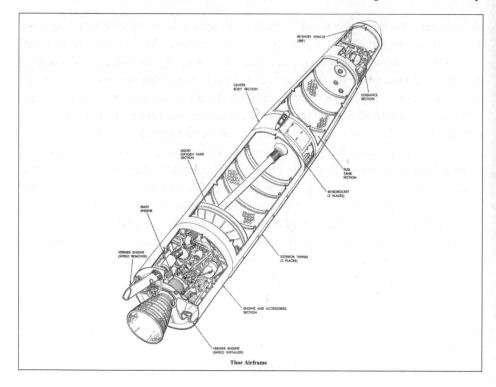

Thor Airframe

which was built to more conventional methods. While the oxidant tank was cylindrical, the upper portion was formed as a frustum of a cone with a blunt nose. This gave the vehicle its characteristic appearance and improved the aerodynamics. It also reduced the diameter of the missile body to the width of the RV. The missile was divided into six different elements:

Re-entry Vehicle (RV) and Warhead

Thor was deployed with a MK 2 Re-entry Vehicle (RV) manufactured at GE's Missiles and Ordnance Systems Division (MOSD) in Philadelphia. The MK 2 was the first USAF heat sink RV and was based on blunt body design, essentially the same as the proposed Atlas warhead.[6] The blunt nose design inevitably contributed to drag during powered flight. Although much of the heat of re-entry was deflected away by the shock wave in front of the RV, there was still considerable heat build-up and this was absorbed on a heat sink basis by a layer of copper and beryllium below the outer surface of the RV.[7] The forward cone of the RV had an included angle of 105 degrees and was 60 inches wide. The MK 2 had a low ballistic coefficient, or *beta*—a product of mass, drag, and cross-section. The MK 2 started slowing down in the upper atmosphere. This resulted in less heat build-up, but only over a longer period of time. A further disadvantage was that the slowing RV produced a trail of ionised gas which had a high radar signature, although efforts to reduce this signature were made by using plastic laminates with a depth half that of predicted Soviet radar wave-lengths. While a high *beta* design was seen as preferable, the greater re-entry velocity of such a design produced a much higher temperature, requiring a thicker layer of copper, the weight of which was inversely proportional to the weight attributable to the warhead. Contained within the RV was the W-49 warhead, with a yield of 1.44 megatons. This warhead, which was also used on the Jupiter IRBM and the Atlas and Titan 1 ICBMs, was derived from that of the MK 28 nuclear weapon[8] with which it is believed to have shared a common W34 Python primary.[9] A panel on the launch officer's console allowed immediate selection of one of two targets pre-stored within the guidance system. A further selection of air burst or ground burst could also be made. The W-49 was 20 inches in diameter and weighed *c.* 1,650 lb. It was produced by the Los Alamos Scientific Laboratory (LASL) and was selected in preference to the W-35, itself an earlier LASL design.

Guidance Section

Responsibility for the choice of inertial guidance can be attributed to Colonel Benjamin P. Blasingame.[10] He had been appointed by Major-General Schriever to the position of Chief Guidance and Control Project Officer in the WDD and was convinced that a workable inertial guidance system could rapidly be developed, even though others considered it too experimental. His confidence was justified when AC Spark Plug, the Electronic Division of General Motors based at Milwaukee, with assistance from the MIT developed a workable system, the AChiever, which was validated by its use in the Martin Mace and Chance Vought Regulus II cruise missiles. The unit was situated below the RV and had a conical indent at its forward end into which the RV was placed. Within the Guidance Section could be found the Control Group, including the Main Flight Controller and Platform Group equipment, with three acceleration sensing fluorolube-coated gyros set at right-angles to each other and covering range, pitch, and track. These gyros had to be kept within a precise temperature range at all times, a feature that was to be particularly demanding during the air transport of the missiles to-and-fro between the US and the UK. Mounted on three gimbal rings cast in light alloy, the whole system weighed about 700 lb. Signals from the gyros were transmitted to the digital computer in its air-conditioned housing. During transport of the missile, a gyro heater power pack (figure on p. 24) was attached to the nose of the missile and this maintained an ambient temperature within the gyros. To provide power for this unit, the C-124's outboard engines had to be run at a minimum of 1,200 rpm at all times when the aircraft was not hooked up to a ground power supply. The machining accuracy required of this inertial guidance system was of an entirely new order. Aero-engine machinists, accustomed to working inside 1,000th of an inch, were now required to work inside a micron.

> The machine shops were like medical laboratories with machinists dressed like surgeons, looking into microscopes at the job they were machining. The traditional machinists began to crack up with the stress of what they were attempting to do. So Douglas recruited 16-year-old schoolgirls who didn't know a micron from a hole in the head, showed them what to do and they just did it.[11]

Three panels provided access to the equipment and guidance installation, while a further three covered the RV latches. As well as the umbilical connectors for RV, electrical and air conditioning systems, two hinged panels were provided for siting the long- and short-range theodolites.

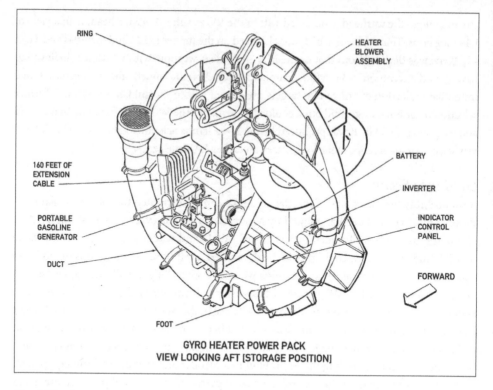

GYRO HEATER POWER PACK
VIEW LOOKING AFT [STORAGE POSITION]

Fuel Tank

Capacity: 4,812 US gallons. This contained the RP-1 fuel.[12] This was a light-cut petroleum, consisting primarily of aliphatic hydrocarbons, to military specification MIL-F-25576A. Fuel reached the engine via a lagged and heated fuel transfer line which passed through the centre of the LOX tank.

Centre Body

This provided an interface between the fuel and LOX tanks. On the outside were two retrorockets placed at 180 degrees to each other. Each vernier engine developed 1,000-lb thrust and was mounted inside a protective fairing. These vernier rockets provided the fine adjustment necessary to the trajectory to place the missile onto its final ballistic path (see below). This section also contained the LOX relief valve and vent, as well as electrical connectors. Manufacture of the valves was subcontracted to the Southwestern Valve Corporation.

Liquid Oxygen (LOX) Tank

Capacity: 7,420 US gallons. This contained the LOX oxidiser to military specification MIL-P-25508. The C-124s transporting the missiles had to reduce their rate of descent to allow both the fuel and LOX tanks to adapt to the changes in pressure. Electrical and plumbing conduits connecting the sections ran externally in two diametrically opposed glassfibre tunnels running up the side of the missile.

Engine and Accessories Section

The aft section was based around the Rocketdyne S-3D rocket engine, but also included the Accessories Pack including the Pneumatics Systems, Gas Generator, and Auxiliary Power Unit (APU). The engine was described by one of the NCOs on the first RAF training course as 'the fearsome and impossibly-powerful Rocketdyne engine, whose thrust to weight ratio was about 70:1, a working life of about 3 minutes and dangerous fuels.'[13] External to the aft bulkhead of the missile were the open end of the thrust chamber and the turbine exhaust duct on which were mounted four large steel spheres pressurised with nitrogen before launch to 3,000 psi; they released this pressure through regulators at about 60 psi to the tops of the propellant tanks, to force liquid into the pumps. There was also a heat exchanger, used for generating gaseous oxygen for pressurising the LOX tank. If propellants were just fed to the engine by gravity alone and then ignited, thrust would only be about 8,000 lb, as in the starting sequence. But the turbopump's turbine, mounted immediately above the injector, was fed with a separate, fuel-rich mixture when ignition was initiated, spinning its coaxial pumps at extraordinary speed. Thrust very rapidly increased to maximum in about one second, a controlled explosion of energy which frightened those who saw it. Anything less and the missile was at great risk of toppling over, as a number of archive films reveal. As propellants were consumed this pressure was maintained until engine cut-off, when vents opened in the tanks and thrust decayed. On the early flight missiles, four small triangular fins were mounted at the base of the aft section. These were to stabilise the missile during its initial passage through the atmosphere, but as this was only a small component of its total flight path, it was later decided that these fins would be removed to reduce weight. There was also concern that the fins were falling off shortly after launch. Showing scant disregard for safety measures that would undoubtedly be applied today, two Douglas engineers, Jay Simmons and Al Ressor, witnessed a lift-off from a bunker a mere 200 yards from the launch pad. They confirmed that the fins remained attached![14]

The choice of rocket engine was very much determined by the short timescale. North American Aviation Rocketdyne Division's Air Force model designation LR79-NA-9 (Model S-3D) was the chosen design and it produced a nominal 150,000-lb thrust.[15] The propulsion package consisted of the MB-3 Block III main engine and two vernier engines (Air Force model designation LR101-NA-11). Again following the needs of rapid development, this engine was basically half of the booster package being developed for Atlas; although *pro rata* it developed a greater thrust as a result of an improved combustion chamber profile. Design and engineering took place at the Rocketdyne Headquarters at Canoga Park, near Los Angeles. Rocketdyne's pre-eminence in the field of large liquid fuelled-rocket engines dated back to 1945, when North American decided to invest in missile research and development, which it presciently recognised would play a major part in future defence programmes. The remains of three V-2 engines retrieved from Germany provided the initial information from which development took place, and a twelve-man group was formed to study advanced aerophysics and all available information about the German rocket programs. The Rocketdyne Division was subsequently formed for the study and development of propulsion systems. In this it was helped by North American's Technical Research Laboratory, which had been involved with the post-war A4 tests. Based on their research, North American had been awarded the contract to build the USAF's Navaho supersonic cruise missile. Though plagued with problems and ultimately cancelled, Navaho was a significant, if still largely misunderstood stepping stone in the development of guided missiles. Experience with the Navaho engine led to the evolution of the engine which was selected to power Thor. The engines were manufactured and production tested at the company's Plant 65, a 228,000-square-foot production facility allied to a 200-acre test facility in Neosho, Missouri.[16] The facility was managed by J. P. Macnamara, under whom worked 600 employees. The design, with some modification, was also to be the engine for the Jupiter, a fact which some critics of the IRBM programme were only too keen to emphasise.[17] Should there be a problem with the engine, it would affect both missile programmes. There was one stage in the development where this would become alarmingly clear. Engine manufacture was under similar pressure, as was the whole programme. A mock-up engine was supplied in February 1956, with the first of an initial batch of six flyable engines being delivered on schedule in September. Engine testing was undertaken at a specially build test stand at Edwards AFB in California. Initial engines were rated to 135,000-lb thrust. The significant features in the design of the engine were the shape of the bell chamber, the injector plate, and the turbopump to feed propellant at high pressure to the engine. The chamber was constructed of brazed flat tubes of nickel, shaped empirically to a convergent/divergent shape and size to maximise the expanding gases to useful thrust at the choke point of the nozzle. Fuel was forced at very high pressure through the tubes before routing to the injector to cool the chamber during flight. The choice of RP-1 fuel was conservative, but it was both readily available and easy to transport and store. The RP-1 used in conjunction with LOX produced a specific impulse of about 260.[18] There was one flaw in the engine's design, although this was not realised at the time: the hot exhaust gas from the turbopump was vented directly through a tube adjacent to the bell chamber, contributing nothing to the total thrust and a loss of around 5 per cent in the efficiency of the propellant. In contrast, Valentin Glushko, the Soviet Union's chief rocket engine designer, recycled the exhaust into the main thrust chamber. This feature was incorporated into the design of the RD-107 engines used on the Soviet Union's first ICBM, the R-7. Glushko used four optimised thrust chambers for each turbopump, but this required exceptional engineering not available to the US until much later.

The engine was a single-start, fixed-thrust, liquid-bipropellant rocket engine providing both thrust and directional control via a gimballing action of the main thrust chamber (see the figure on p. 27). Main engine movement was 7 degrees in pitch and yaw. The engine nozzle was bell-shaped and the thrust chamber a tube-walled regeneratively-cooled design. Each engine was hot-tested for a 15–30-second run at the Neosho plant before being certified for flight use. Periodically the test rig was recalibrated with a 110-second test firing. The engine could be broken down into two major assemblies. The upper assembly was fixed while the lower assembly was the section mounted on gimbals. In addition, there were seven engine subsystems:

Main propellant subsystem
Turbopump lubrication subsystem
Gas generator and exhaust subsystem
Pneumatic control subsystem

Start subsystem
Main thrust chamber and engine thrust frame
Electrical subsystem

Two vernier rockets provided fine tuning to the trajectory. They were mounted on the backplate of the missile and could be moved 45 degrees in pitch and from 6 to 36 degrees outbound in yaw.

Also on the aft bulkhead were six sockets into which fitted worm-driven pins to hold the missile on the launcher. Each socket was stressed to exceed one sixth of the weight of the missile, to allow for the effects of wind while the missile was in the vertical position.

Various pyrotechnics/explosives were used on the vehicle. These were:

RV Latch squibs x 3—used for separating the warhead[19]
In-flight cable disconnect squib for the warhead x 1
Retrorockets x 2—slowed the main body to achieve separation distance from the warhead
Retrorocket Igniters x 2
Gas Generator Igniters x 2
Vernier Engine Igniters x 2
Main Thrust Chamber Igniter x 1

Until needed, these were stored in the special purpose Pyrotechnics Buildings found on each launch site. The total weight of an operational Thor, fully fuelled and with warhead fitted, was *c.* 110,000 lb.

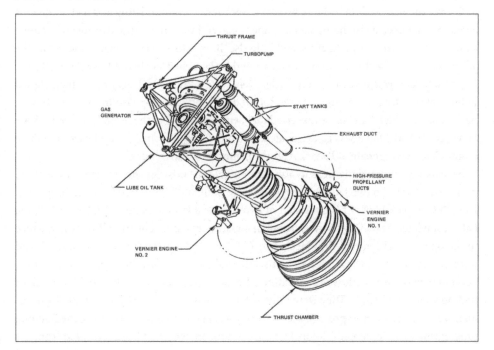

Failures and Successes

On 26 October 1956, the first Thor (Serial T101) was air-lifted aboard a Douglas Globemaster to Patrick Air Force Base in Florida.[1] This location had become the Air Force's missile flight testing range. Missile tests after the war had initially taken place at the White Sands Proving Ground in New Mexico. It was here that the German rocket scientists under von Braun had been based and it was from here that the A4 (V-2) missiles collected under Operation Paperclip had been fired. However, the range, though extensive in area, was soon compromised by the increasing reach of the reconstructed A4s fired from it.[2] Anticipating this development, the Committee on Long Range Proving Grounds had been formed in October 1946 and eleven months later identified two preferred sites. The first was El Centro in California, conveniently close to the major missile manufacturers, with a range at Baja, Mexico; the second was the Banana River Naval Air Station, deactivated after playing its wartime role, with a range at the adjacent Cape Canaveral 15 miles to the north. However, Mexico refused to allow missiles to fly over the Baja Region. Britain, however, was more accommodating and had no qualms about missiles overflying the Bahamas. Cape Canaveral was an unattractive area of swampy land inhabited mainly by alligators, and little else. It was close to the Equator and, using the advantage of the Earth's rotation, missiles could be launched safely out to sea. Selection of Cape Canaveral was confirmed on 11 May 1949, when President Harry S. Truman signed Public Law 60 designating the area the Joint Long Range Proving Ground with its base at Banana River, which had been transferred on 1 September 1948 to the recently formed US Air Force. On 11 May 1950 it was re-designated the Long Range Proving Ground Base, and three months later it was renamed Patrick AFB, the name it holds to this day.[3]

No existing launch pads were in any way suitable for missiles the size and range of the proposed IRBMs, so two launch complexes were built and configured for launching Thor. Launch Complex 17 (LC-17) consisted of two identical launch pads, LC-17A and 17B, the latter completed first. They were substantial concrete structures bearing little resemblance to the operational Launch Emplacements (LE) on which Thor would be mounted, and were in fact based on the design to be used for Atlas—such was the urgency with which development of the missile was proceeding. These two were 'wet' pads that could be used for tied-down engine firings. They were fully instrumented with large red and white, 110-foot-high servicing gantries to provide access to all parts of the missile. Overseeing the building programme was Lieutenant-Colonel Charles Mathison, who had been seconded from the

WDD for the purpose. He was an imposing man who had previously been involved in the flight test programme of the first weaponised hydrogen bomb, the Mk 17. Despite the high-tech public image of 'The Cape' when it became home to the American Moon Programme, the task Mathison faced was considerable. The whole area was a mass of swamps, home to snakes and alligators, and an ideal breeding ground for mosquitoes. Plagued initially by labour disputes, steel and component shortages, despite the high national priority of the Thor programme, LC-17B was only just ready in time for Thor's arrival.[4] A launch control blockhouse was also built using the Army's Redstone blockhouse design as a starting point to save time. Also used was LC-18B on the adjacent complex to the north, Launch Complex 18. This was a 'dry' pad only usable for live launches. LC-18A was reserved for the US Navy's ill-fated Vanguard launch vehicle. The necessary missile assembly and checkout facilities for the Douglas engineers were provided in Building 'M', and it too was only just finished in time by astute management juggling. When Lieutenant-Colonel Edward N. Hall[5] visited Patrick AFB in December 1956, he reported:

> [...] the work being accomplished in facilities, instrumentation and the missile itself—is amazing, both in quantity and quality. All people are pushing themselves to the utmost[6]

Another problem was that the maximum range of the missiles previously launched had been 200 nm, so no Atlantic Missile Range tracking facilities existed for longer-range ballistic missiles expected to splash down in the region of Antigua. These too had to be provided with unprecedented speed. The launch operations were under the control of Project Director Dr Dolph Thiel from Space Technologies Laboratory (STL). Thiel had been one of the A4 engineers brought from Germany, so had some experience in the complexities of a missile development programme. Associate Director was Arnold Anchordoguy, later to become the Atlas Program Manager. Overseeing operations was Dr Ruben Mettler, Director of System Engineering and Technical Direction for the Thor programme.

The first Thor was erected on LC-17B in November, which allowed for the engineers to start making the numerous checks now possible on a 'live' vehicle. T101 was radio-guided and fitted with an aerodynamic nose cone, but, under concurrency, was a quasi-production vehicle.

The first pre-launch engine firing test was scheduled for 20 December—less than a year since the initial contract had been signed. The launch was a joint effort between Douglas and Rocketdyne personnel, but sadly a failed relay in the sequencing system in the primary ignition circuit prevented main engine ignition from taking place. Any hopes of bringing Thor to life in 1956 were thus dashed. Other problems were also identified, and with Christmas imminent and the concurrent shut down of the range it was decided to postpone further pre-launch testing until the New Year. The first launch would take place in January. In many ways the demands of the concurrency programme had dictated a launch very early on, using a very basic launch vehicle. Minimum requirements were set for the early launches, if only to show the basic viability of the design, and T101 was in many ways a simple engineering vehicle. It was therefore not surprising, albeit frustrating, when problems arose. A revised launch date was set for 22 January 1957, but also had to be aborted and was re-scheduled for the 25th. By then it was increasingly desirable that a successful launch should be achieved. The countdown had been rehearsed time and time again, but luck was against the Douglas team. Engine ignition took place and the missile lifted off Pad 17B, rose about 6 inches, then fell back onto the launch pad, through the launch ring, and exploded on the exhaust deflector plate, causing significant damage to the pad.[7] The cause was traced to a contaminated liquid oxygen pipe which ruptured, triggering a failure of the LOX fill and check valve. The fault was identified when footage from a promotional film being made was examined and the LOX pipe was seen to be dragged through the sand. The lesson was learned that LOX had to be handled more carefully, as the slightest contamination could cause an instant explosion. Launch failures were the price to pay at that time for the development of complex rockets, and the American public did not take readily to them. But this failure also exposed the potential risks of the concurrency programme. Gaseous oxygen was used to pressurise the LOX tank. Gaseous nitrogen, arguably safer, had been eliminated as a choice because of fears that it would contaminate the LOX, but no proper test had been conducted to prove or refute the theory. There was simply no time.

As LC-17A was still not complete, and with an estimated two months needed to repair and refurbish -17B, further launches had to be postponed. In due course the second Thor (T102) which had been airlifted to Cape Canaveral in November of the previous year was taken to a refurbished LC-17B. Similar in configuration to T101, it was launched on 20 April and seemed to presage success when the missile began its trajectory out to sea. However, from the depths of the windowless command bunker, the Range Safety Officer's (RSO) telemetry indicated that the missile was flying inland at 180 degrees to its anticipated, and in fact actual, flightpath. With no view of the outside world to see that the missile was in fact on its correct trajectory, he initiated the destruct command after 35 seconds of flight.[8] A simple wiring fault in the DOVAP plotter had reversed the reading.[9] Yet again a Thor fireball lit up the sky over the Cape; still, the flight had demonstrated the potential for success. The offending RSO suffered the anger of Mettler and was criticised for too quick a response and failure to counter-check his other instruments before destroying the missile—he soon found himself posted to Alaska. Such was the establishment's resolve to succeed.

T103 was, if anything, less successful that the previous two launch attempts. On 22 May it exploded four minutes before launch, when fuel tank overpressure resulted in the tank's rupture—an embarrassing moment for Major-General Schriever. There was a strict rule that no countdown could last more than twenty-four hours, as it was considered that the resulting fatigue would encourage mistakes by the launch crew. After a day of frustration, Mettler considered the launch was at last close, even though this would exceed twenty-four hours, and ordered the launch countdown to go ahead. However, a weary technician failed to notice the pressure building in the fuel tank.

By now people began questioning the wisdom of the concurrency concept, as Thor was not the only missile being launched from the ETR. Also on site were the ABMA team and their test firings of Jupiter were proving much more encouraging. The Germans had the advantage of practical experience and were also testing many of the components using Redstone before committing them to Jupiter. They also had significant telemetry coming back from their missiles, which allowed faults to be quickly identified and resolved. Jupiter's launch successes had the potential to threaten the Air Force's tenure on their ICBM. If their simpler IRBM programme was experiencing difficulties, what might be the corollary for the ICBM? Major-General Medaris and his Germans could in theory make a strong case to follow Jupiter's success with their own ICBM to displace Atlas, even if they still would have to hand over the finished missile to the Air Force—Medaris already had a reputation for not letting obstacles deter him from his objectives. Von Braun must have personally warmed to that possibility, as such a missile could have been developed into the space launcher that was still dearest to the German's heart. The Army team also wished the specification of the IRBM to include the ability to increase the range to 2,000 nm. They knew that Thor, with its existing heavy RV, would be unable to achieve an increase in range without significant lightening of the copper heat shield on the RV. However, the Air Force was also keen to point out that Jupiter was merely as yet only a missile in isolation: its necessary operational infrastructure had yet to be developed, and this would take time. Thor, on the other hand, was an integrated weapons system. Furthermore, Jupiter would have to be manufactured by a commercial aircraft company, as the prototypes had been made by the ABMA in-house and it had no capability for mass production. As for the Germans, they were witnessing history repeat itself: the early A4s had been manufactured at Peenemunde for testing, but mass production had to be set up under a separate organisation.

Thor T104, the first launch from LC-17A on 30 August, was deemed a 'partial success.'[10] It started off in a promising fashion, but broke after, 92 seconds in, when it suffered an interrupted electrical signal to the yaw actuator. Finally, on 20 September, T105 soared upwards, arced onto its nominal trajectory, and plunged into the Atlantic 1,100 nm from LC-17B. It was the success that Douglas and the Air Force had long been waiting for, and indeed desperately needed for the programme to maintain credibility. T105 was a Phase 1 missile with radio guidance and a dummy warhead—still far from an autonomously guided missile with a live warhead, but progress nonetheless.

Meanwhile, the Thor *vs* Jupiter controversy still rumbled ominously in the background. Even as T104 was being readied for the next launch, SecDef Wilson was announcing production and overtime limitations on the Thor programme until the decision on 'which missile' had been resolved. Thor production was limited to two per month. The aim was still to determine which of the two IRBMs should be selected for production. To assist him in the decision, Wilson appointed an *ad hoc* committee to assess both missile designs. This committee was chaired by William M. Holaday (Special Assistant to the Secretary of Defense for Guided Missiles), with Major-General Schriever representing the Air Force and Major-General Medaris the Army. The Committee was tasked with considering 'all aspects of Jupiter and Thor programs including specific consideration of the basic design of each missile, the overall programme status as well as flight test results, and the manufacturing and test facilities of the various agencies now contributing to both missile developments.'[11] Perhaps with the prestige and reputation of both services so publicly at stake, not to mention the valuable commercial contracts that would be placed in jeopardy, it was hopelessly optimistic to anticipate either the Air Force or the Army giving way. The committee was deadlocked and Holaday could only report back that both missiles had their individual advantages and could be made into a viable operational weapon. Unable to make a decision, Holaday recommended that 'both programs be continued until successful flight tests are achieved by either missile in order that greater assurance of the early availability of an operable missile system may be achieved.'[12]

Thor launches did at last show signs of improvement. T109, launched on 24 October 1957, was the first flight that could be described as fully successful. This missile, stripped down of all unessential components, flew with a nose cone weighing 1,000 lb and was designed to test the missile structure above its maximum acceleration. This it achieved, and also flew a full range of 2,350 nm. The launch of T115 from AFETR on 4 June 1958 represented another significant step towards operational capability. Although this was an R&D Phase 2 missile configured to test the Bell guidance system for the Titan ICBM, it was also the first launch from the IOC Pad (LC-18B) which in design was closer to the tactical configuration planned for the UK. The missile

[…] rose ponderously aloft from a tremendous backlash of smoke and flame at [16.17EST]. The Thor launching was more spectacular than usual because of some of the special operational equipment used.[13]

It was deemed a success apart from the loss of two of the four fins, which were in any case to be deleted from operational missiles. Douglas sought to put a further stamp on its missile's supremacy with the launch of T138 on 5 November 1958. The launch took place from LC-17B and the missile was the first DM-18A IOC configured vehicle, operational in all respects except for a dummy warhead.[14] Lift-off was successful, but soon thereafter the autopilot failed and the RSO destroyed the missile after 35 seconds. Nevertheless, the manufacture and launch of operational Thors was another milestone in the programme.

The press showed considerable interest in the launch of T114 on 28 January 1959. On 14 January, Major-General Schriever had confirmed that Thor would be the booster used for a military reconnaissance satellite programme which would use a recoverable capsule. With Donald Douglas Jr looking on from the VIP stand, T114 lifted off at just after 3.00 p.m., and all appeared to be well until the exhaust, visible to observers, appeared to

[…] swerve back and down. A solid particle seemed to fall from it, and a puff of white smoke suggested that there had been a further explosion.

Notwithstanding this evidence which seasoned observers noted had not characterised the previous Thor launch on 19 December, the Department of Defense claimed that the missile 'flew its prescribed course and landed in the pre-selected impact area.'[15] In fact, the missile had lost guidance and had been destroyed by the RSO at T+152 seconds. The launch from LC-17A was significant in one other respect: an operationally configured launch mount had been used for the first time.

A British IRBM?

It had originally been the intention of the United States to assist Britain in the development of a British IRBM rather than embark on its own IRBM programme. This would allow the US to concentrate on the development of an ICBM—essential to its nuclear armoury. The US Army and the USAF were at that time pursuing differing paths in missile development. Under the leadership of von Braun and his team of Germans based at the Redstone Arsenal, the Army was concentrating on short-range tactical missiles leaving the Air Force to contend with the very much more demanding, and expensive, ICBM. The concept of an IRBM did have a place in US planning, but such a missile would be made obsolete by the arrival of the ICBM, expected somewhere in the late 1950s. An IRBM, however, would be a useful adjunct in the European theatre and, with the much reduced ranges involved, would be capable of a quicker response to target and would not be made redundant by the ICBM. Britain, for instance, would have little use for a weapon of such extended range. The presence of US forces in the United Kingdom was nothing new, but there was always political uncertainty about how far the Americans could go in pursuit of military objectives, and the presence of their nuclear weapons on British soil was always going to be sensitive. President Truman had given Prime Minister Clement Attlee his personal assurance of consultation should the US ever wish to use atomic weapons. Truman indicated that

> [...] he would not consider the use of the bomb without consulting with the United Kingdom. [Attlee] asked whether this agreement should be put in writing, and the President replied no, that it would not be in writing, that if a Man's word wasn't any good it wasn't made any better by writing it down.[1]

But personal assurances may not have reflected US Government thinking. On 20 January 1953 Dwight D. Eisenhower assumed the American Presidency and on the following 6 March Foreign Minister Anthony Eden and US Secretary of State John Foster Dulles met to discuss the joint decision-making process on the use of atomic weapons, although Dulles sought to keep the discussions to the more general subject of the decision to go to war. A year previously, Truman and Churchill had agreed that

> Under arrangements for common defense, the United States have the use of certain bases in the United Kingdom. We reaffirm the understanding that the use of these bases in an

emergency would be a matter of joint decision by His Majesty's Government and the United States Government in the light of circumstances prevailing at the time.[2]

Eden was keen to obtain confirmation that this understanding still existed under Eisenhower. Dulles assured Eden of the status of the UK as its major ally,

[and the] United States clearly did not wish to take any action that would endanger the safety of the United Kingdom. To the extent that time and circumstances permitted, the United States would of course wish to consult with the United Kingdom on situations that may arise and might lead to general war.[3]

Dulles could only comment on the official line taken by the US Government. Any personal assurance from the President, should he so agree, would have to be given to Churchill personally. This was broadly the on-going basis of the US presence in the UK.

The initial approach on the siting of missiles in the UK was made during the NATO Council in Paris in December 1953, when SecDef Wilson indicated to the British Minister of Supply, Duncan Sandys, that a visit to the US could be arranged to discuss missile co-operation. The plan in question was for a UK IRBM programme to be developed with US support, an idea that was attractive to Sandys, who was well aware that the Treasury could not continue to support UK defence spending at the then rate. However, an assessment of the technical capability of British industry by the Aircraft Industries Association was to identify many weaknesses in Britain's industrial capability.[4] Britain, already about five years behind the US, would be unable to cope with the technical demands of such a complex missile programme, although with US assistance the gap could perhaps be narrowed to three years. Computer capacity alone was considered inadequate.

Notwithstanding this, Britain was keen to establish itself in the brave new world of guided missiles. The country had after all suffered directly from the effects of the V-2s launched against London and other English cities. Joint talks took place in June 1954, leading to an agreement—the Wilson-Sandys Agreement—dated 12 August in which elements of a joint collaboration programme were itemised. In early autumn 1953, Assistant Chief of the Air Staff (Operational Requirements) Air Vice-Marshal Geoffrey Tuttle CB, DFC, had already requested that a specification for a 2,000-nm ballistic missile be drawn up. This led to Britain's MRBM programme being officially started in 1955 under Ministry of Defence Operational Requirement OR 1139. Work on such a project had in fact already been underway for some two years and the lead contractor, de Havilland Propellers, already nominated. The requirement called for a 2,000-nm range missile (initially 1,500 nm, with development increasing this to 2,500 nm) which was to become Blue Streak. Assuming a ten-year development period leading to operational deployment of the initial six sites by 1965 with full operational capability by 1968, the Air Ministry saw the missile as initially complementing the manned bomber squadrons and superseding them when, like the Americans, they could foresee a time when conventional aircraft became increasingly vulnerable to Soviet air defences, thus compromising the basic concept of deterrence which the manned bomber at that time embodied. The missile had to be capable of taking a warhead in the 'megaton range' to unspecified targets in the western USSR with a CEP of 8,000 feet.[5] The design borrowed heavily on US technology, but in many areas UK skills improved on information received. De Havilland had obtained a license from Convair to build large stainless-steel rocket components and the rocket engines were to be built by Rolls-Royce under the expert leadership of the Rocket Division's chief engineer, Val Cleaver.[6] These RZ-2 engines were essentially improved, updated versions of the Rocketdyne S-3D which was to power Thor, Jupiter, and Atlas.[7] While accepting the value of sharing US knowledge, the Air Ministry was keen that this would not also represent reliance on the US, and in a note to Sandys (who had taken over as Secretary of State for Defence in January 1957) noted:

> We are getting help in developing Blue Streak as a result of the Wilson/Sandys agreement. We should aim to get all possible assistance from the Americans, but we should insist on continuing to keep it in our programme not only because we want it but also because, politically, we cannot afford to be dependent upon America for this vital weapon. Operationally and technically we must be free, since the continuing interplay of counter-measures and counter counter-measures will be involved, to develop and modify the weapon to meet our appreciation of the operational situation.[8]

Blue Streak found favour within the Air Ministry because it provided a path to UK nuclear independence, a policy vigorously pursued by the Air Staff, but also because it could undermine unwelcome Royal Navy murmurings about putting missiles in submarines. In its early stages, Blue Streak enjoyed a 15-per-cent contribution to its costs from US Mutual Weapons Development Program (MWDP) funds. As part of the Thor agreement, however, it was proposed that this support would stop and this change also signalled a lessening of US support for the UK missile, which was by then seen as wasteful duplication of the US IRBM programme.

From the start, Blue Streak's warhead was a key determining factor. The outline parameters for Thor were known by this stage, but concerns over the possible weight of the conjectured Blue Streak warhead determined that a one-engine missile may only have an insufficient range of 1,200 nm. By then the Air Staff considered 2,000 nm to be the minimum acceptable. This would require a two-engine missile with a possible total weight of about 200,000 lb. Recognising Thor's vulnerability by nature of its storage and launch on the surface, Blue Streak was to be sited in underground launchers which would protect it from all but a direct nuclear hit, but also added considerably to the technical challenge of the programme.[9] The initial projected cost was £70m—somewhat optimistic as it turned out. In 1956 Sir Frederick Brundrett, Chief Scientific Adviser to the Ministry of Defence, concluded:

> [...] the warhead for Thor is being designed to a weight of atomic core of 1,500 lb, but the weight of the warhead itself must include the metal sheathing designed to act as a heat sink. The total weight including this sheathing will be 2,600 lb if the sheathing is steel and 3,100 lb if the sheathing is copper. The comparable figures for our own design are 2,250 lb, 3,600 lb, and 4,500 lb.[10]

Like the ICBM and at that time all missiles of any significant range, Blue Streak was to be liquid-fuelled, with all the attendant problems and disadvantages that this entailed. Blue Streak was also underfunded from the start—in part at least because of the optimistic cost projection—a critical shortcoming in such a fast developing environment, where to fall behind the racing progress of rocket technology in the US and USSR was all too easy. There was every possibility that the US ICBM would be operational well before Blue Streak reached the squadrons. However, the British aerospace industry, still optimistic about its future, was keen on rocket development—more so perhaps than the Air Ministry, as is evidenced by an IRBM design put forward in 1958 by Armstrong Siddeley. In essence this was an enlarged Black Knight rocket, a project running in parallel with Blue Streak and designed to define the characteristics of nuclear warheads re-entering the atmosphere at high velocities. Further support for the role of missiles in the future defence of the UK had come in the 1957 Defence White Paper presented to the House of Commons by Sandys. This had outlined in fairly unequivocal terms the central function that missiles would in the future play over the traditional role of fighters and bombers. Sandys was by no means a popular figure, particularly within the Air Ministry, but he had shown the ability to take tough decisions and carry them through. His White Paper was designed to cut the cost of Britain's defence budget. National Service was to be brought to an end and reliance for defence was to be placed on nuclear weapons and a policy of deterrence. Maybe Armstrong Siddeley had been encouraged by this declared policy, but little interest was taken in their IRBM proposal, possibly because by that time the true costs of missile development were becoming alarmingly apparent to the politicians.

Meanwhile, the US had been giving full consideration to what was threatening to become a proliferation of missile programs, as the three services considered what roles each one wanted missiles to play. Within the State Department John Foster Dulles was still advocating the ICBM programme, but Eisenhower, along with Air Force Chief of Staff General Nathan F. Twining, wanted an insurance policy and maintained an interest in basing IRBMs overseas—although any missiles based in Europe would be under the control of SACEUR. The list of possible client countries being considered at that time was somewhat more holistic and indicates a more global approach to the IRBM programme than has been traditionally understood. The list in fact included only two European countries, England and Germany, the others being Libya, Turkey, Formosa, South Korea, the Philippine Islands, and Japan. Locating the missiles in these countries would provide coverage of a large percentage of strategic targets in Russia and the Soviet Bloc while providing 100-per-cent coverage of current and anticipated theatre targets for both general and local war conditions.[11] SecDef, Charles E. Wilson, defined two IRBM programmes, Air Force (#1 IRBM) and Army-Navy (#2 IRBM), on 8 November 1955, but had not given a clear-cut assignment of operational responsibility for the missiles, nor the mechanism for agreeing basing rights in countries identified as suitable for forward locations. Wilson's directive had been surrounded by caveats to keep a number of options open until a final decision was made, and in no way suggested excluding the Army from the final operational decision. On 1 December 1955, the National Security Council considered both the ICBM and the IRBM programmes. They noted that

The President had stated that the political and psychological impact upon the world of the early development of an effective ballistic missile with a range of 1,000-1,700 range would be so great that early development of such a missile would be of critical importance to the national security interests of the United States.

The NSC accordingly granted highest priority to both missile programs 'above all others'. This gave the green light to Air Force aspirations. USAF Director of Plans, Major-General Richard C. Lindsay, advised VCAS, General Thomas D. White, that these matters must be addressed as a matter of urgency as both aspects could delay the ultimate deployment of the missiles. He also pressed the point that the Air Force must be the custodian of the IRBM force:

> [The] Army's employment of the IRBM is considered to be in violation of the present roles and missions which clearly indicate this to be a responsibility of the Air Force.[12]

General White, in a handwritten note, observed, 'this is highly controversial, nevertheless I think we should smoke this out—early rather than late.'[13] This must have reflected a certain concern on the ability of the UK to field its own MRBM. However, in the background to these early discussions there remained the restriction on the exchange of atomic information between the two countries, still controlled by the McMahon Act. Under pressure from Eisenhower this had been relaxed by the passing by Congress of the Atomic Energy Act of 30 August 1954. Congress was not against the development of peaceful applications of atomic energy, but would not sanction the exchange of information on atomic weapons. Britain was fortunate to have as its ambassador in Washington, Sir Roger Makins, who had already served in the British Embassy in Washington from 1945 to 1947, and clearly understood the American point of view on sharing information with its allies. The exchange of data on weapons had always been contentious. The limited progress made on this subject for all intents and purposes ended when the British atomic scientist Klaus Fuchs, who was working at UK Atomic Energy Research Establishment at Harwell, was being arrested as a Soviet spy on 2 February 1950. The unexpectedly rapid advances in atomic weapon capability made by the Soviet Union could at least in part be attributed to Fuchs, although the exact value of the data he transferred is still not clear, if only because much of his research is still classified information. Fuchs was not the only one who had been in touch with the Soviets, but his arrest undermined the case for closer co-operation between the two countries, particularly because the US was becoming increasingly paranoid about the Soviet threat. Eisenhower, however, continued to press for a freer exchange and on 15 June 1955 a bilateral civil agreement was signed. Concurrently, another bilateral agreement allowed for the sharing of information on the evaluation of enemy nuclear capability and defence plans to counter these and also the training of personnel in the use of nuclear weapons. Though not specifically included for the training of RAF crews in handling nuclear weapons, this latter clause may have been of help in paving the way three years later for the training of RAF crews on the complexities of Thor.

By mid-1956, progress on the Atlas missile was such that the USAF had to start planning for its operational deployment. The draft plan proposed the initial use of IOC missiles being fielded before the full testing programme was complete. In this respect the missiles would still essentially be advanced prototypes, but hopefully advanced enough to impress the Soviets. One complex of three launchers would be in place by March 1959 with a full deployment of a complete wing of 120 missiles in three bases by March 1961. The concurrent deployment plan for the IRBMs was to have two squadrons of 15 missiles operational by June 1959 expanding to a complete wing of eight squadrons—120 missiles—within the following 12 months. Although the US Air Force had already considered the idea, actual discussions regarding the placing of its IRBMs in Britain had already started in early 1956, albeit at a somewhat unofficial level. It was not until 16/17 July 1956 that SecAF Donald A. Quarles raised the subject at an official level during a visit to London with Sir Walter Monckton, the British Minister of Defence, and Sir Frederick Brundrett, the Ministry's Chief Scientific Adviser. The discussions took place in Room 60 of the House of Commons, under the somewhat vague title of 'Missile Situation'. Monckton had been warned of the topic for discussion in a telegram from BAFS[14] Washington which advised that Richard E. Horner, Acting Assistant Secretary to the Air Force for Research and Development, had made reference to recent correspondence between himself and representatives of the Ministry of Supply concerning a suggestion to establish operational USAF IRBMs in the UK.[15] BAFS had also warned Chief of the Air Staff, Air Chief Marshal Sir Dermot Boyle about USAF expectations. He was advised that both the US ICBM and the IRBM programmes seemed to be proceeding rapidly and the IRBM should be available well before Blue Streak.[16] Quarles therefore outlined his proposals, adding a cautionary note that, as yet, there was no official Government approval for the idea. Nevertheless, it was no longer a tentative proposal as had been suggested before and the USAF was now anxious to take discussions to the next stage and initiate planning in anticipation of official approval being granted. Quarles was respected in the USAF for being a pragmatist and not a career politician, and had earned similar respect within the Air Ministry. Only a broad outline was at this stage considered, but certain ideas had been formulated within the minds of the Air Force planners. Once operational ICBMs became available, the USAF would transfer the IRBMs to the RAF. Occasional live firings with dummy warheads would be undertaken to prove the system. Furthermore, a failure rate of one in ten was anticipated for the IRBMs and this needed to be factored into target planning. He was also asked to ascertain how many missile sites were planned. Clearly Quarles had come armed with some substantive initial ideas. Seven sites were anticipated—six operational ones and a seventh one, possibly on the Atlantic coast of northern Scotland, for the live firings.[17] Monckton was warned in advance that this would present potential difficulties, as live firings of Blue Streak from the UK had already been vetoed. Trial launches of the British missile would take place at the Long-Range Weapons Establishment at Woomera in Australia and provision would be made in the draft understanding that Thor, too, could be test-fired from Woomera if required. The ideas were viewed with interest as the deployment of Blue Streak was still some five years or so away and a US missile would give some coverage to this gap in the defences of the UK. Political difficulties were anticipated, but the RAF was increasingly concerned about shortcomings in the UK's all-weather fighter defence after 1958, and very quickly bargaining possibilities began to develop within UK minds. Certainly, when Prime Minister Anthony Eden had seen the minutes of the meeting, he commented:

> [...] is this not a chance for a quid pro quo. I thought we had plans for this. Please let me know.[18]

He possibly never got a reply.

Eden fell victim to the first of two events which were effectively to seal the deal on the placement of IRBMs on British soil. In July 1956 the Egyptian Government of President Gamal Abdel Nasser, intent on advancing the cause of pan-Arabism in the Middle East, nationalised the Suez Canal, an event which seriously prejudiced British military and economic interest in the region. In concert with France and Israel but, crucially, without informing the US, British forces invaded the canal area on 29 October. Operation MUSKATEER Revised was not fully supported by all the military chiefs, not properly carried out, but above all was a diplomatic disaster. Angered that the action had been taken without their knowledge, the US response was distinctly unfavourable. The USSR, keen to protect its growing interests in the Middle East, threatened to retaliate. Faced with this response and the threat of a run on sterling, Britain had to back down and suffer the consequent humiliation on the international stage. It was a brusque warning of US global influence, but it was also a costly lesson which would influence Britain's military planners for some time to come. The 'special relationship' between the UK and the US came under severe strain, reaching perhaps its lowest ebb. While events in Suez were grabbing world attention, the Soviet Union took the opportunity to invade Hungary on 4 November. Hungary had been showing worrying signs of failing to toe the Communist Party line. In the wake of Suez, Anthony Eden, who had waited in the wings for so long, to take over the premiership from Winston Churchill, was forced to resign owing to his failing health and political moves by R. A. (Rab) Butler and Harold Macmillan to oust him. His premiership had lasted a mere twenty-one months.

Although most people expected Butler to take over from Eden as Prime Minister, it was the quietly but ruthlessly ambitious Harold Macmillan who had acceded to Number 10 on 10 January 1957. So tenuous was the political situation in the country as a result of the Suez Crisis that he confided to the Queen that he could not guarantee that his Government would last six weeks.[19] But he was unduly pessimistic, and was in fact to head two successive Conservative Governments ultimately brought down by the unwise dalliances of his Secretary of State for War, John Profumo. The perceived representative of a bygone era in the British way of life, Macmillan was nonetheless an astute politician who was responsible for formulating future British nuclear policy. On taking office, his priority was to repair relations with the US. In this context it was fortunate that Macmillan already knew Eisenhower well, having acted as Churchill's liaison officer with the future President in North Africa during the Second World War when he was Minister Resident in the Mediterranean. The two had got on well together. Macmillan knew that despite the fiasco of Suez, a stable relationship between the two countries was essential to the integrity and authority of Britain within the NATO Alliance. America, aware that anti-US feeling in

Britain was significant, needed to reinforce the relationship which it viewed as vital to its own needs. The first rumblings of an anti-nuclear movement were starting to be heard and a public display of unity between the two nations was urgently required. Macmillan had appointed Duncan Sandys, Churchill's son-in-law, his Minister of Defence four days after he took office. With the emphasis on restoring good relations between the two countries, Sandys visited America between 28 January and 1 February for discussions on defence-related matters. On the afternoon of 29 January, Sandys met Secretary of State John Foster Dulles, who was keen to learn how the discussion on IRBMs had gone. Sandys replied that they had been very satisfactory, to which Dulles indicated that there were certain political aspects to any agreement that might be reached, particularly the conditions of use which might be attached to any such agreement. These would be of interest to Congress. Sandys responded that the warheads would be subject to similar controls to existing US nuclear bombs for RAF aircraft, but he cautioned that if the red tape surrounding the warheads became too complex, the deterrent value of the missiles risked being lost.[20] During this visit Sandys had seen a presentation that had earlier been given to the National Security Council (NSC) on 11 January. This covered the subject of ballistic missiles in general, including a discussion on possible deployment of IRBM units to the United Kingdom. However, at that time no decision was being sought as to the nature of such a deployment.

> [The] presentation was based upon the Thor missile, but it was pointed out that the final selection might be the Jupiter, for which approximately the same factors would apply. While no promises or commitments of any sort were made or sought on either side, the British [had] indicated that they [were] receptive to the whole concept.[21]

The NSC meeting further considered that, bearing in mind the urgency attached to establishing an IRBM capability, a programme to establish an IRBM capability in the UK should proceed as soon as possible. A proposed meeting between the President and newly appointed Prime Minister Macmillan at Bermuda in March would afford an excellent opportunity to finalise these details. Macmillan was therefore happy to accept this invitation to meet with Eisenhower.[22] By this time it appears that American support for Blue Streak was fast evaporating.

Over the next two months, sufficient progress had been made that a formal approach to the Foreign Office to start negotiations was recommended. By then the Americans had developed the operational concept to encompass ten sites. Nine of these were to be on existing USAF bases, and the tenth, a new site, would be built in the extreme north of Scotland, from which live firings could take place despite the indicated misgivings of the Air Ministry about such events. Construction work would begin in July 1957, with the first squadron operational by 1 January 1959.

During Sandys' visit to the US, he had taken with him a brief on the IRBM discussions from George Ward, Under-Secretary of State for Air. Unknown to most at the time, Sandys was formulating his thoughts on his forthcoming defence white paper in which missiles were to feature prominently and Blue Streak was a key component. Ward also advised that current thinking within the Ministry was that the American IRBMs should be manned and operated by British troops and that the necessary manpower should be found. A clear concern at the time was that the presence of missiles would make the UK a more attractive target. This would be true of both Blue Streak and Thor, but the reality was that the Soviet Union had almost certainly already saturated the UK in terms of targets. The Air Ministry wished to play this card because there was considerable concern that the continuing indecision on defence cuts was adversely affecting the RAF's defensive fighter capability.[23] Perhaps, however, there were too many political cards in play and quid pro quo arrangements, and Soviet targeting disappeared from the agenda (although the targeting issue was later taken up by CND activists). Both the Air Ministry and the Ministry of Supply agreed to consider the nature of the proposals so that there would be no unnecessary delay when the formal offer from the Americans arrived. Yet it seems that the American offer arrived somewhat quicker than had been expected, and consequently neither ministry had completed its examination or was prepared to make a specific recommendation. It was agreed, however, that while the advantages of taking Thor were obvious, the disadvantages needed to be examined. These were broadly: the range of the missile, which might be insufficient to reach certain desired targets—unless Britain developed its own warhead it would merely be operating a component of the American deterrent and a decision on the ability to produce a home-grown warhead could not be made until after the GRAPPLE tests;[24] the manpower involved, which might drain much needed capacity from other areas of the RAF; and finally, that Thor might interfere with the Blue Streak programme.[25] Clearly at this stage, growing US indifference towards Blue Streak had not been recognised or was being ignored.

The Sandys meeting was productive, although no commitment, financial or otherwise, was made by either side. It was also noted that no political considerations had been included, these being the subject of separate discussions. Sandys had been informed that such was the importance of deploying the missiles at the earliest possible date that a 'crash programme' had been considered. This programme would probably involve the use of contractor personnel and deployment of an experimental squadron of five missiles, subject to UK agreement, at a US air base in the United Kingdom as rapidly as possible. If decisions were taken soon it was hoped that such a squadron could be deployed by July 1958. This part of the programme would be fully paid for and wholly manned by the United States. Thereafter, four other sites would follow as rapidly as possible, the experimental squadron being disbanded as these became available. The first two would be constructed by the US and manned initially by US service personnel. It was hoped to have these operational by 1959. Meanwhile, the UK would undertake construction of the third and fourth sites with a view to bringing them into operation with British personnel at the earliest possible date. The target date for completing these would be December 1960, at which point the two US sites would be transferred to British control. While the cost of the missiles, their support, and spares—basically anything originating in the US—would be borne by the US, Britain would be responsible for acquiring and building the sites and all costs associated with this. Training would be undertaken in the US, with only subsistence costs borne by the UK.

On 14 February 1957, Sandys met with the French Minister of National Defence, M. Maurice Bourgès-Maunoury. Their discussions included the subject of missiles. Bourgès-

Maunoury confided that France had considered ballistic missiles and had deemed them too expensive, but as an alternative they were now considering an unmanned bomber.

All this was to provide a background to the March 1957 Bermuda Conference between MacMillan and Eisenhower. Internally, Washington was seeking guidance on the line to be taken on missiles. The Foreign Office had informed the Ambassador that 'subject to settlement of technical details between experts, we shall be glad to accept firm proposals for THOR.' M. J. Dean from the Air Ministry wrote to Sir Richard Powell, Deputy Secretary at the Ministry of Defence, 'I hope you don't mind me stressing how important it is that we should drive the hardest bargain we can with the U.S.'[26] Estimates—and they could at that stage have been only rough figures—indicated a manpower need of 3,000 personnel, a cost of UK-sourced equipment of £12 million, and unknown running costs: 'All this in order to enable the Americans to site here, and for many years to control the use of, a weapon which is useless if sited in the United States.'

Sandys knew that significant cuts had to be made in the armed forces—difficult but essential decisions that his predecessor seemed unable to make. He was unashamedly a supporter of the IRBM/MRBM, as indeed was MRAF Sir William Dickson, who as Chairman of the Chiefs of Staff Committee was moulding the shape of the V-force and supporting elements of which he saw Thor as being one.[27] MRAF Dickson's support for an IRBM, which he saw as a potentially cheap option, was partly at the expense of Blue Streak, in his opinion an expensive project which would divert funds from a projected supersonic bomber whose specification was covered by OR 330. Air Ministry concerns, however, lay in major part with the Gloster Javelin, a delta-winged, all-weather interceptor which was failing to live up to expectations to such an extent that the Americans had refused to pay for the 177 Javelins they had contracted under the off-shore purchase scheme. The Air Ministry saw the possibility of linking any forthcoming agreement on Thor to the supply of a suitable Javelin replacement. They had in mind either the Convair F106-B, a two-seat all-weather trainer which retained the operational capabilities of the single-seat F-106A and could therefore be adapted to RAF needs, or the Avro Canada CF-105 Arrow. There was considerable pressure from various directions to use Thor as a lever to acquire either of these interceptors. Convair, however, was already under immense pressure from its existing contracts with the USAF and was unlikely to welcome an extra commitment, even from a close ally. This focused attention on the Arrow, an aircraft that was being developed on a similar basis to concurrency with no prototype stage. Coincidentally, Avro Canada had already approached Britain with a view to selling them the Arrow, but was turned down on the basis of protection of 'national interest'. But just as Britain was living beyond its means on defence expenditure, so too was Canada, and the Arrow project was to end up summarily cancelled on 20 February 1959. Despite the robust words initially used in support of a *quid pro quo* arrangement, the idea quietly evaporated, although the reason why is not clear.

Still, Macmillan was a seasoned politician, and keen to use an IRBM agreement as a political tool to reinforce Anglo-US relations. In theory this may have seemed simple but with the number of different agencies that would progressively be drawn into the IRBM debate it was inevitable that a multitude of conflicting interests would soon become apparent. The

Bermuda Conference was therefore a key element in keeping relations on a steady course. It took place from 21 to 24 March 1957 at the Mid Ocean Club at Tucker's Town. Macmillan was accompanied by the Foreign Secretary, Selwyn Lloyd (retained by Macmillan despite his involvement with Suez), Sir Norman Brooke, Sir Richard Powell, and Patrick Dean, Deputy Undersecretary at the Foreign Office. Included in the wide-ranging agenda of items of mutual concern was the plan to place US IRBMs on UK soil. The IRBMs in question, whether Thor or Jupiter, were not at this stage identified, and in any case the US was still undecided on which missile to select. This would be a public display of military co-operation between the two countries and an overt countermove to the Soviet missile developments which were causing so much concern in the military intelligence community. While the UK delegation was enthusiastic about the proposal, Eisenhower was reticent in giving total commitment to the deployment. His administration was increasingly keen on fiscal prudence and Eisenhower himself was not totally committed to the IRBM programme, conscious that once Atlas was operational, the IRBMs would be effectively redundant—at least, from an American point of view.[28] Eisenhower was not even sure that the IRBMs would become operational, and perhaps a better piece of equipment might become available in the future. He further indicated his desire to refer only to 'guided missiles' and not specifically IRBMs. Had he been fully aware of the vital intelligence that Thor might gain as a satellite launch vehicle, he may have been more enthusiastic. Accordingly, the post conference communiqué stated,

> Agreement in principle [had been reached] that, in the interest of mutual defense and mutual economy, certain guided missiles will be made available by the United States for use by British forces.[29]

The detail of the offer was to be agreed later. This satisfied the State Department, but the lack of unity between State and Defence was exploited by Macmillan who presented a much more definite face to British interpretation of the discussions either through a possible misunderstanding of what had been agreed or, more plausibly, because Macmillan's political skills had allowed him to take the initiative.

Despite the agreement there were still a number of agencies with an interest in the actual outcome. The USAF was keen to establish improved nuclear capability at its forward bases in the UK and theirs was perhaps the most straightforward agenda. It was still extremely wary of the Army's ambitions in the wider sphere. The US State Department, however, was keen to limit the expansion of nuclear capability among its NATO allies and to take in a European-wide view of defence which could include a much wider deployment of IRBMs. But this implied control of the missiles being placed in the hands of SACEUR, a recurrent theme during the subsequent negotiations. This was not a path that the UK wished or was indeed prepared to follow. The State Department also believed that the money Britain was spending on Blue Streak—which was already lagging behind in technological terms and likely to worsen—could be better spent on other defence projects to the wider benefit of NATO. This debate further widened when Britain moved towards a greater reliance on nuclear weapons in its defence plans at the expense of conventional forces.

As far as Britain was concerned, any agreement would reinforce the 'special relationship', but while certainly to the benefit of Britain, this relationship was not so appreciated in the US. While Britain was considered its strongest and most reliable ally, this did not mean that their military interests were the same. Britain was also keen to establish a better nuclear relationship with the US, although the likelihood of giving Britain, let alone any other country, independent control over any US nuclear weapons in its arsenal was never going to happen.

The RAF, as we shall see, was divided on the subject of missiles in general. Blue Streak was being promoted as a future requirement but there was also a strong vote for manned aircraft for both defence and offence, a view supported by the head of the RAF. But Blue Streak, even if it enjoyed a trouble-free development programme—a somewhat unlikely prospect when the US missile programmes were looked at—was not going to come on-stream until the mid-1960s, by which time the V-force, which was significantly an independent UK deterrent, would have become vulnerable to Soviet air defences. Some considered that the US IRBMs were short on range for UK needs; hence Blue Streak's required range of 2,000 nm. The Americans were aware of this and reference was made by Holaday to a range of 2,000 nm in a meeting of the National Security Council on 10 October 1957.

> The President pointed out that the early NSC directives on the development of the US ballistic missiles program had emphasized that one of the first requirements was for the achievement of a workable intermediate range ballistic missile. If an attempt to develop an IRBM with a 2,000-mile range was slowing up the achievement of an IRBM with a 1500-mile range, [he] was altogether against it.[30]

But in RAF hands, an operational missile, even of 1,500-nm range, would provide valuable knowledge which could benefit Blue Streak. Incorporating IRBMs into its ORBAT would represent a significant manpower cost, but would provide a base of experienced personnel who could later move on to Blue Streak. Others, however, saw the IRBM as presenting a potential threat to Blue Streak's continued development. Nonetheless, missiles were very much the flavour of the month for Sandys. He was shortly to deliver to Parliament his defence white paper, entitled 'Defence: Outline of Future Policy', which took a radical view of Britain's defences.[31] It planned to give relief to the country's sorely strained economy and produce compact, all-regular forces of the highest quality. Fighter aircraft would be gradually replaced by air defence missiles, while

> British atomic bombs are already in steady production and the Royal Air Force holds a substantial number of them [perhaps a somewhat generous claim]. A British megaton weapon has now been developed. This will shortly be tested and thereafter a stock of them will be manufactured. The means of delivering these weapons is provided by medium bombers of the V-class whose performance in speed and altitude is equal to that of any bomber aircraft now in service in any other country.[32]

It also revealed that 'these will in due course be supplemented by medium-range ballistic rockets of the American Thor type, a substantial number of which have been offered to Britain by the United States.'[33] It is interesting to note that Thor was specifically identified, as at that stage the Americans had still not publically identified which missile would be destined for England. But although the defence budget could not be sustained at its previously high levels, the Chiefs of Staff were alarmed at what Sandys outlined. Then, on 11 June, an event took place which moved towards strengthening the arm of those ambivalent about Thor's future: the first Atlas Series A launch took place from LC-14 at Cape Canaveral. After twenty-four seconds the missile lost thrust before cart-wheeling to the destruct command of the RSO. Unsuccessful though it appeared to have been, the launch did, however, prove certain aspects of the airframe design. But missile technology remained high-risk and unreliable.

The second event which determined the Thor agreement was another launch far away, this one of even greater international importance than the failed Atlas. On 4 October 1957, the Soviet Union launched an R-7 Semyorka rocket from 'Site-1' at its remote Baikonur Cosmodrome in Kazakhstan.[34] The launch vehicle deposited in Earth's orbit the world's first artificial satellite, 'Sputnik-1'.[35] The lights in the Pentagon burned late into the night as the traumatised American nation faced Soviet superiority head-on. In fact, the warning signs had been seen by some Americans and, impressive though the achievement was, it did not indicate an immediate ICBM capability. Nonetheless, the world could see that the Soviet Union had the capability to launch a long-range missile. More significantly perhaps in military terms, it was immediately obvious that the shadowy Chief Designer Sergei Korolev had mastered the dynamics of guidance by placing Sputnik into a satisfactory pre-determined orbit. It was not thereafter a great technical leap forward to place a nuclear warhead anywhere on the Earth's surface. Shocked by this unexpected move which mocked US expertise in advanced technology, the only politically acceptable decision for the National Security Council was to endorse Holaday's recommendation to proceed further with both IRBM programs. This they did on 10 October, the day after Neil H. McElroy was sworn in as the sixth US Secretary of Defense. McElroy gave his endorsement on 31 October, instructing both Thor and Jupiter to go into production. He further indicated 31 December 1958 for the UK Thors to be at operational readiness. Once again the missile faced an ambitious timeline. Douglas was instructed to manufacture a maximum of six missiles per month to support a four-squadron IOC.[36] Although the Sputnik launch had appeared to give ample proof that the Soviets had ICBM capability, it was in fact an understandable misinterpretation of the real Soviet capability (although the USAF in particular used it to further the Missile Gap argument). On 28 August, just thirty-eight days before the Sputnik launch, a high-flying U-2 reconnaissance aircraft had returned with an IMINT photograph of the Site-1 launch pad which provided Eisenhower with evidence that the Soviet Union did not as yet present an ICBM threat to the US. The CIA-sponsored Lockheed U-2s, developed under the codename 'Project Aquatone', flew at above 70,000 feet, above all Soviet air defence capability. All flights were part of Operation Overflight and were individually authorised by the President. The programme was a derivative part of a 'Sensitive Security' (SENSINT) programme authorised by the President in early 1954. The resulting photography was divided into two theatres of operations, CHESS (European) and CHURCHDOOR (Asian). Intelligence of this type was top-secret and, despite the evidence it produced, could not be the subject of a public announcement. Whatever the reality of actual Soviet capability, the public perception was quite clear. It was a body blow to US morale and sent ripples of concern throughout western nations.

Eisenhower's public response was muted—too muted for many who were unaware of the secret programmes that were being developed and were in many cases well ahead of the Soviets—and ill-advisedly dismissed Sputnik as little more than a publicity stunt. He was accused by his political opponents of putting fiscal budgets before the defence of the US.[37] The American people were not satisfied and demanded that something be done to restore confidence. It was not a time to pull back on technological programs of any nature whatsoever, and this included IRBMs. To demonstrate US capability Assistant SecAF for Research and Development, Richard E. Horner, requested that the Department of Defense approve a space programme that would furnish an early demonstration of space capability and 'provide important development test vehicles leading to larger reconnaissance and scientific satellites.' Three Thor missiles, T114, T116, and T118, 'could be made available in a relatively short period of time with minimum interference to the IRBM program.' These boosters could be used to orbit a recoverable animal satellite prior to 1 July 1958. Thor, it was also suggested, would be a practical vehicle to furnish the Air Force satellites with specific military capabilities.[39] On 10 October the NSC met to discuss the 'Implications of the Soviet Earth Satellite for US Security'. Despite the advent of Sputnik—or arguably because of it—Holaday reported that it was still impossible to make a choice between Thor and Jupiter. Eisenhower cautioned Holaday to

> [...] watch [the] problem of inter-service rivalry all the time. The objective of the program was not to achieve a missile which a particular service desired, but instead to achieve the most efficient missile system. The President felt that such matters as deployment, the character of the ground installations, methods of employment desired by the different military services, and similar matters, were completely secondary to the determination by the United States to fire a 1,500-mile missile and hit something.[40]

Meanwhile, the ever astute Macmillan saw the launch of Sputnik as a lever towards achieving The Great Prize—the relaxation of the McMahon Agreement on the exchange of nuclear information. Indeed, wasting no time, in a memo dated three days after the Sputnik launch Sandys wrote to Sir Richard Powell:

> The launching of the Soviet satellite has produced a powerful psychological shock in America; and this is bound to cast doubts in their minds about the wisdom of continuing to refuse co-operation with us in the nuclear field.[41]

Through the Embassy in Washington Macmillan sought to test the US reaction to the event. Sir Harold Caccia responded that Secretary of State Dulles

> [...] did not believe it had much military significance, although the Russians were trying to make political use of their Russian scientific achievement [...] there was an element

of bluff in the Soviet attitude. They had probably decided to skip a stage in their weapon production.

Dulles did not believe the Russians would produce ICBMs in quantity for some time. That left a gap, he thought, of some five years, during which the Russians would be in a position of comparative weakness.[42] Nonetheless, political pressure would determine that a significant and visible response would have to be made to re-establish US confidence in itself. Notwithstanding all this, the continuing indecision over 'which missile' still acted as a backdrop. On 28 December 1957, Killian reported back to Eisenhower on the status of the various US missile programs. He acknowledged that the US was behind the Soviets, principally because the country started later and not because of inferior technology. He reflected on the much publicised flight failures that seemed by some to typify US efforts, but these, he said, were

[…] normal and unavoidable occurrences in the development of complex mechanisms, many functions of which can only be tested in flight […] the development programs of the IRBM are moving ahead very rapidly. There have been flights of both JUPITER and THOR which were complete technical successes. The regular production of IRBM's [sic] is soon to begin.[43]

On 4 February 1958, Killian reiterated his belief that only one IRBM should go ahead. He declared a preference for Thor, not because it was necessarily better, but because its progress was nearer quantity production—a possible vindication of the concurrency concept.[44] However, a classified USAF memo about the situation had been leaked and the contents, though based on planning assumptions only, had led to speculation about the relative status of Thor and Jupiter development. This memo proposed that the previously promulgated deployment of four Thor and four Jupiter squadrons be revised to nine Thor and three Jupiter squadrons. This by default suggested a closed contract for Jupiter and an open-ended contract for Thor, placing the UK deployment on a much firmer footing. The Pentagon was annoyed, believing this to be essentially an example of bad reporting. However, the British Joint Services Mission (BJSM) in Washington—from their viewpoint closer to the US end of things—suggested that it could be turned into an advantage:

[…] with assistance from our US opposite numbers it should be possible to leak the new THOR proposals to a suitable pressman (and I have in mind Chapman Pincher)[45]. I am discussing the possibilities of doing this with Brigadier Hobbs.[46]

Ultimately, continued US indecision was to lead to an unwanted stockpile of Jupiters, putting pressure on the State Department to find a place to deploy them, which resulted in an ill-judged and unsatisfactory placement in Italy and Turkey.[47] Unforeseen at the time, this later weakened the US position in arms limitation talks and was to lead indirectly to the Cuban Missile Crisis.

By late April 1958, the National Security Council approved the decision which finally achieved Thor's ascendancy over Jupiter, when production of the Douglas missile was increased and Jupiter production curtailed to the three squadrons to be based in Europe. By then it was known that the Thors would come to Britain, but the Jupiter basing was still to be settled. This was not entirely the victory which the Air Force sought. It wanted full cancellation of the Jupiter contract: 'The Air Force [had] long argued that more IRBMs could be turned out at lower total cost if production [was] confined to the Thor.'[48] On 2 March 1958, *The New York Times* quoted an authoritative source as claiming that the Air Force expected to have Thor combat-ready by June, if not earlier. The source also revealed that the Pentagon was hatching plans to base further Thors in Alaska and Libya, and that it eagerly awaited confirmation of Thor's readiness, for it would redress the imbalance that was the current missile gap with the Soviet Union. At this stage the first operational squadron was still planned to come under RAF, as opposed to USAF, Command by December 1959, but it seemed increasingly unlikely that this deadline would be met.[49] A no doubt innocently made, but ill-judged remark by McElroy further exacerbated the situation. At a news conference at the Pentagon on 8 May 1958, a seasoned *Newsweek* correspondent, Lloyd Norman, asked him to comment on the technical bugs that were affecting Thor and Jupiter. He replied, 'the only thing I can tell you is that it has to do with certain parts of the propulsion system,' and the *Daily Express* duly reported, 'the Thor missile has faults and needs further testing'—a comment quickly picked up by the anti-Thor lobby.[50] At the same press conference, Charles Corddry of *United Press* had further enquired whether there were plans to increase Thor production, cut back on Jupiter, or terminate the Jupiter programme altogether. McElroy answered that nothing had changed since the 'decision made during the previous December to proceed with the production of both missiles, as there was not a sufficiently clear answer to the development programme of both missiles.' He was therefore at that time still unwilling to place an exclusive bet on the success of either missile. BJSM reported from Washington to the MoD that it was not, in their opinion,

> [...] sufficiently clear as to which one, if either, [was] the one on which to make an exclusive bet for us to do anything more than we have determined to do, which is to make a planning exercise on certain assumptions, now, what apparently has happened is that a classified memorandum setting up certain bases for this planning exercise has found its way out of departmental channels into someone's hands and the only thing that [we] can say is that this is a classified memorandum; it suggests certain assumptions for planning purposes only.[51]

All this was somewhat confusing, and at variance with the advice of Dr Killian's President's Science Advisory Committee (PSAC), which had already firmly argued against the continuation of both programmes. The SecDef nonetheless refused to accept this recommendation. He was 'not yet ready to resolve this needless competition between the Army and the Air Force.'[52] But to all intents and purposes, the decision had been made. Thor would be the selected missile.

The Thor Agreement—
Substance and Interpretation

It is interesting to note that the Bermuda Joint Statement made specific reference to the guided missiles being available 'for use by British Forces.' This is clearly not what Strategic Air Command (SAC) had in mind. SAC bombers operated out of US bases in Britain, and the thinking was that SAC IRBMs would operate on a similar basis, secure within a US base on English soil, but perhaps as part of a linked SAC/Bomber Command strike force. The understanding that there was 'the intention of ultimate transfer to the RAF as soon as our own longer range ballistic missiles are available' evidenced some degree of flexibility.[1] The wish to use existing US facilities was understandable, but some of these potential sites were inland, and from the start the British expressed a wish that the missiles be sited as close to the coast as possible. Not only would that put them closer to the target and effectively increase their range, but it would also minimise the time spent flying over the English countryside with the attendant risk to the population in the event of an accident. Bermuda gave the authority to deal formally with the question of basing the missiles and the US view was put forward when Major-General John P. McConnell, Director of Plans for Headquarters SAC, visited the UK from 27 to 29 June 1957 and gave the Ministry of Defence full operational details of what was at that stage planned.[2] The ground for these discussions had been prepared in advance when Sandys had written to Wilson the previous week,

> [...] we warmly welcome your proposal. We much appreciate the spirit in which you have made it and we are confident that this project will make a valuable addition to the strength of the Western Alliance.[3]

Sandys confirmed that the draft proposal was acceptable to the UK as a basis for detailed negotiation, although there were several matters of policy and detail which would require further discussion. However, a damper was put on the impending talks two days later, when George Ward wrote to Sandys with reference to the proposed timeline of events which showed the Americans flying in the first missile at the end of August.

> You and I both made statements in the House intimating that by the time the weapons were deployed they would be an effective addition to the deterrent. We certainly could not make such a claim at the moment without being confronted by the known results of American test

launchings to date. The Air Ministry understand from American sources that the series of test launchings which will enable the performance and reliability of the weapon to be established will not in fact be completed until August, 1959. It would be reasonable to accept some missiles before they are proven for testing the installations which are now under construction. But it may well be 12 months before we are able to point to a series of successful test launchings as proof of operational performance of the weapon for deployment in RAF squadrons. This is too long a period to explain away by reference to the need to test ground installations.[4]

However, Thor's track record threatened to become its Achilles heel. The Chiefs of Staff remained unconvinced and at their meeting on 29 January expressed concern that the UK could find itself committed to an unsatisfactory weapon.[5] They also raised the question of SACEUR's control of IRBMs deployed in European countries, citing the dangers of the possible misuse of what was a strategic weapon as a tactical weapon and also the profound difficulties of gaining the approval of fifteen Governments to allow use of the weapon. They did, however, concede that this problem may be overcome if European missiles were under the control of General Norstad as a national commander and not as SACEUR. But the view on the UK IRBMs was quite clear: they must be treated as a supplement to the RAF's Medium Bomber Force with a UK right to veto their launching.

On 7 November 1957, Eisenhower received a report from the Security Resources Panel of the ODM-SAC on 'Deterrence and Survival in the Nuclear Age'.[6] In an Appendix headed 'An Early Missile Capability', it was noted that

> The early acquisition by SAC of an ICBM capability and the implementation of an IRBM capability overseas will greatly increase this country's offensive posture and deterrent strength.

Furthermore, with an early decision, a major effort, some extra funding, and some intensive training, it was considered possible to have one squadron be operational by the last quarter of 1958 and a full deployment of sixteen squadrons be in place by the end of 1960. This implied a total of 240 IRBMs.[7] This number remained somewhat fluid. Exactly a month later *The Daily Telegraph* was able to report under the heading 'Four Missile Squadrons for British Isles—Anglo-American Agreement',

> The United States and Britain have agreed to establish four squadrons of I.R.B.M. missiles in [the] British Isles. The cost of building the site[s] is estimated at £30M to be borne largely by Britain. Three of the squadrons will be British and the fourth will come under the USAF. This became known today as Mr McElroy, Secretary of Defense, left New York by 'plane for talks in London.'

The article furthermore claimed that the first squadron had been promised by the end of 1958. This idea had been discussed in general terms during the first meeting between Powell and Quarles.

From the Air Ministry viewpoint this was out of the question, on the basis of any American ideas about THOR so far considered. This has been made plain to the Ministry of Defence, who indeed have never been in doubt about it. It is however conceivable that the Americans will have some kind of crash programme to propose.[8]

From the start there had been a significant difference in how the two countries envisaged the dispersal of the Thor bases. The USAF favoured a concentrated deployment with all fifteen missiles of one squadron in the same place. Initially they had even considered concentrating the missiles on one or possibly two significantly large sites. They envisaged four USAF squadrons and four RAF squadrons fielding 120 missiles—although this was soon halved to sixty missiles in four squadrons. The USAF squadrons would be the 672nd, 673rd, 674th, and 675th Strategic Missile Squadrons. The first two RAF squadrons would initially be manned by US personnel, while the third and fourth squadrons were manned by RAF crews from the start. The RAF would subsequently take over the first two squadrons.[9] The USAF particularly favoured Sturgate and East Kirby, where they already had a presence. The RAF, which envisaged eventually controlling all the sites, had from the start shied away from centralised and thereby essentially vulnerable sites, and rejected both airfields. They considered that there were insufficient nearby sites to provide a network of dispersed sites when they took over from the USAF, and the road network was completely inadequate for the bases to be used as the central maintenance and domestic sites for a dispersed complex. Furthermore, domestic accommodation at both sites did not conform to contemporary RAF requirements and an upgrade was considered to be prohibitively expensive. Notwithstanding these factors, Sturgate would in the fullness of time be used as an accommodation facility. Instead the RAF offered Hemswell and Feltwell. Both were stations with substantial brick-built hangars suitable for conversion into the RIM Building and Technical Stores. At this stage, too, they envisaged the nearby RAF Methwold being used as an additional site in support of Feltwell. The existing nature of these two stations would allow the necessary works services to be achieved in line with the US deployment schedule for the first squadrons. The Ministry of Works had made a provisional costing in September 1957 for both concentrated and dispersed deployments, and total cost worked out at £7.15 million for either method of deployment. At this time in early 1958, the operational date had slipped but the plan was still for the first two squadrons to be manned by USAF crews and only later handed over to the RAF as follows:

First squadron forms July 1960—handed over to the RAF in January 1962
Second squadron forms November 1960—handed over to the RAF in June 1962
Third squadron forms March 1961 (RAF manned)
Fourth squadron forms July 1961 (RAF manned)

But the caveat to all this was that, to ensure these dates, LOX tanks would have to be ordered immediately (in January 1958), a generating plant by March, and work started in the late spring.[10] This at best seemed an ambitious target and most large projects had a habit of slipping. But it was a timeline that both sides then seemed to find acceptable. Things were in due course to change, as the Americans sought once again to bring forward the start date by a considerable margin and the question of the first two squadrons being US-manned brought serious political problems.

From these, at times tentative beginnings a deployment plan emerged which provided for four squadrons each consisting of five sites located on active or disused airfields belonging to the Air Ministry in Norfolk, Lincolnshire, and Yorkshire. The final choice of sites would depend on the results of a detailed survey. The concluding agreement indicated that the first squadron would be operational between July and December 1958, the second by mid-1959, and the remaining two by March 1960.

Once again Thor was the subject of a very ambitious timeline. No sites had been identified or surveys conducted; no contract tenders had been issued for the site construction; no personnel had been selected, let alone any training programme drawn up. And yet, an initial operational date in the second half of 1958 had, it seemed, now been agreed. There were also a number of secret provisions within the agreement which were not to be made public, and would be the subject of a private exchange of letters between the two countries. These would outline the duration of the project and an understanding of the allocation of responsibilities.

The US would provide, at its own expense and in a quantity appropriate to five years of operation: the missiles, training missiles, training facilities, specialised equipment, spare parts, modification kits, and modified components and assemblies. The UK would provide, at its expense: land, appropriately prepared sites and supporting facilities—including utilities, buildings, and other fixed installations—and supporting equipment—including such items of common ground support equipment for units and bases as may be agreed upon, and such items of a technical nature as may be agreed should be produced in the UK.

Regarding the financing of the project, it was understood that funds already earmarked for the UK in support of the RAF's Plan K would, wherever practicable, be utilised. While most of these secret provisions may seem relatively innocuous, the five-year-term of the agreement should be noted. This provision was not widely known at the time, as would become apparent later.

Despite the degree of work already done, the Air Ministry at its highest level remained culturally resistant to the IRBM proposals. The RAF's senior officers had served in a war where aircraft had, in their view at least, reigned supreme, albeit for Churchill's reluctance to publically recognise the contribution made by Bomber Command—which still rankled with many. To downgrade the functions of air defence and bombing to batteries of missiles was not the way ahead. Considerable funds were being invested in the V-force bombers: the Vickers Valiant, Avro Vulcan, and Handley Page Victor. The supersonic English Electric Lightning was to be the backbone of Fighter Command. Manned aircraft and their future would remain uppermost in the minds of these senior officers. Chief of the Air Staff MRAF Sir Dermot Boyle wrote a note in January 1958, 'on the unsatisfactory state of affairs which now exists regarding the establishment of American IRBMs (THOR) in this country.'[11] He claimed that the Ministry saw itself being rushed into an agreement which largely benefitted the Americans rather than the British, and which was being concluded with insufficient concessions by the Americans for the privilege of basing their missiles on UK soil, one of the few countries where they could be operationally effective. He cited as his objections: lack of control over the warheads, overall costs—both financial and in terms of personnel—vulnerability of the sites, unreliability of the trial missiles already launched, and finally the possibility, still unresolved, that the missiles would be assigned to SACEUR. This latter condition, while politically reconcilable, was militarily anathema to the RAF. Such differences inevitably made for difficulties in presenting a united front by both nations. In February 1958 the British ambassador in Washington, Sir Harold Caccia, whose appointment had been occasioned to repair the post-Suez relationship, signalled the Foreign Office:

> The Americans have given careful thought to the Saceur issue. They emphasise strongly that they have no desire to see this issue raised, still less to allow any sign of difference between us to emerge. In these circumstances they would expect the decision to place the missiles under Bomber Command to be a United Kingdom decision, which it would be for Sir Frank Roberts [UK Permanent Representative on the North Atlantic Council] to defend. If Mr Burgess[12] were questioned he would point out that the agreement with us had preceded the December NATO meeting. [...] So far as he would be concerned, the less said the better. But the United States could not go so far as to state that there is an understanding between us to the effect that the missiles will not be placed under Saceur. The State Department also fear, of course, that they may be asked straight out whether they have ever suggested to us that the missile be committed to Saceur.[13]

In practice, the SACEUR issue was more a fear in the minds of the two nations than a reality. The UK stuck to its declared position and the issue gradually receded. Of far greater impact was the basic acceptance of the missiles and deriving from this the question of their warheads. As regards the operational use of the missiles, this would be a matter of joint decision between the two countries, but the nuclear warheads would, in accordance with United States law, remain in American custody and under American control. The missiles could therefore not be considered an 'independent' British nuclear deterrent, a recurring political theme in the years to come—not only in the context of Thor, but also subsequently over the Polaris missile system and its successor, Trident. The warheads, however, would always be in a fully assembled state and would normally be permanently positioned on the missiles. There would be a number of safety features incorporated in the design to prevent an inadvertent nuclear activation.

But words of caution still came from the very top levels of the RAF. MRAF Boyle was advised by the Air Council:

> [...] so far only 10 THOR missiles have been fired with the complete assembly and none of them have been fully successful. It is estimated that the weapon has progressed 25 per cent of the way to operational effectiveness and yet a production order has been placed for

147 missiles. The deduction is that these weapons will be wholly unreliable and will require extensive and costly modification. It is by no means clear if the modification programme will be adequate and how it will be financed.[14]

Boyle had flown with Bomber Command during the war and his previous appointment had been AOCinC Fighter Command. A committed believer in the efficacy of manned warplanes, it was perhaps inevitable that he should seek to counter, at least in part, Sandys's move towards a missile-led RAF, an idea which he believed had 'come out of Sandys [sic] head.'[15] Recognising an impending 'done deal' when he saw it and aware of the increasingly parlous financial state of the service, Boyle was not, as has sometimes been portrayed, wholly against missiles *per se*. He did, however, stress that the missiles should be accepted only on one of the following conditions: either that the missiles be treated on similar lines to the US bombers stationed in the UK, financed by the US but under joint control, or that, if the proposed joint funding arrangements were accepted, both weapon and warhead would have no strings attached and would be completely under British control.[16] In saying this he must have known that the last option was unlikely ever to be allowed under US law. MRAF Boyle was, in the end, supportive of Thor, which he saw as a necessity in keeping up to technological par, particularly in view of the role that would be played by Blue Streak when it entered service with the RAF in the mid-1960s. The deal just had to be on the right terms. But the quality of the missile based on the initial test firings results remained a stumbling block. These concerns were further reinforced by a memo to Sandys from the Chiefs of Staff, who were concerned

> [...] that we may find ourselves committed to an unsatisfactory weapon. This point was also made to you by Sir Richard Powell in his recent minute of 27th January.[17]

The Chiefs of Staff were also energised over control of the missile as the SACEUR issue once again was raised. At their December meeting the Atlantic Council had recorded: 'In view of the present Soviet policies in the field of new weapons, the Council has decided that the IRBMs will have to be put at the disposal of SACEUR.' Supreme Headquarters Allied Powers Europe (SHAPE) was planning its disposition of IRBMs and DSACEUR Field Marshal Bernard Montgomery—not noted for his political savvy and about to retire from his albeit illustrious military career—had advised that SACEUR saw the missiles as an adjunct to his forces and would use them accordingly. The Chiefs were culturally averse to any such restrictions being placed on the UK missiles which, they believed, should be targeted jointly by SAC and Bomber Command. They cited as principal objections: that the missiles could be used tactically in support of NATO ground forces, and the conundrum that, unless SACEUR was delegated authority to use them, it would be necessary to obtain agreement from fifteen Governments, which to all intents and purposes negated their military credibility. They did, however, concede a scenario whereby General Norstad as US CinC Europe could control and coordinate the use of the weapons, which seems in part at least a *volte face*. But overall they saw a scenario whereby the UK at great expense would be forced to accept a weapon which was untried operationally, of as yet proven unreliability non-operationally, and highly vulnerable to attack. It increased the attractiveness of the UK as a target at a time when the UK's air defences were being reduced and, despite the considerable burden to the UK defence budget, the only control the UK would have over the weapon was the negative one of veto. While contributing to the Western deterrent, it would in no way contribute to UK nuclear independence. But, no doubt accepting that the agreement was already in train, the British senior staff declared in summary that the weapons should be accepted if they were treated 'similarly to US bomber units stationed in this country, i.e. that they be financed, manned and operated by the USA, but can only be launched by joint agreement between the two countries.'[18] It has to be remembered, too, that among them was the powerful Lord Mountbatten of Burma, who never missed an opportunity to manoeuvre the pro-naval vote towards custody of the deterrent and away from the RAF. Inter-service rivalry was in full swing on the British side of the Atlantic.

These objections were all very well, and the issues raised justifiable, but it was in reality too late to reverse the situation. On 17 February DCAS Air Marshal Sir Geoffrey Tuttle was able to inform Sandys that 'we appear to be on the verge of a satisfactory understanding with the Americans,'[19] and on that basis, the Thor programme was finally ratified on 21 February 1958 by the laying before Parliament of a document entitled 'Supply of Ballistic Missile to the United Kingdom by the United States'. The document, originally somewhat tersely entitled 'Intermediate Range Ballistic Missiles', was subject to a number of drafts during which Sandys liberally exercised his red pen. However, what the agreement did confirm was that the missile in question was the Douglas Thor and that

> The squadrons would be manned and operated by the Royal Air Force as soon as sufficient officers and men had been trained in America; if missiles were ready for deployment before this stage had been reached, the United States Air Force would man some of the squadrons until the RAF were ready to take them over. The Americans would provide the missiles and specialised equipment free of cost; Great Britain would meet the cost of constructing the sites.

So that in the space of little more than a month there was a subtle move towards RAF manning from the start—if at all possible. The main published elements of the agreement confirmed that: the Americans would supply the missiles and specialised equipment and would provide appropriate training of British personnel in the United States. Britain would provide the sites and certain supporting facilities, such as communications, the capital cost of which was estimated at about £10 million, although this was a figure subject to revision. In return for this, the US took over a dollar commitment roughly equal to the purchase of Corporal SSMs for the British Army.[20] These would now be provided free of cost under the Military Assistance Programme. At the press conference after the parliamentary announcement, Sandys left no one in any doubt about his commitment to the project. Construction of the missile sites would start soon and training of the RAF crews delegated to operate the missiles would begin almost at once. '[There was] certainly a possibility that the first Thor launching sites [would] be installed in this country before the end of the year,' Sandys said.[21] They had been much public speculation about where the missiles would be based and Sandys to some degree answered the question by stating that the bases would mainly be in East Anglia, Lincolnshire, and Yorkshire. He quelled concerns about the possibility of bases being established in Scotland by confirming that there would be no bases north of the Border. Rumours about Scottish bases had been circulating for some time and had generated much constituency correspondence in the areas deemed to be affected. This was possibly a result of the original US plans for a test facility in the extreme North West, but some information surrounding the intention to base the first Blue Streak squadron at the former Royal Naval Air Station at Crail may have contributed to the speculation.[22] Such was this speculation about the siting of missiles in Scotland that when the Scottish Secretary of State, John Maclay, gave an 'off-the-record' briefing to the editors of the main Scottish newspapers in February 1958, authority was sought from the MoD to confirm that, although no firm decisions had been reached on locations, the editors were not to assume that there would not be any such bases in Scotland.[23] Sandys refused to be drawn in on the number of missiles, or indeed the number of bases:

> Of course people will see these sites, but they won't know if they have seen them all. It is a well-established principle of security to let foreign intelligence services work for themselves and not hand them information on a plate.[24]

Regardless of his words, many people, including James Harrison, MP for Nottingham North, appeared to believe that a declaration about Scottish bases had already been made. Harrison raised the issue of basing during the defence debate in Parliament on 5 March. Ward denied that such a declaration had ever been made and confirmed what Sandys had said the previous week; that the bases

> [...] would be dispersed throughout Yorkshire, Lincolnshire and East Anglia. That has always been the plan and it still remains so.[25]

Marcus Kimball, MP for Gainsborough, added helpfully: 'from a farming point of view, a rocket base takes up less land, there is no noise from practice flying and there is no more danger than from the present Air Force bases.'[26]

Progress then began in earnest. At the invitation of Major-General William H. (Butch) Blanchard,[27] Commander of 7AD, a party of twelve senior RAF officers and representatives from the Air Ministry arrived at Offutt AFB on 17 March 1958 for a three-week visit to various Thor-related facilities. The purpose was to provide a greater understanding of the weapon system and the facilities it would require. The delegation was led by Air Commodore John H. Searby DFC, Director of Operations (Bombing and Reconnaissance),[28] although after Air Commodore Searby's unscheduled recall to London, Group Captain Patrick Sands MBE DFC (DDO1) was instructed to take over.[29] Sands was to be appointed OC RAF North Luffenham on 9 September 1959.

So by this stage, the final parameters of the deployment were largely known and agreed. Sixty missiles would be sited at twenty bases. It was time to search for suitable sites. On the face of it this should not have been difficult. The eastern counties of England were liberally covered with the RAF stations from where Bomber Command and the US Eighth and Ninth Army Air Forces had conducted the bombing campaign against Nazi Germany. Many of these were still in use, but a number, though they had reverted to other uses, were still in reasonable condition. The first proposal was to use Class 1 airfields. This caused AOCinC Bomber Command Air Chief Marshal Sir Harry Broadhurst consternation, but by the time he expressed his concerns to DCAS Air Marshal Sir Geoffrey Tuttle, the idea had already been dropped and he had been given the assurance of his involvement in the future planning stage.[30] An initial siting plan (see the figure on p. 58) showed four groups of five sites each (in each case the first site was chosen as the Main Base for the Group with the others being termed Satellite Units).[31] Each group of sites would constitute a squadron. The satellite sites would be called 'Flights'. This was later changed to give all sites autonomous squadron status. Each group of sites was seen as constituting a wing.[32]

Group 1	Feltwell, Marham, Watton, Honington, Witchford
Group 2	Hemswell, Caistor, Ludford Magna, Bardney, Waddington
Group 3	Driffield, Full Sutton, Leconfield, Holme-on-Spalding-Moor, Riccall
Group 4	Dishforth, Scorton, Leeming, Marston Moor, Sherburn-in-Elmet

Interestingly, with the exception of the Dishforth Group, this plan conforms fairly closely to the final list of twenty chosen stations. The inclusion of Witchford in the first group was at the request of the Americans and a detailed layout plan was even drawn, but as the land was owned by the Church Commissioners it was deemed prudent to replace it with nearby Mepal. Consideration also had to be given to the road network connecting the outlying sites with the wing headquarters.[33] Any variation in the road gradient of more than one in seventeen was considered a potential grounding hazard to the missile transporter. There is also evidence in official correspondence that there was now a tacit acceptance, though not perhaps universally approved, of US involvement as the pressure to field operational missiles was clearly urgent and full training of RAF personnel had to take place before any RAF units could operate the missiles. By this stage as well, a draft set of operational dates had been set for the twenty sites:

The First Squadron: (Norfolk area)
Feltwell, Honington, Witchford, Marham, Watton—between 1/7/58 and 31/12/58.

The Second Squadron: (Lincolnshire area)
Helmswell, Caistor, Ludford Magna, Waddington, Bardney—between 1/1/59 and 30/6/59.

The Third Squadron: (E. Yorkshire area)
Driffield, Full Sutton, Holme-on-Spalding Moor, Riccall, Leconfield—by 30/10/59.

The Fourth Squadron: (E. Yorkshire area)
Dishforth, Scorton, Leeming, Marston Moor, Sherburn-in-Elmet—by 31/3/60.

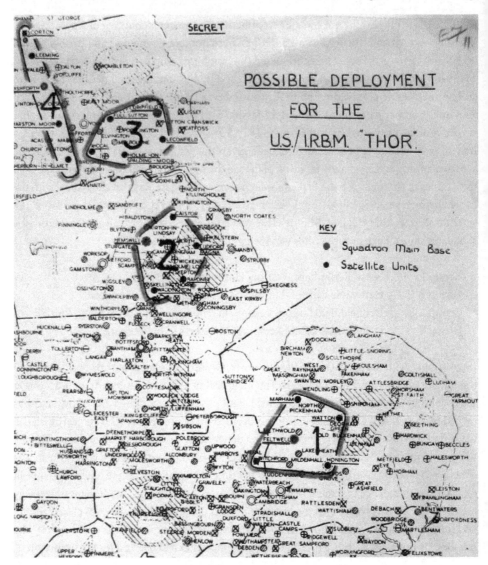

It was noted that

> [...] it would not be practicable to keep secret the existence and location of the Thor sites.
> But we want to keep secret the reason for the choice of particular sites and certain technical
> features of the sites, especially the arrangements for the operational control of the weapons.
> At the moment we do not tell Parliament the detailed deployment pattern of the bomber force
> although we do not prevent the local press from talking about their nearby bomber station.[34]

However, the growing anti-nuclear lobby were never going to help keep the location of the sites
secret. In June 1959, the *Daily Express* revealed that the Air Ministry were studying a document
distributed by an anti-nuclear group identifying, correctly, the sites of the Driffield Wing.[35]

Further consideration of the proposed sites revealed that radar scatter in the Yorkshire dales could be a problem and a search was made for a suitable replacement for the Dishforth group. This was found in a group of sites based on North Luffenham with outlying sites at Harrington, Polebrook, Melton Mowbray, and Folkingham. This group was possibly not ideal as it extended west into Northamptonshire and would require the missiles to fly over populated areas, but no satisfactory alternative could be found.

Having now consolidated the deployment plan, before the final layouts were agreed it was necessary to link the sites dispersal with the target list. With a range of 1,500 nm, only a percentage of the desired targets were ever going to be within range and within that target list, even those targets covered would be further governed by the alignment of the pads. Inherent in any fixed ballistic missile system is the problem of achieving optimum target coverage by staggering the pad orientation, dispersing the pads to ensure maximum survivability in the event of attack, and allocating primary and secondary targets. Once set there is only a limited amount of azimuth freedom. Targets comprised cities, with Moscow considered an essential target, and a selection of secondary targets covering defensive airfields, missile sites, and command and control centres, accepting, however, that the accuracy of the missile would only be appropriate for relatively large target areas. The original plan for pad orientation relative to north was:

Feltwell	60 degrees
Hemswell	78 degrees
Driffield	42 degrees
North Luffenham	68 degrees

This was initially considered to be the best orientation to give maximum target coverage, though it was not perfect: there was poor coverage of targets in the middle and too great a coverage of the northern targets, but more seriously, bad coverage of the southern targets.

Strategically, NATO planners had identified a total of 525 strategic targets of varying importance and vulnerability to ballistic missile attack. Although some of these were beyond the IRBM's 1,500-nm range, some 450 could realistically be reached if additional launch sites in NATO countries were established. However, only certain counties were considered likely to be politically agreeable to the basing of missiles on their territories. In addition to the UK, those expected to be willing to take the missiles were identified as West Germany, France, Italy, and Turkey. These countries could cover 440 of the 450 targets. Of these West Germany was considered too sensitive to be included, whereas Turkey was the least likely to be affected by political veto. Although there were advantages in basing IRBMs in Scandinavian countries, political considerations there were deemed to be adverse to such a plan. The target coverage afforded by the four countries was as follows:

UK	(West Germany)	France	Italy	Turkey	Targets covered	% of 450 covered
✓		✓	✓	✓	425	94%
✓				✓	420	93%
✓		✓	✓		380	84%
✓		✓			360	80%
✓					340	76%

In the end of course, both West Germany and a recalcitrant France had to be excluded, leaving the final Thor and Jupiter IRBM deployment thus: sixty in the UK, thirty in Italy, and fifteen in Turkey, which provided good coverage, if ultimately restricted by the total number of missiles available. By the time that this seems to have been fully realised, the construction of Feltwell and Hemswell was too far advanced to make any alterations to the orientation, but it was not too late to alter the latter two wings, which were accordingly changed to:

Driffield and Full Sutton	retained at 42 degrees
Carnaby	55 degrees
Catfoss	60 degrees
Breighton	70 degrees
Harrington and Folkingham	75 degrees
Melton Mowbray	80 degrees
North Luffenham and Polebrook	85 degrees

The relative improvement in coverage by changing the orientation is outlined in Appendix 7. As there were concurrent deliberations taking place over the possible sites for Blue Streak bases, a cautionary note was added—'the experience with Thor illustrates the need for careful planning to provide the launcher orientation to give the maximum target cover and flexibility.'[36]

Notwithstanding all this, the design and layout of the sites had then to be agreed. Douglas provided an outline of what was required based on its boilerplate site at Culver City, but it lay with the Air Ministry to define the requirement and to design the final layout, launch pads and ancillary needs for an operational site in a UK context. The responsibility for turning the outline into a final design was given to Rowland Hall, who after serving in the Royal Navy had studied architecture and civil engineering before joining the Air Ministry's Directorate of Works. He was helped in his task by Mr Villars. They worked from an office in the Air Ministry's Sentinel House in Holborn, London, which had to be kept locked at all times and with the windows papered over to thwart prying eyes. The LEs were clearly the major feature of each site and evolved from an early squarer design to the final one that was to be the basis of all twenty sites.

Hall was instructed to work to an operational date for the first site of August 1958 which was in line with the US expectations at the time.[37] It was at this time too that the project acquired its name. Hall remembered,

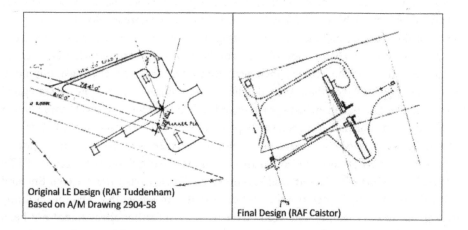

Original LE Design (RAF Tuddenham)
Based on A/M Drawing 2904-58

Final Design (RAF Caistor)

The United States Air Force occupied an adjacent room whose main function was administration and sanctioning what we were achieving. One day [Lieutenant-Colonel Woodruff T.] Sullivan came into the office and having decided that the project needed a name asked us if we had any ideas. I had been given a calendar with a scantily clad female on it with the name of Emily in small print. I decided to stencil her name in large letters and then pinned it on the notice board. The Colonel asked to borrow it and that is how Project Emily got its name.[38]

Sadly the calendar and indeed the identity of Emily, who almost certainly never knew the part she played in the programme, have been lost in the mists of time.[39] While it was an American that gave the British end of the project its name, the USBMD adopted the codename 'Operation Go Away' instead. Consignments thus labelled often took time to reach their destinations as the handlers in the UK failed to recognise the relationship between the two names. Apart from the final shape of the LEs, it is apparent that the other essential elements of the launch complexes were defined early on and changed little thereafter, other than defining their precise locations. Understandably, wherever possible, existing runways were utilised to minimise additional road-building, particularly in the case of access to the LEs. Existing hangars were essential for providing the RIM Building and for housing the Technical Section. Two of RAF Driffield's four Type-C hangars were used to provide the RIM Building (No. 1 Hangar, Bldg 59), Technical Section (No. 2 Hangar, Bldg 61), and MT Section (No. 3 Hangar, Bldg 62), while the fourth was used for a variety of recreational purposes.[40] American influence was evidenced by the two-lane bowling alley and a cinema converted from the old gym. Hall worked on the final configuration for the North Luffenham Wing in August 1958. The Thor compound was at the south-east corner of the airfield and some of the perimeter fence followed the boundary of the Air Ministry land. The three LEs were sited so as to use as much existing concrete, in the form of dispersal areas, as possible. Extra 18-feet-wide access roadways had to be built, along with the hardstanding for the Launch Control Area and the radiusing of some of the corners. At the western end of the complex was the separate US compound accessed via a gate and picket post within the security fence. Inside this compound were situated the Surveillance and Inspection Building and the Classified Storage Building, protected by an L-shaped earth revetment. Two of the existing Type-J hangars to the north-west of the airfield were used for the RIM Building and the adjacent Technical Storage Building.[41] An existing ammunition storage building situated on the airfield, Building 89, was converted to become the segregated pyro storage. North Luffenham had a proud record of service having served as a heavy bomber station during the war and once again was to play a vital part in the defence of the UK.[42,43]

First, the sites had to be surveyed and this was undertaken by 13 Field Survey Squadron, Royal Engineers. Captain Robin Gardiner-Hill, assisted by NCOs Sergeants Riffel and Dyall and Corporal Everett, and seventeen civilians, started the 'Eastern England Task' in May 1958. By September the captain was able to report that 'Operation Emily was well ahead of schedule,' and would have been even further ahead had it not been for the appalling weather.[44] By October, the second squadron (Hemswell) was almost complete and the survey party expected to return to their headquarters at Fernhurst for training and refitting. The Driffield complex was completed in May 1959, after which the team moved to North Luffenham, which was completed on 20 July 1959. At that time astrological observations still had to be completed at Carnaby. Short nights and cloud slowed down the rate of progress, but the team stood by at all times and every favourable opportunity to complete the task was exploited.[45]

The logistic operation to construct the missile bases and bring them to the point of operational capability was immense. From the start it was decided that much of the equipment would be flown into the UK, although some, mainly the heavier items, was to be brought in by sea. In February, the US Third Air Force based at South Ruislip Air Station had been nominated to oversee the UK end of the operations. The SAC base at RAF Lakenheath, home to the 3910th Air Base Group, was the prime candidate for the reception of the equipment, missiles, and personnel arriving in growing numbers from the US.[46] Because of its close proximity to Lakenheath, RAF Feltwell was a natural selection as the main site for the southernmost complex of bases. It would also act as a 'prototype' for the whole project. It was, however, a grass-strip site first used by the Royal Flying Corps (the predecessor to the RAF) in 1917 as a training depot. Its lack of runway meant that no items could be airlifted in—but this was no real problem, as the distance to Lakenheath was only 6 miles. A complete survey of the site was undertaken. There were five Type-C hangars, two of which would be needed for the RIM Building and the MT Section (Buildings 72 and 71 respectively). There were also existing administrative offices and a limited amount of barrack accommodation, although this was to prove far short of the eventual needs. One disadvantage was that, being a grass-strip airfield, the only surfaced area was the perimeter track which circumnavigated the airfield. Other Thor sites were to use existing runways and airfield roads to minimise the construction of access roads to the LEs (although two, Caistor and Coleby Grange, were also only grass-strip airfields). An area to the south of the airfield was identified as the location for the three LEs and two alternative layouts were drawn up.[47] These used the edge of the runways as the northern perimeter of the missile enclosure.

The facilities required at Feltwell had already been established and were determined by the reception, handling, servicing, and onward movement of the missiles. This was essentially covered by the two designated hangars. The main one was the RIM Building. On arrival, the missiles mounted on their Transporter Erector Launchers (TELs) would be taken to this facility, attached to an air-conditioning unit, a Missile System Checkout Trailer, and a Missile Launching Equipment Simulator Trailer. Provision was made to handle two missiles at a time, with provision for a third being made ready. Because of the specialist nature of much of the equipment, the RIM Building was subdivided into various sections. Provision was also made for maintenance of the various Ground Support Trailers. Different areas were constructed using breezeblock walls within the hangar and air conditioning and temperature control added—these features being to US specifications but manufactured by UK subcontractors. To ensure a dust-free environment there was a slight overpressure in these areas, as evidenced by a contemporary news film which shows the simple homemade paper frieze positioned above the door to allow those entering to check that the overpressure system was working. These separate areas covered:

Propulsion Test Shop
Component Test Shop
Electrical Equipment Shop
Inertial Guidance Shop

These test shops surrounded a central open area where the missiles could be dismantled for subsequent specialised servicing. By mid-1958, the final selection of sites had been made.

The contract for the first site was awarded to the civil engineering firm of Sir Alfred McAlpine, with work starting in August 1958. The magnitude of the operation should not be underestimated, nor should the success of the project as a whole. To spread the load of construction, contracts were to be awarded to three more contractors: Taylor Woodrow (Hemswell), W&JR Watson (Driffield), and A. J. Monk (North Luffenham). Feltwell was to replicate the prototype LE at Culver City—5,500 miles away. This Douglas site, constructed in a car park, was itself still being modified as practical experience demanded. Further consideration had to be given to the launch complex at Vandenberg, where modifications were being incorporated as well. The further three UK sites were undoubtedly to benefit from the experience of constructing the Feltwell complex, but there was from the start a major challenge in logging modifications and ensuring that they were correctly communicated and applied as construction continued across the dispersed sites.

Further equipment was flown in to RAF Burtonwood near Warrington, which was a base for the US Military Air Transport Service (MATS).[48] Cargo-handling was undertaken by the Air Freight Section of 1625th Support Squadron. When Burtonwood closed as a USAF facility in April 1959, the squadron transferred its operations to RAF Mildenhall which, from Thor's viewpoint at least, was a more convenient transit point as it was adjacent to Lakenheath. A further advantage of Lakenheath was that it had accommodation suitable for the 500 or so contractor personnel that it was estimated by Douglas would be necessary in the construction,

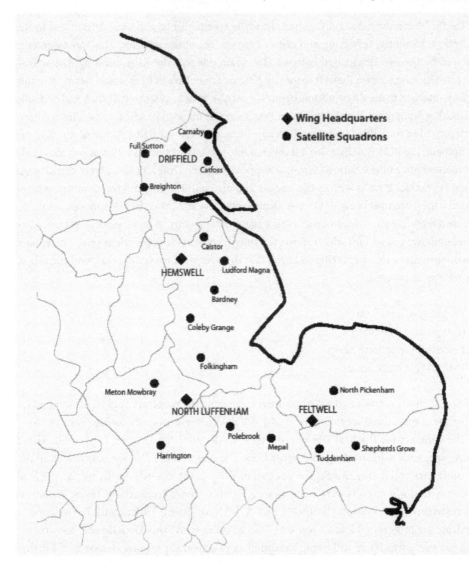

commissioning, and handover of the sites. The arrival of the US personnel started in the second quarter of 1958. The set-up and check-out of the sites was handled by contingents from Douglas, GE, Rocketdyne, and AC Spark Plug with Douglas providing the largest number. By the end of 1958, an estimated total of 406 Americans, not including their families, were in the UK, dedicated to the project. Roughly half this number would be retained during the operational phase to provide technical support to the twenty sites. Instructors from field training detachments started to arrive by the summer with contract technical service staff arriving late in 1958, as the sites became commissioned. The question of accommodation for these personnel was a recurrent problem during the construction phase, and in fact one that was never satisfactorily resolved. In addition to the housing available at Lakenheath, local hotels had to be used and some personnel even found themselves living in the fading grandeur of Lynford Hall, Brandon Park Great House, and North Court Guest House.[49] Such pressures on personnel required that both air forces second some of their staff to supplement the civilians—not strictly legal, but deemed necessary to keep pushing the project forward. Sometimes the transfer to England could be at very short notice. Douglas employee Harvey Mathis, one of the first to be sent to England, remembered that one morning when he checked in at work in Sacramento, he was told to go down to the Douglas Santa Monica plant where, on arrival, he was handed a passport application form;

> I was told to take it down town Los Angeles to the passport office and wait for it. Two hours after I arrived they gave me my passport. I think that was the fastest anyone ever received a passport. The next morning four other employees joined me and we were on a plane headed for England.[50]

Being early on the scene, Mathis was lucky to be housed in the officers' quarters at Lakenheath. Many Douglas staff arrived under cover of darkness after a long transatlantic flight. Invariably it was raining. Many didn't really know what they had been recruited for, and when they arrived didn't know where they were.[51] It wasn't only men who answered the call: Vernita Laws was the second person allocated to Project Emily. At first there was not even a project office at Douglas,

> [...] so we sat in a vacant office over tool cribs where they were assembling planes on the floor below us at Gate 50, the main gate to the Douglas Aircraft plant until they opened up the project office about two or three weeks later. That was in late May or early June 1958. I went to England on the second flight in July 1958.[52]

Tony Yanez flew to the UK on an SAS flight which went via Copenhagen, which gave him a break in the Danish capital before travelling on to England. On arriving he was billeted in the accommodation at Lakenheath, heated, he remembers, by a pot-bellied stove.[53] The majority of Douglas staff crossed the Atlantic on specially chartered Pan American World Airways flights arranged by Douglas. As more and more arrived the problem of accommodation became increasingly acute. Initially, preference was given to unmarried personnel as these were easier to accommodate, but the specialist engineering knowledge required meant that some older, married personnel also arrived, some with families. Various billeting solutions were put forward but the problem was never truly resolved. The idea of using accommodation ships was also considered, but it is difficult to see where these might have been conveniently berthed. In the end the decision was taken to house those who could not be otherwise accommodated in trailers (caravans in English parlance), in large trailer parks on RAF stations. Fortunately the trailers in question were large US-style mobile homes, and therefore suited to US expectations. Putting value into the UK economy, they were manufactured in the UK, although originally it was thought that they too would have to be shipped from America. Residents local to RAF Sturgate soon became accustomed to the sign pointing to 'Santa Monica in the Wolds'. On arrival newcomers would find the trailers parked neatly in herring-bone formation. The accommodation situation was little better for the RAF junior NCOs as they started arriving on the bases. For the married ones there was little chance of securing one of the limited married quarters and private lettings were hard to find or too expensive, so the bases spawned RAF caravan sites—not, however, quite up to the US standards.

Fortunately there was much to divert the newly arrived Americans' attention from the British weather, somewhat different to the balmy Californian sun. There was also the quaint novelty of adapting to the English way of life, while RAF personnel at Feltwell warmed to the newly built bowling alley. Many Americans took instruction in the game of darts at their local pub, while supping the mandatory pint to accompany their meal of jugged hare. Many brought their own cars with them; some bore the names famous American motor manufacturers, but many were the ubiquitous Volkswagen Beetle. Warren Howard was accommodated near Newmarket and, shortly after his arrival, while driving near Newmarket was pulled over by the police and informed that the exhaust noise from his VW was such that if he spotted any of the Queen's horses being exercised, he was immediately to stop and switch off his engine until they had passed. One of the American civilians, Frank 'Z', worked at the North Luffenham site, mainly in the RIM Building. He had a left-hand drive Triumph and lived in Leicester, not far from where Jnr Tech Ronald Muggleton lived in Wigston:

> I often prevailed on him to give me a lift in to the middle of Leicester from which point I was able to catch a bus home. Nothing remarkable in that except that Frank was a bit of a demon driver and overtook anything and everything on the A47 road to Leicester. I, being in the passenger seat on the right hand side of the car was able to see oncoming traffic long before Frank saw it. It made for some hair-raising rides home but it did save me the train fare one way![54]

Suffice to say that not all were so lucky: a number of Americans had accidents on the road.

Various other contractors also moved staff to England. Robert Hallbauer had joined the GE Arming and Fusing Department in April 1957 as an Engineering Technical Assistant at GE's Philadelphia facility. Fred Kurth headed up GE's UK-bound team and invited Hallbauer to join him. Before leaving for the UK, however, a number of months were spent in equipment-handling and nose cone compatibility and mating trials. Some of these trials took place at the Douglas Culver City plant and involved consolidating the design of the holding, raising, positioning, and lowering trailer that was used for handling, transporting, and attaching the warhead to the missile. The latching mechanisms for holding the warhead in place were also tested. Flown over to England in a USAF aircraft, Hallbauer's first memories of arriving in England were of 'the buses and taxis,'[55] and of the paperwork necessary to process them into the country; 'The people were efficient and patient and very helpful.' Hallbauer had arrived in time to enjoy two exceptionally good summers, not quite the 'traditional' British weather that many expected. Presumably because of the classified aspects of their work, the GE group was kept largely apart from the other contractors, except where the necessary exchange of technical information or physical warhead mating exercises was required. Fortunately these restrictions did not apply to off-duty hours. Initially Hallbauer stayed at a hotel in Newmarket and he remembers enjoying the music and dancing that took place there on various nights, as well as visits to local pubs and dance halls. Later he moved to a flat in Norwich which involved a daily commute; fog and black ice were daily hazards in the winter months. GE's project headquarters were in London, where Hallbauer used the facilities of the RAF Officers Club. 'Great club with great staff,'[56] he remembers. The workload was demanding and on many occasions he slept overnight in the Warhead Storage Facility to avoid driving home exhausted. Most of the Douglas staff had been working long shifts since the start of the Thor programme and this proved particularly trying for the accompanying families; many wives would see their husbands off to work at 6.00 a.m. and not see them again until 8.00 p.m. Recreational arrangements were necessary and these fell to Dennis Raz to coordinate. Raz had flown directly into Lakenheath in August 1958 and was accommodated at Lynford Hall, colloquially known as 'The Dungeon'. With the assistance of Master Sergeant Goss, he obtained limited funds to undertake some much needed refurbishment. Gardeners who had previously worked at the hall were enticed back to tidy up the gardens. Typical of the married staff recruited were Peter Portanova, who brought over his wife, Carolyn, and his daughter, Jaye-Jo, and electrical engineer Charles Ordahl, who was accompanied by his wife Eileen. Both families arrived in August 1958.[57] Some of the single Americans found love among the local girls and were to return to the US at the end of the project accompanied by their new wives—known colloquially as the 'Feltwell Wives'.

RAF Hemswell had meanwhile been chosen as the headquarters of the second group of sites. Corporal Neil Trotter who worked in the supply section remembers that prior to Thor's arrival, life on the station had become rather tedious:

> No. 542 Squadron's Canberras [B.6] had been deployed to another Unit and No. 1321 (Lincoln Conversion) Flight [had been disbanded on 31 March 1958]. So there were no operational aircraft remaining on the station, save for the occasional Canberra arriving for modification which was carried out in No. 4 Hangar by a lodger unit, namely a Bomber Command Modification Centre (BCMC).[58, 59]

But instead of numbers reducing, as might be expected, the personnel posted to Hemswell were increasing, including those in the supply section. Freight destined for Hemswell was usually delivered by rail to the nearest railhead, which was Kirton-in-Lindsey, 6 miles to the north.

> Each morning a 3-ton lorry with a civilian MT driver would go to the railhead and remain there until lunch-time. Any freight that had arrived for RAF Hemswell, would be brought back, delivered, unpacked, identified by the Receipt and Despatch section and finally delivered to its appropriate location in the main store. After lunch, the same driver would return to Kirton-in-Lindsey railway station for the afternoon to await any further freight for […] Hemswell. This was the daily routine.[60]

One morning there was a call from the Kirton-in-Lindsey freight manager advising that a number of rail trucks had arrived with freight for Hemswell. Hearing the word 'trucks' Corporal Trotter was a little suspicious, as freight for Hemswell never involved more than one truck. He decided to go to the station to see exactly what was there. On arriving at the railway goods yard, he asked the freight manager what he had for Hemswell. He was taken to a siding full of railway wagons.

> My first thought was that someone in 'Provisioning' had made an awful mistake and had over-ordered. I returned to RAF Hemswell and reported to my OC Supply to advise him that I thought there had been a 'bit of a mistake' and told him that we had numerous trucks at Kirton-in-Lindsey loaded with screw pickets and barbed wire.[61]

With a wry smile on his face, the OC Supply said, 'it is time to briefly tell you what will be happening with this Unit.' The general lack of productive activity at the station had for some time been the subject of much speculation among the station personnel, but no one had come up with the reason why, so the explanation came as a complete surprise. 'I was told that we were about to become a Missile Unit and the freight which had arrived at the railway goods yard was for temporary security fencing [to be erected while the launch pads were installed].'[62] The sheer volume of equipment was such that the limited capability of the existing Supply Squadron had to be rapidly supplemented by No. 2 MT Company who had the staff and capability to cope with the task. Even then it would be some months before they were relieved of duties at Hemswell, due to the volume of freight movement, a situation made more difficult as the runway was out of commission while the contract work was being undertaken. During this period RAF Scampton was used as an airhead for regular Globemaster flights which brought in some of the consignments. No expense was spared, as was evidenced by the fact that most of the US freight was delivered in custom-made wooden crates. Those items destined for the launch facilities were identified by a letter 'A' and were often quite heavy, requiring special handling. Corporal Trotter remembers the complex and time-consuming identification process for incoming consignments. Consisting of numerous boxes, there would be a number allocated to each consignment, such as 'Consignment XXX, Boxes 1-40.'

> In box No.1 would be all the transfer documents relating to everything in the whole of the rest of the consignment and it was my staff's task to find the document—or voucher— and then go through all the rest of the boxes in that particular consignment to find the equipment to go with the voucher.[63]

This method was extremely time-consuming and wasteful in the number of man hours it used up. Corporal Trotter appealed to his CO to ask if the consignors—of whom there were many, including civilian contractors such as Rocketdyne and Douglas—could attach vouchers to the equipment to which they referred, but this didn't happen.

Instead, three men from the USAF were posted in solely to identify and 'match up equipment to vouchers' ready for progression in the supply procedure. One of these was a [former] US Marine, now a Sergeant in the USAF. His nick-name was 'Boot-Neck'—I wonder why![64]

Other USAF personnel also arrived at the various sites and were involved in the commissioning of the LEs. One of these was Sergeant (E-4) Lee Wise. After four weeks' further training at Patrick AFB, Wise received amended orders to proceed to McGuire AFB, New Jersey, to be flown to England. In late August he and three other classmates left for England aboard 'the Bucket', a USAF Douglas C-118, a military version of the DC-6 airliner. After arriving at RAF Burtonwood they took a train to London and after changing trains headed north to Lakenheath. Taking a taxi from the station they reported to the Personnel Centre. Perhaps unsurprisingly, no one knew they were coming. After an inspection of their travel orders and

> [some] phone calls they were assigned quarters in transit accommodation and told to report back the next day to determine what they were going to do. After staying a couple days on Lakenheath they were transferred to RAF Feltwell and assigned to the 672nd Technical Training Squadron.[65]

This was located in one of the large hangars jointly used by the USAF and RAF.

> We soon were assigned to barracks on Feltwell and started reporting to our individual Section Shops. There was no chow hall for the USAF troops, so we were given an allowance of $2.57 a day and [were] required to buy our food in the RAF NAAFI. There's no way we could buy three meals for $2.57 so we had to lighten up on breakfast and lunch to save for a decent dinner meal![66]

By this time a substantial number of Douglas employees had arrived and embarked on the construction of the missile bases. The basic civil engineering works were completed by the four UK companies. This involved laying the substantial concrete foundations and grillage for the LEs which had to be constructed to very fine tolerances—a demanding requirement in itself. The sites were then handed over to Douglas and USAF personnel to install the launch equipment in preparation for the arrival of the missiles. Sergeant Wise remembers twelve-hour shifts, seven days a week, as the urgency of the project increased. He spent a good deal of time at Shepherds Grove, the second of the Feltwell Wing sites.

> I spent most of my time at [the] Shepherds Grove Site building the three Missile shelters and since I had received training on Thor missile and AGE (Aerospace Ground Equipment) Systems I also was involved in installing various pieces of stainless steel plumbing. These systems were used for hydraulic, GN2 (gaseous nitrogen), Liquid Oxygen and RP1. The weather was cold and wet most of the time. I remember well many times we would arrive

on site in the morning and the seagulls would have covered the whole area with excrement and we had to clean equipment, tools and whatever before it could be used. Also when the sun finally came out (some days) around noon and start warming the area up the smell was very bad to say the least. We soon learned to cover as much of the equipment as possible before we left the Pad at the end of the day. It was a totally new experience for most of us to witness the almost morning daily fog that was so thick you couldn't see 50 feet away. I recall riding the Air Force bus from Feltwell to Shepherds Grove many times and I don't see how our bus driver who was a small 120-pound guy could see 20 feet in front of the bus travelling through the narrow streets in the small towns. He always got us there and back safely and he should have received a medal for his effort.[67]

By the very nature of the project, upgrades and modifications were the subject of constant review and implementation. Coordinating this from California across all twenty sites was challenging and at times frustrating for those on the ground in the UK. Major Warren S. Woirol who was in charge of the Modification Program indicated these frustrations when he wrote to W. F. Shaver, DAC Engineering Chief at RAF Hemswell:

In order to accomplish pertinent engineering evaluations, which can be properly interpreted, and provide engineering recommendations, which can be successful incorporated into the Modification Program, it is requested that the obvious practice of omphaloskepsis used by the DAC Engineering Department in completing evaluations and arriving at recommendations be employed to a limited degree, if at all.[68]

Although work generally progressed well, the contract was a demanding and complex one and produced many tensions among those working on it. Homesickness and long hours were taking their toll. On 10 January 1959, the *Daily Mail* reported problems on its front page under a banner headline: 'Thor Rocket Hold-Up'. The previous month, DAC Vice-President Leo A. Carter had paid an unscheduled visit to Britain to take stock of the situation. Errol M. Neff, DAC's European representative for the Thor programme had sacked two trouble-making engineers and sent them back to the US. On 19 December, however, Carter relieved Neff of all his duties. Two days later Neff suffered a heart attack, but was subsequently able to tell reporters from his hospital bed at the USAF 7510 Hospital at Arrington, south-west of Cambridge, that he had been replaced because of his physical state. 'I have no complaints about my treatment by Douglas, and I hope to return to California and take up a less exacting post with them', he told reporters. He declined to reveal the number of DAC workers in Britain or to name the two he had sent back to the United States but did comment, 'it is true that there has been some dissension among Douglas workers in Britain but that is not why I have been replaced.'[69] The widespread dissatisfaction among the Douglas staff was vehemently denied by a spokesman for 7AD.[70] In an exchange of letters between D. Hanson, Private Secretary at the Air Ministry, and H. Godfrey at the MoD, the former gave assurance that:

The American technicians engaged on the Thor programme are concerned solely with the installation of equipment. Consequently the works programme has in no way been affected by the labour troubles referred to in the *Daily Mail* article. The works services for the Feltwell complex were completed slightly ahead of the overall target date, which was 31st December, 1958, while the construction work on the sites for the Hemswell squadron is proceeding according to plan. Nevertheless there has been some slippage on the installation programme and the Feltwell squadron will not become fully operational until March. This slippage has resulted from several factors, of which perhaps the most important was the Douglas Aircraft Corporation's underestimated the size of the problem in installing and checking their equipment in the field. The installation teams originally sent over did not have enough high-grade technicians and some of the work was beyond their capacity. As a result there was considerable discontent among the firm's employees and this was heightened by certain minor accommodation and general welfare problems.[71]

By the late spring of 1959, delays were, perhaps inevitably, occurring causing 7AD representatives to visit the Department of Works. At that stage the problems seemed to centre on RAF Full Sutton, but Air Commdore J. Searby, DofOps (B&R), admitted that problems also existed at Breighton, where extensive piling was needed resulting from unforeseen drainage problems which had been encountered, adding eight weeks to the building programme, further hampered by demonstrations, albeit peaceful, by the Direct Action Committee. RAF North Pickenham had been a particular target for demonstrations where the protesters somewhat underestimated the robust countermeasures, such as high-pressure hoses, implemented by the construction workers. There were also construction problems at North Luffenham and Harrington, although these two were caused by the delays in agreeing the formation of the Fourth Wing. But the USAF's concerns were centered on more than just these sites. When the commissioning of the first site at Feltwell had earlier fallen behind, it had been necessary for Douglas to bring in additional higher grade supervisors. DAC was now concerned that these highly skilled workers were without sufficient useful employment. The delays would result in peaks and troughs in the labor deployment rather than a steady rate, as had been anticipated. The monthly DAC costs were in the realm of $1.5 million, and where these were incremental costs, it was feared that the US Government may have to pick up these extra costs. In a worst case scenario, DAC had warned that they would have to dispose of a proportion of the skilled personnel and negotiate a new contract which it was projected would delay completion until July or August 1960. After full discussion with the Ministry of Works, a revised schedule of completion dates was agreed. Carnaby, Full Sutton, and Harrington would be subject to a two-week delay in completion. Breighton was the worst site, having already suffered a three-week delay due to the pads having to be realigned. This would be delayed by four weeks due to the poor nature of the subsoil, which was the underlying cause of the extra piling needed. Inevitably this meant that for a short period there would be little for DAC employees to do, but 7AD accepted the revised schedule which brought the date for completion of the groundworks for the last site, Harrington, to 28 October 1959.[72] Many of the US contractors were working extremely long hours and inevitably there was friction with the more restrictive working hours of the senior RAF officers involved with the project. Regular progress meetings took place at the Air Ministry on Fridays, starting with coffee and biscuits followed by the morning meeting. Lunch was usually a relaxed interval before a further meeting in the afternoon followed by afternoon tea and dispersal. Frustrated by what he saw as a lack of engagement by the RAF, one DAC representative suggested that perhaps they could reconvene the following day to move matters forward. The senior RAF officer present apparently looked askance at the proposal. 'We're not at war you know,' he commented acerbically before heading for his staff car and his weekend.[73]

By this time it had become apparent that the operational dates embodied in the Technical Agreement were now unrealistic and a revised schedule of dates was agreed on to align with the revised completion dates.[74]

Feltwell	Early December 1958
Shepherds Grove	24 December 1958
Tuddenham	25 February 1959
Mepal	25 February 1959
North Pickenham	25 February 1959
Hemswell	21 March 1959
Bardney	30 April 1959
Caistor	31 May 1959
Coleby Grange	30 June 1959
Ludford Magna	31 May 1959
Driffield	31 July 1959
Catfoss	20 August 1959
Carnaby	14 September 1959
Breighton	7 October 1959
Full Sutton	15 October 1959
North Luffenham	1 November 1959
Harrington	7 December 1959
Polebrook	14 January 1960
Melton Mowbray	21 February 1960
Folkingham	31 March 1960

Opening for Business

Once Feltwell was in a 'presentable' state it was only natural that it should become the focus of attention for politicians and senior officers who were involved in the project. Paving the way was AOCinC Bomber Command ACM Sir Harry Broadhurst, who toured the Feltwell installations on 25 February 1959 under the guidance of Squadron Leader Stanley Baldock DFM, OC designate of No. 77(SM) Squadron and USAF Detachment Commander Colonel William A. Delahay. On 24 March the first full VIP visit took place when Duncan Sandys arrived at Feltwell at 11.30 a.m. accompanied by DCAS Air Marshal Sir Geoffrey Tuttle, Commander 7AD Major-General Blanchard, Donald Douglas, AVM Kenneth Cross, and Air Commodore William Coles CBE, DSO, DFC, AFC-SASO 3 Group HQ, under whose control the Feltwell group of sites was to come. Squadron Leader Baldock was once again the escort officer. After a briefing on the organisation of the station and its satellite locations, the VIPs moved to 'A' Flight, where a complete RAF/USAF operational crew was lined up for inspection. After lunch in the Officers' Mess, the party visited the RIM Building before departing at 3.00 p.m. Families of those serving at the station were also included when a 'Meet the Missile' day was held on 12 April. This included films and demonstrations to show what was going on 'behind the wire'. Some months later Feltwell arranged an unusual 'salute' for SACEUR, General Lauris Norstad. Feltwell's Wing Commander (Ops) learned that the general was flying from Burtonwood to Mildenhall en route to Germany. As his aircraft flew over Feltwell, all three Thors were raised to the vertical in his honour.[1] Nor were the 'old and bold' forgotten. MRAF Sir John Salmond GCB, CMG, CVO, DSO, who had retired from the RAF as long ago as 1933, was a guest of No. 220(SM) Squadron at North Pickenham. He arrived in a staff car still resplendent with a five-star plate on the front.

Speculation naturally increased about when the first missile would arrive and where its destination would be. *Daily Express* reporter Gordon Thomas reporting from 'somewhere in Norfolk' claimed he had seen the first missile base. 'It's so secret even the residents don't know,'[2] he claimed. Construction workers who with overtime could earn an impressive £20 a week were told they were building a car park. Although the workers treated this as a private joke, it seemed that few of the locals, when questioned, were aware that they were about to have missiles as neighbours, but 'accepted it in the phlegmatic way of Norfolkmen.'[3]

The first RAF Thor (T139)—the second production missile, but still essentially at this stage non-operational—which was to test the compatibility with the Feltwell LEs, was airlifted into Lakenheath without any ceremony on 29 August 1958.[4] On 1 September 1958 No. 77(SM) Squadron was officially formed at RAF Feltwell. (At that time it had an establishment of fifteen missiles as it was not until 22 July 1959 that the four outlying Flights became autonomous squadrons, whereupon No. 77 Squadron's establishment was reduced to three missiles.) However, the public and perhaps more importantly, the media would have to wait until 19 September to get its first sight of Thor's arrival at Feltwell. On the day, Colonel Delahay gave a brief overview of the project before officially handing over the missile to Group Captain Frank Willan DFC, OC RAF Feltwell. Also in attendance were Major-General Blanchard and Air Marshal Kenneth Cross CBE, DSO, DFC, AOC 3 Group. Anticipating the event, on 9 September *Daily Express* readers were treated to a scoop preview under the headline 'No. 1 rocket site—first picture'.[5] Apparently taken with a long lens from outside the perimeter fence, Robert Haswell's photo was accurately captioned to show the major components of one of the launch pads, although the fuel tank, still to be put in place, was positioned where the missile would eventually be sited. Chapman Pincher wrote in an article accompanying the picture,

> This is the first picture of Britain's first ballistic missile launching site near Feltwell in Norfolk. [...] more than 100 American technicians under Colonel Harry Zink are moving into the old married quarters at the RAF station near Feltwell. They will teach the RAF men how to handle Thor, fuel it and run up the gyroscopes which keep it stable during its 1,500-mile flight. Group Captain Frank Willan commander of the RAF's first ballistic missile squadron hopes to have the first site ready for operational use before the end of the year.

Efforts to keep the sites' locations secret were fine up to a point, but Pincher went on to reveal that although permission would not be granted to a Russian diplomat to travel near the sites, no such restrictions applied to Polish, Hungarian, or Czech diplomats.[6] Likewise, although every effort was made to keep a low profile on the transport of the missiles to their squadron locations, in practice the movement of a 65-foot missile, even when shrouded under its protective cover, was hard to conceal from an inquisitive public. The original US M-52 tractor units had all evidence of the US origins of the trailers obscured by a coat of RAF blue paint, and suitable RAF markings were later replaced by Leyland 19H Hippos. Furthermore, Pincher had two weeks previously alerted the public to 'what the rocket base will look like if one is built in your area'[7] by way of a drawing of a typical Thor installation, so by the time the first Thor made its media debut as it trundled into Feltwell, the public were well briefed on what to look for. The following day, Pincher wrote yet another article about the missile and its arrival at Feltwell. It is purely speculative to suggest that he was used as a unwitting conduit for deliberate disinformation, he may simply have misunderstood what he was told, but he reported:

> [...] some of the [...] rockets [...] will be fuelled up and ready for firing, complete with their H-bomb warheads AT ALL TIMES.... The US experts showed me how the Thors,

with their completely mobile equipment, can be switched from site to site so that foreign agents will never know which are operational. Dummy rockets will be used in the deception.[8]

Fully fuelled missiles were certainly never intended and technically presented an impossible scenario. Likewise there is no evidence of any of the UK missiles apart from T110 being other than fully operational. Placating existing public fears about warhead safety, he continued,

[…] while I inspected the concrete launching pads, Group Captain Andrew Willan, commander of the Strategic Missile Squadron, assured me that the warhead cannot explode accidentally.

At the time of the first Thor's arrival at Feltwell, only one of the three pads was finished. It was not until 16 September that concrete pouring was complete on LEs 2 and 3, still at that time designated A2 and A3. This event was marked by a ceremony at which Colonel Delahay formally handed over responsibility for Thor to Group Captain Willan.[9] Once again Major-General Blanchard and Air Marshal Cross were in attendance. A significant milestone was achieved when, on 27 November, the first Thor was successfully raised on its launch pad. Much of the credit for this event went to Douglas propulsion engineer Tom Rehder who drew on his experience of the Thor tests at ETR.[10] By the end of the year, the authoritative *Flight* magazine had published an 11-page article, complete with photographs and diagrams, comprehensively covering the whole Thor system.[11]

By early autumn of 1959, Feltwell was nearly fully up to speed as far as handling the missiles was concerned and had become the focus for visits by the 'interested and uninitiated' as the Squadron's ORB reports. On 4 September AVM W. C. (Wally) Sheen CB, DSO, OBE, Commander RAF Staff, BJSM in Washington visited with C. A. Warner from the US Embassy and Dr W. A. Offutt from the Office of Directorate of Defence Research Engineering. Six days later, Air Marshal Sir John Whitley KBE, CB, DSO, AFC*, Inspector-General of the RAF visited. The following day it was the turn of US mission to NATO led by Lieutenant-General T. Larkin of the US Army. Each visiting group saw a specimen launch crew and a simulated countdown.

The process of bringing the missiles to the various sites had to be meticulously planned. Moving the 65-foot missiles on their transporters around the wide open spaces of California was not generally a problem. Manoeuvring them through narrow English country roads and villages was a completely different matter with little or no margin for error. Firstly the various routes were the subject of a full reconnaissance to identify any problems which required work to be undertaken on the roads. Even following the routes today on better roads is not always easy. The access to RAF Folkingham for instance seems particularly tortuous and there is the well-known photograph of the Thor convoy negotiating Rothwell village en route to RAF Harrington to emphasise the difficulty. Naturally, the convoys attracted much attention from a curious public but, as with most of the Thor programme, photographs were 'discouraged'. Corporal Neil Trotter recalls,

On one occasion when, returning from RAF Scampton with a Thor Missile mounted on a low-loader, suitably 'shrouded' and under escort by both RAF and Civilian Police, the convoy of vehicles necessary to transport these weapons[12] suddenly halted and a civilian policeman hurriedly passed the vehicle I was in and [approached] a civilian on the roadside. I wasn't able to hear what was said, but what I did notice was that the policeman had taken a camera from this man, opened it and unrolled the film to expose whatever had been photographed. I can only assume the policeman had spotted this man taking photographs of our [convoy]![13]

All road movements had to be alerted to the police and the County Surveyor at least forty-eight hours in advance.[14] All transfers had to be made in daylight. Similar but more stringent security surrounded the warhead convoys.

Warheads remained at all times under strict USAF control and management. They were transported in curtain-sided trailers normally attached to a Leyland 19H tractor unit. Their movement started and finished at the appropriate Surveillance and Inspection Building, at which point the convoy commander would ether assume or relinquish responsibility after his F.1250 identity card had been authenticated against the movement order. Strict instructions referred to the convoy's progress on public roads. No vehicle was to be allowed to come between the rear of the trailer carrying the warhead and the convoy commander in his following Land Rover, and no overtaking of the convoy was permitted until the road ahead had been established as clear enough to permit the overtaking manoeuvre to take place. On transferring a warhead from the S&I Building to a LE, the convoy escort was not to be dismissed until successful mating of the warhead had taken place, in case of problems necessitating the warhead's return to the S&I Building. As Senior Technical Representative to the USAF, Robert Hallbauer was responsible for training the US personnel in the handling and mating of the warhead with the missile. Having completed the training at Feltwell, he moved to Driffield. He remembers being graciously greeted on his arrival by the Station Commander. Initially housed in the Officers' Mess, he was impressed by finding his napkin in a silver napkin ring waiting for him at mealtimes. He enjoyed great hospitality in the Mess, even when his fellow representative Leon Weiss beat the standing record for downing a 'yard of ale', a record which the RAF rapidly sought to regain![15]

Strict rules covered the handling of the warheads. Anyone dealing with the warheads had to have SECRET or equivalent security clearance, and only a minimum of absolutely essential staff had access to the warhead. Whenever possible, the warhead was to be mated to its RV. When separated from the RV, an extra series of safety rules applied: when being transported, the warheads had to be in sealed containers guarded by at least two armed personnel, and when stored had to be in a locked and guarded facility. This facility consisted of a special building known as the 'Classified Storage Building'. At each of the Wing HQ sites there were two 'semi-detached' Classified Storage Buildings which, along with the Pyrotechnics Store and the Surveillance and Inspection Building, were contained within a separate fenced area, access to which was controlled by a US guard accommodated in a picket post at the gate to the compound. Access to the US compound was via the main missile site. At the dispersed sites there was a single storage building and pyrotechnics store, contained within the site, but not requiring a separate fenced compound. Early US warhead design had allowed for special nuclear parts within the warhead to be transported separately. This was not possible for the Thor warheads which were of an integrated sealed design.[16] There was no suitable British special container in which the warheads could be transported and the Americans deemed it unnecessary in any case, as the warheads were generally being transported only over relatively short distances. However, custody of the warhead would remain firmly in US hands at all times. This covered all transport, mounting of the warhead on the missile, and removal when the missile was non-operational for routine maintenance or deep fault modification.[17] A minimum of two qualified personnel had to be present during all maintenance checks which had to be supervised by an officer at all times.[18]

On 25 August, just before the first Thor arrived, the Ministry of Defence had announced that the 'nuclear warheads for Thors would remain in possession of the American forces and would only be issued following joint agreements between the British and American Governments.'[19] This was the principal on which Project 'E' was based; however, if Thor was to be seen as a credible weapon system, the warheads needed to be in place on the missile (unless removed for maintenance).[20] The missiles were never to be fuelled except 'in anger'. This was not disclosed to the public, but there was assurance that the complexity of the launch sequence and the number of people involved effectively eliminated any possibility of an inadvertent or mischievous launch. American assurances were given that there was no possibility of an accidental explosion of the assembled warhead, but there were differences in requirements relating to the security and safety of nuclear devices between Britain and the US, so this was to be the subject of extra assurances by AWRE.[21] Air Marshal Sir Geoffrey Tuttle, DCAS at the Air Ministry, was informed by Air Chief Marshal Sir Harry Broadhurst:

> I consider that detailed investigation should be made by our scientific and technical safety experts, who should then be asked to provide clearance for [the warheads'] movement, assembly, period of assembly and disconnection, as has been done for our own weapons. I understand that the Ministry of Defence is trying to arrange for the USAF Engineering Liaison Office which handles Project 'E', to act as the contact point for these discussions, but my concern is that unless the highest priority is given on both sides to the completion of the work, it may be many months before there is enough information to go on.[22]

There was also the concern that rogue elements would try to detonate the warhead during normal configuration, with the warhead mated to the RV. In effect, the warhead had been developed quickly to meet the IRBM and ICBM timetables, but a 1961 report revealed that

> [...] this warhead, like all other warheads investigated, can be sabotaged, i.e. detonated full-scale.... Any person with knowledge of the warhead electrical circuits, a handful of equipment, a little time, and the intent, can detonate the warhead.[23]

Tests had indeed shown that the arming and firing mechanisms in the warhead met rigid standards of reliability and it was estimated that five hours of complex actions involving disassembling the RV would be required before any nuclear detonation could be achieved. What was seen by the Americans as deliberate delaying tactics by the British did not impress those who were keen to confirm that Thor was operational at the earliest opportunity. The issue was raised by DCAS Air Marshal Sir Geoffrey Tuttle when he met US SecAF James Douglas in early May a few days after the sudden death from a heart attack of Donald Quarles, whose 'strength and wisdom [was] greatly missed.' Douglas confirmed to Sir Richard Powell that a suggested date of sometime in June for an announcement of Thor's operational status was mutually acceptable, although this in reality had the flavour of an agreement between people who disagreed.

In the spring of 1959 Douglas, a man widely respected by the Eisenhower administration, had visited Feltwell. Shortly after his return to the US, he addressed the Business Advisory Council:

> For me the important discovery in England was recognising the importance of our joint effort in the Thor intermediate ballistic missile program. I visited the first site and saw missiles on their launchers. These missiles and launchers are being used for training purposes, but the first site, and other launch sites of the first squadron could be brought to quick reaction status in case of emergency. Within a year the four-squadron program will be completed and will give the Royal Air Force, under joint control with us, a very significant ballistic missile system with large nuclear warheads. The progress made in this program may well be one of the most significant military accomplishments of the last year. Great Britain stepped up at the earliest opportunity to acquire the most modern nuclear weapons. This step is a fine contribution to the strength and morale of the western world.[24]

Momentum on the project gradually increased and on 7 July 1959 the RAF agreed to show off their new weapon system to a selected press audience. There was a fine line to be drawn between American desire to suggest to the Soviets that Thor now had an operational capability and the British reluctance to reflect this when they felt there was still some way to go before this was the case. One of the resulting articles, in the American *Missiles and Rockets* magazine, set the cat among the pigeons when it published a summary of the visit to Feltwell. Unfortunately, much of the detail given in the article had previously been withheld from the British media, who had been barred from speculation about Thor's operational readiness by a Government D Notice. As a result of the article, the D Notice had to be relaxed to cover only the operational relationship between the sites. The MoD had refused to comment on the article, claiming that statements in the British press—that the Thors had been stood down in order to help the international atmosphere or that Britain had protested strongly to the Americans about the publication of this information—had no foundation and were purely speculative.[25]

Although SAC had handed over operational control of the Feltwell Wing to Bomber Command on 22 June 1959, it was not until the beginning of 1960 that Feltwell was fully ready for its 'operational' public debut. A full media briefing for around seventy British, Commonwealth and US correspondents took place on 10–11th February at Feltwell; the first day for the photographers, the second for the reporters. The visit was recorded in the ORB as the squadron's main task for the month.[26] True, the day was cold, grey, and rain-soaked, but whether the local Norfolk population would have warmed to the description of their county as 'the bleak plains of South Eastern England'[27] is debatable. 'PAD1. POSITIVELY NO ADMITTANCE' warned the sign. But for the benefit of the newsmen, 'Fifteen men with one [USAF] lieutenant staged a simulated count-down of a single squadron of three Thors.'[28] What the press saw was every major event on a full countdown except the loading of the fuel and LOX and the final commit to launch. It was enacted with a 'grim realism,' reported the *New York Times* correspondent, Walter H. Waggoner;

> The hangar-like 'environmental shelters' moved back on their tracks to expose the white Thors with the RAF's red, white and blue bull's-eye emblem on their sides. The horizontal missiles slowly rose on their bases and pointed skywards. The screeches of signals and crisp voices over the loudspeakers resounded through the otherwise silent base. In a tense fifteen minutes, three Thors were all but launched.[29]

At the ensuing press conference, AOCinC Bomber Command, Air Marshal Sir Kenneth Cross, accompanied by AVM Michael Dwyer, AOC 3 Group and AVM Gus Walker, now the RAF's newly appointed Chief Information Officer, left the reporters in no doubt about Thor's capability when he advised them that 'operational means capable of going to war.' The point was driven further home by Feltwell's station commander Group Captain Frank Willan, who added, 'we must be capable of launching the missile at any hour of the day or night in fifteen minutes.'[30] What was not said was that none of the missiles was fitted with a warhead. AVM Walker came up with a new version of an effective deterrent force for the visiting Americans, 'when Russia sets up a war game against the West, plays it and *loses*—then you have an effective deterrent.' He also proudly reminded the Americans that the part played by Bomber Command in this deterrent force was several times as large as the SAC contingent stationed in Britain[31] and would be the first manned force to strike the Soviet Union in the event of war.[32] At that stage the location of the other main bases was still secret, but the *New York Times* reported that it had been published that the others would be at Hemslow [*sic*], Lincolnshire, and two near Driffield, Yorkshire.

The question of Thor's operational capability was by now becoming increasingly urgent. To move this forward, arrangements had been made for a three member scientific team from the Operational Research Branch of Bomber Command to visit the US in a two-week programme of visits to STL and AFBMD HQ in Los Angeles. The aim of the visit was to assess the overall performance of the Thor system to date and to make a formal recommendation for operational acceptance. To do this it was hoped that maximum disclosure of all relevant data would be provided by AFBMD officials to permit confidence in the system before responsibility was handed over to the San Bernardino Air Materiel Area (SBAMA). The team were to use as a benchmark an achievable 2-mile CEP at 1,500 nm and were satisfied in their investigations that this degree of accuracy could be expected to be achieved. They did, on the other hand, accept that missiles then in the UK would not necessarily achieve this same level of accuracy without a modification programme. A further concern and one perhaps more related to the UK environment was the demonstrable ability to hold a missile in the vertical position with bad visibility, 'when a missile frame reference would have to be used to preserve azimuth alignment and also the reliability of the Operational Flight Safety System which monitors the guidance and only arms the warhead when certain conditions are satisfied.'[33] The team were satisfied by the claims that at that stage the CEP for the last successful thirteen firings was 1.8 miles, although it was also accepted that a lack of accurate weather data in the vicinity of the target could also account for deviation from the correct trajectory on re-entry. Their remit did not extend to aspects of nuclear safety.

What was still missing in the complex jigsaw to achieving operational capability were Bomber Command operational procedures for training and maintenance countdowns. Douglas had provided documentation (200 copies at $200 per page), but this just provided the procedures for setting up a missile launched in anger with a nuclear warhead and was of little practical use for day-to-day operations where practice countdowns would be the norm with 'the taps turned off'. When it was realised that the lack of procedures would mean that Thor could not become operational and that these procedures could not be developed in the UK, a hurried mission set off to SBAMA to explain what was actually needed. The mission was successful and agreement for developing the required procedures (which involved additional budgeting) was reached. The new procedures which had been vetted for nuclear safety issues arrived in time.

In August 1958, Bomber Command began moving in the right direction with the establishment of an Ops BM officer at High Wycombe. Squadron Leader Bob Broad, who had attended the second training course in the US, became Ops 1d. As the programme gathered momentum, Wing Commander Ed Haines DFM, who had briefly been OC No. 150(SM) Sqn at Carnaby, took up the newly created post of HQBC (Ops BM) in March 1960 with Squadron Leader Broad as Ops BM1.[34] 'Wing Commander Haines had a very clear idea of what had to be done and played a very significant role in Thor achieving operational status. The Ops BM Section set up the routine Thor Exercises, RESPOND, RECLAIM, and REDOUBLE. In addition, it wrote the Bomber Command Missile Orders Book.'[35] Section responsibilities were far-ranging, covering everything from establishments, the complexities of health and safety (different for both nations), nuclear decontamination, and establishing an initial training budget, to security issues and the release of data. Also to contend with was the unwelcome rivalry between the senior officers of Nos. 1 and 3 Groups, under whose control the squadrons came: AVM John Davis, AOC No. 1 Group from June 1959 to December 1961, was particularly memorable in this context. Squadron Leader Broad also took on responsibility of organising the forthcoming CTL programme. Like many who worked quietly in the background, the true nature of Wing Commander Haines's invaluable contribution to the success of the Thor programme received no public recognition.

While interest focussed on Feltwell, building continued apace at the other sites. Apart from some local coverage, mainly when the nascent CND made their presence known, there was little real publicity to affect their progress. As far as the satellite sites were concerned, all were superficially at least, broadly similar but their layouts encompassed considerable diversity. What, for instance, would visitors arriving at a typical Thor site have found? Where concrete runways existed, these were incorporated into the layout so that there was no such thing as a standard site as such. Three sites, Feltwell, Coleby Grange, and Caistor, only had grass runways where access roads had to be built and these sites may arguably be seen as preferred layouts, where a greenfield approach was possible.

Just before reaching the entrance, there was a lay-by where the Thor convoys could park. The main entrance was the only access to the site and through the sterile area defined by the double security fencing. Just inside the entrance were the wooden huts used as the administrative buildings, while (usually opposite) was a standard RAF fire tender garage with an added wooden semi-detached police car garage. A little further on could be found the brick-built domestic area including the Power Conversion Building. Beyond this was the Launch Control Area or Squadron Control Centre based on a concrete hardstanding roughly in the shape of a right-angled triangle. Here were to be found the Launch Control Trailers (LCT)—colloquially termed 'Large Conspicuous Targets'—the generators and their associated fuel tank, mounted on semi-circular mountings within a low enclosing wall.[36] From the LCA three cable trenches extended out to the three LEs. SI store buildings— Classified Storage Building and the Pyrotechnics Store protected behind an 'E'- or 'F'-shaped earth revetment could be found a little distance from the missile pads.

These facilities were common to the HQ sites as well, with the differences of a two-bay Classified Storage Building and a larger Power Conversion Building (Air Ministry Drawing 7784B/58) to cope with the greater power requirement, which at these sites included the US-controlled Surveillance and Inspection Building.

The LEs were obviously the focal point of the sites. Each was of basically cruciform design oriented roughly east-west. Taking the base of the launcher as a central reference point, to the north and south were L-shaped blast walls, 15 feet high by 5 feet thick. These were designed to offer some protection to the various equipment trailers which were accommodated on the pad. Along the east-west axis of the LE lay the Missile Shelter. This was a 108-foot-long, prefabricated, moveable structure which protected the missile in the horizontal position and, providing an environmentally stable enclosure, also allowed maintenance work to take place on the missile. It was formed of ten bent-column ribs providing the basic structure of the Shelter. The outside cladding consisted of steel honeycomb-filled panels. The Shelter was 20 feet high and 28 feet 10 inches. It was mounted on rails which allowed it be retracted clear of the missile as one of the first stages in the countdown procedure. The western end was fully closed but the eastern end butted onto a free-standing wall which remained in place when the Shelter was retracted. This wall had two doors in it to allow full access to the interior but, also on rails, it could be slid to the side. In practice this seems rarely to have happened. It was held in place by two lock bolts. Within the interior of the Shelter were retractable maintenance platforms allowing access to guidance, flight control, and centre sections. Two half-ton hoists were mounted on 'I'-section beams over the nose section of the missile. The Shelter was retracted via a

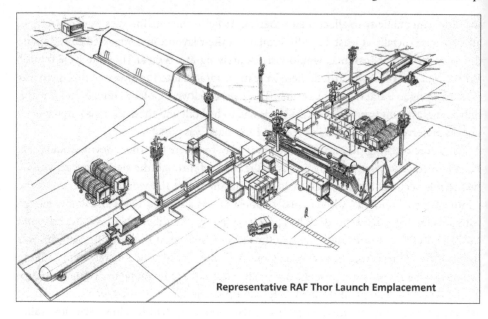

Representative RAF Thor Launch Emplacement

winch driven by a 60-hp electric motor which wound ¾-inch steel cables. The system had two speeds. Once the end of the Shelter was clear of the launch structure, a micro-switch engaged a higher speed. Co-axial drums also reeled in the power and communication lines. In the northern arm of the LE was the RP-1 fuel tank contained within a surrounding revetment which could also contain any fuel spillage. The tank was made of stainless steel, coated with 2 inches of glass fibre and covered in aircraft fabric shrunk with dope. It had a capacity of 6,500 US gallons with a 5-per-cent air space from pressurisation. In the event of over-pressure, a 120-psi relief valve was incorporated in the upper surface. Diametrically opposite on the pad was the LOX tank. This was in effect a large thermos flask. The inner tank was also made from stainless steel and contained within an outer tank of aluminium, the two separated by an 8-inch gap filled with santocel, an aerogel, to absorb moisture. Although delivered to the site on wheels, these were removed and the tank mounted firmly on the ground. Adjacent to the LOX tank were two nitrogen storage trailers which each contained thirty-eight cylinders of the compressed gas (GN2) with a total capacity of 55,000 cubic feet. The gas was used to pressurise the LOX tank during the loading process. GN2 supplies had to be replenished on a regular basis as the gas was used during practice countdowns when the LOX was loaded into the missile. Each wing was supplied with seventy-one GN2 trailers—sixty on site and eleven to allow for replenishing where the fleet of Leyland 19H tractors were in constant use to transport the empty cylinders for refilling. Both fuel and LOX were supplied to the missile through 6-inch stainless steel pipes suspended on gallows to allow for expansion. The northern blast wall protected five trailers. These were: a hydropneumatic systems controller, a power-driven reciprocating compressor, two GN2 cylinder semi-trailers, and a compressed gas storage unit. The southern blast wall protected: an air-conditioning unit, a trailer-mounted launching countdown unit, a hydraulic pumping unit, and a power distribution switchboard, while

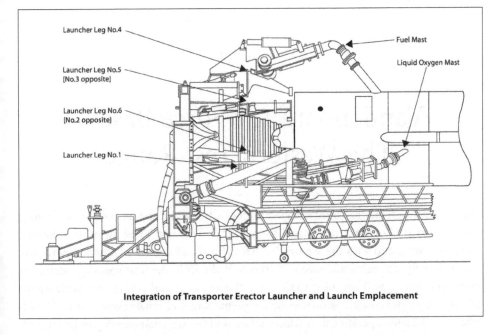

Launcher Leg No.4

Launcher Leg No.5
[No.3 opposite]

Launcher Leg No.6
[No.2 opposite]

Launcher Leg No.1

Fuel Mast

Liquid Oxygen Mast

Integration of Transporter Erector Launcher and Launch Emplacement

parked beside the shelter was a missile checkout unit. Seven floodlight towers provided the necessary illumination to the pad. The missile itself was mounted on a 22-ton launch structure secured on the launch emplacement. The TEL reversed up to this structure and, once secured, the transporter bearing the missile thereafter became the erector.

Security was provided by an inner and outer security fence. The sterile zone between the two fences was patrolled at night by RAF Police dogs. The site was well illuminated, with particular emphasis on the sterile zone. Certainly at Feltwell—and possibly at other sites as well—the inside of the chain link fence was blackened, which considerably assisted the patrols in maintaining an effective watch inside the zone. On at least two sites, Harrington and Bardney, a third lower outer fence was in evidence to protect livestock grazing in fields adjacent to the sites.

Vandenberg Air Force Base— The Western Test Range

The Eastern Test Range had been adequate for the early test launches of Thor, but something more suited to Air Force needs had to be found. This had to be away from heavily populated areas and with the sea over which the missiles could be launched in relative safety close by. Though some favoured staying at the ETR, the west coast was viewed as more convenient, as it was near to the aircraft companies and contractors building the missiles. A further consideration was the requirement to find suitable bases for the ICBMs when they became operational. A selection board under the chairmanship of Lieutenant-Colonel Vernon L. Hastings, the chief of the WDD's IOC Branch, examined around 200 different possible Government-owned sites, but in June 1956 selected a US Army training facility called Camp Cooke on the Californian coast, some 160 miles north-west of Los Angeles. Camp Cooke had been closed in 1953 after the end of the Korean War, so by the time the 82,000-acre site was selected it was largely derelict, but was maintained in a standby state by Army Disciplinary Barracks personnel. It had originally been chosen by the Army in 1941 as a suitable training area for a variety of units.[1] It was remote, there was plenty of space available to build launch facilities at a distance from the administration and accommodation facilities, and the climate was relatively favourable, without seasonal changes that might affect operations. In the wider military context it was essentially the only location in the United States which offered safe launch trajectories into polar orbit. While not significant as such for the IRBM programme, this was a major consideration for the forthcoming reconnaissance satellite programme. Yet Secretary Quarles was initially unwilling to spend a large amount of money on establishing the base. He saw no reason why ETR could not continue to be used. A site selection briefing headed by Colonel Osmand J. Ritland, deputising for Major-General Schriever, took place on 10 August 1956. This proved seminal for the future of missiles within the Air Force. Quarles faced senior officers who presented a strong, united front in support of the Cooke proposal. Clearly riled by the force of the presentation, and still of the opinion that the ETR presented the best option, Quarles stated that the one criteria being used in selecting the site was that whether it permitted systems exercise. This was not an accepted Air Force policy. He had never approved such a requirement and it should not have been used as part of the selection criteria. He stated that this criterion presented a clear bias in favour of the recommendation of Camp Cooke. Nor should the discussion of a west coast impact point have been included as a part of the site selection briefing. General Power then indicated that there would have to be some place available to exercise the operational crews, to explode an atomic warhead and to utilise the thousands of missiles that would be built. To this Quarles responded that he had no intention to build more than a few hundred missiles; no exercise of an operational missile with an atomic warhead would be allowed, and he did not visualise the exercise of the complete system less the nuclear warhead. The Air Force considered the ETR as, broadly speaking, an R&D facility. General Don R. Ostrander, Assistant Deputy Commander for Weapon Systems and formerly the Deputy Commander of the 6540th Missile Test Wing, advised that the US Army experience at the White Sands Proving Grounds—where they had attempted to conduct operational training and R&D—was that the two were not compatible and failed in accomplishing successful operational testing. Two distinct facilities were required. In the face of this continuing barrage, Quarles eventually gave way and signified his approval of Camp Cooke if the Air Staff could present a case justifying the need for a missile proving range. An interesting note in the memo record of the meeting was the comment that, 'during the rather intense two hour discussion [...] WDD personnel remained silent.'[2] The case was duly successfully argued, and so in November 1956 Wilson ordered that 64,000 acres of North Camp Cooke, bounded on the south by the Santa Inez River, be transferred, without public disclosure, from the Army to the Air Force, and although the formalities were not completed until 21 June 1957, Air Force access was permitted immediately so that work on converting the area could begin.[3] This work was directed by 6591st Support Squadron. The area was given the name Cooke AFB, but it was to be renamed on 4 October 1958, Vandenberg AFB, the name it retains to this day. This was to become the Air Force's main missile development complex.[4]

In October 1958, the *Santa Maria Times* reported, 'during the next three months the US Army Corps of Engineers[5] expects the award of [...] $9 million worth of construction at Vandenberg Air Force Base.'[6] This was in addition to existing contracts already placed and would bring to a total of nearly $62 million the value of work contracted for by 31 January 1959.

> Engineers declined to name the projects, but mentioned that they will include fuel storage facilities, additional Thor launchers, missile assembly buildings, and an access road to a launching area [...] Colonel Sanders, Army Engineer in charge of the base construction program, said that it would be a few more weeks before the first Atlas launcher itself is complete. All of the Thor launchers, however, have been completed and turned over to Strategic Air Command.[7]

An 8,000-foot runway had also been built to facilitate the transport of the missiles and components to the base. From the start it was planned to conduct static firings and live launches. Siting criteria required the pads to be at least 5 miles from any inhabited building and away from any populated areas because of the high noise levels. Dry-flame deflectors were to be developed for static firings. However, for early static firings, cooled-flame deflectors would be used. This would allow for firings of between five and ten seconds but would require a water flow of between 7,000 and 10,000 gallons per minute.[8] It was further recommended that test equipment be developed so that the 'motor and pressurisation systems [could] be tested to some extent and that the frequency of the static fire test [could] be reduced to reasonable proportions.'[9]

In total, seven Thor launch pads were constructed at Purisima Point in what was known as 'Area 75'. A further two pads, on a complex designated 75-4, were planned but construction of which was subsequently deemed unnecessary. Two were two-pad complexes and one was a three-pad complex essentially trialling the operational layout in the UK, to which they remained largely similar (apart from a few features necessitated by their nature as re-useable pads, and which the 'one use' UK pads did not require). They were, however, development pads and were modified as the full operational configuration design was consolidated. As the downrange flightpath of the missiles was over the Pacific, i.e. to the west, this differed from the UK downrange direction, which was to the east. This therefore required that the orientation of the Vandenberg pads be approximately 180 degrees to their UK equivalents. The two 75-3 pads were used by Douglas and Lockheed for the USAF satellite programme and were orientated to allow for southerly launches which enabled satellites to be placed in polar orbit.

> [Area 75] sat amongst sand dunes just a short distance from the ocean. Wind was an ever-present factor that was dealt with on a daily basis.

Dave Prebish remembers,

> [...] our pad work areas, even inside the vehicle shelters, were not environmentally sealed like modern systems are. The weather inside was the same as the weather outside; all the dust, cold wind and fog from the ocean leaked in through big gaps in the shelters. [...] Pretty much all operations took place out on the drafty launch pads.[10]

> Despite abatement efforts such as deer grass being planted and snow fencing being constructed, shifting sand was always a problem.[11]

The pads designations were as follows (there was no Pad 3):

Pad Number Initial Designation	Pad Number From Sept 1961	Pad number Final 'Slick'	First Launch	RAF—IWST	RAF—CTL
75-1-1		SLC-2E	16 Dec 1958	IWST-3,6	CTL-2
75-1-2		SLC-2W	17 Sep 1959	IWST-5, 7, 8, 9	
75-2-6*	LE-6	SLC-10W	14 Aug 1959	IWST-4	
75-2-7	LE-7	SLC-10E	16 Jun 1959	IWST-2	CTL-4, 7, 8, 9, 11

75-2-8	LE-8	SLC-10N**	16 Apr 1959	IWST-1	CTL-1, 3, 5, 6, 10, 12
75-3-4		SLC-1W	28 Feb 1959		
75-3-5		SLC-1E	25 Jun 1959		

* Also referred to as 4300 B-6.
** This designation is rarely used.

The first two pads to be constructed (75-1-1 and -2) were 'wet pads' about 2,000 feet apart that would allow not only actual launches, but captive launches as well. Because of this, the protection for the various pieces of equipment required for the launches was more robust than the simpler blast walls incorporated in the operational design. A flame bucket was accommodated where in the final design the LOX tank was to be sited. This required the LOX tank to be offset by 45 degrees. Each pad complex had a Control Centre (CC) or blockhouse from which the launches were conducted.[12] In addition a RIM Building was constructed to handle the missiles on arrival before transfer to the launch pads. Two DAC technical teams covering service and technical functions were based permanently at Vandenberg. A later team was to be added to handle the refurbishment of the launch pads after launches. The RIM Building was approximately 7 miles from the launch complexes and this caused serious logistic problems, firstly in the movement of personnel between the two locations and secondly in the provision of technical backup to missiles in place on the launch pads.[13] Captive launches covered all aspects of the countdown except the actual launch as the missile was held captive on the pad with the flame pattern deflected into the water-protected flame trench. In August 1958 Thor T142 was used as a facilities check vehicle on the first pad to verify the missile's compatibility with the launch emplacement. It obviously had a rigorous life as on 5 February 1959 it was declared 'Bent—No Launch on Pad 2'.[14] The first two pads, although differing in a number of ways from the final layout, did not prevent them from being used by RAF crews for seven of their sequence of launches of live missiles.

As can be seen, the twenty-one Thors launched by RAF crews took place from five of the seven pads with all but one of the later Combat Training Launches (CTLs) concentrated on LE-7 and LE-8 within Space Launch Complex 10 (SLC-10). 'Slick 10' therefore played an important role in the development of Thor as an IRBM and later also in the early stages of the satellite and anti-satellite programmes. Its significance was recognised in 1986 when SLC-10 was designated a National Historic Landmark 'possessing national significance in commemorating the history of the United States of America.' It was refurbished by 4315th Combat Crew Training Squadron to become the Vandenberg AFB Space and Missile Heritage Center. The three pads on the original 75-2 complex covered 138 acres and were set out in much the same way as a typical UK site. Orientation was roughly east-west with west, over the Pacific Ocean, as downrange. Rather than an open Launch Control Area the complex featured a 'T'-shaped Blockhouse approximately 500 feet from

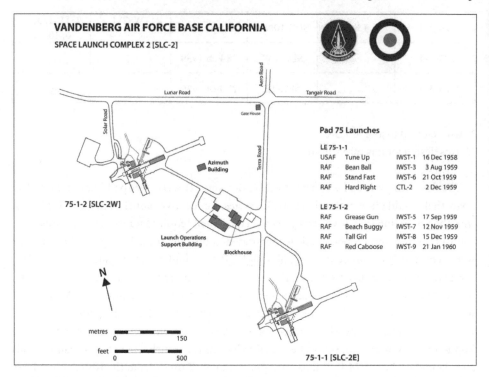

each pad from which launch operations for all three pads were conducted.[15] This replaced the mobile trailers that were a feature of the operational sites. Alternatively known as the Launch Control Center or Launch Operations Building, it was of hardened construction to withstand any explosions on the launch pads. Made from heavily reinforced concrete with a roof made from layers of steel embedded in high strength concrete, entry was via a steel blast door. Outside, a shale revetment gave some protection against mishaps on the launch pad and also against winds blowing in from the Pacific. Inside, the building was divided into four rooms. Apart from the main launch operations room there was a communications room a mechanical room and a latrine, all accessed off a main corridor. In case of some problem with the main door, an emergency escape hatch was located in the roof. By late 1961 the later RAF launch crews had an additional wooden 'penthouse' mounted on the roof.[16] This provided an additional two-room facility which was officially used as a study area, although Sergeant Maurice Botley remembers it being used for recreational table tennis.[17] His memory is echoed by Douglas employee Larry Kasulka, who was always happy for an excuse to visit the launch area when the RAF were there—

> We liked going over to their complex as the RAF types had built a club house on top of their launch control center where they could relax, have a game of billiards, draughts, watch TV and have a drink. Sort of like a NCO club.[18]

Kasulka had been on an USAF exchange posting to the UK, during which time he had visited one of the Thor sites.

I remember the shelter was there but not a lot more than that. [...] Because of my exchange with the RAF and the great reception I received from the people I decided when I graduated to interview with Douglas and try to get on the Thor Program and be sent to the UK to support RAF facilities.

Although successful in being taken on by Douglas, Kasulka never made it to the UK as a result of the termination of the Thor programme, but continued to be involved with Thor and its derivatives for some thirty years. In the midst of this modern launch facility there remained a remnant of Camp Cooke's former role in the Second World War and the Korean War. The area had previously been the site of an infantry infiltration training facility that was called the 'Indian Village' and comprised various wooden structures representing a native village, albeit in a much dilapidated state. (The rubble from this facility remains to this day on the dirt road between CC-3 and LE-6.)[19]

The two dry pads on 75-3, neither used by the RAF, were later re-configured to support the CORONA optical surveillance satellite launches which used Thor-Agena two-stage launchers. Although publically described as a research programme, the DISCOVERER series of launches—later identified as the CORONA programme—were conducted under a secret CIA-Lockheed agreement to develop the KH-1 reconnaissance satellite programme to provide imagery of the Soviet Union.[20] The pads were used for rigorous checking out of the complete systems, a procedure not always without incident. On one occasion, the programme to simulate the flight sequence was being tested—ostensibly a low-risk operation. However, unknown to a civilian technician who was installing a loudspeaker on a pole, the test crew had forgotten to disconnect the squibs and the retrorockets which duly fired at the appropriate time in the flight sequence, much to the alarm of the technician, who left his safety harness attached to the top of the pole in his haste to escape.[21] The main structural features of SLC-10 during the RAF era were:

Launch Emplacement North (LE-8)—Facility 1661.
Launch Emplacement East (LE-7)—Facility 1651.
Launch Emplacement West (LE-6)—Facility 1658.
Blockhouse—Facility 1654.
Maintenance Support Building—Facility 1664, adjacent to LE-7.
Located on the hardstanding of LE6 were a Power Substation—Facility 1669—Storage and Administration building—Facility 1663—and a Tank Farm.

Added later were:

Metal Building—Facility 1656. A former 1940s Army building re-located.
Office and Administration—Facility 1657. Also a former 1940s building.
Technical Support Building—Facility 1659.

Cooke had officially become an Air Force Base on 1 January 1958 when Lieutenant-

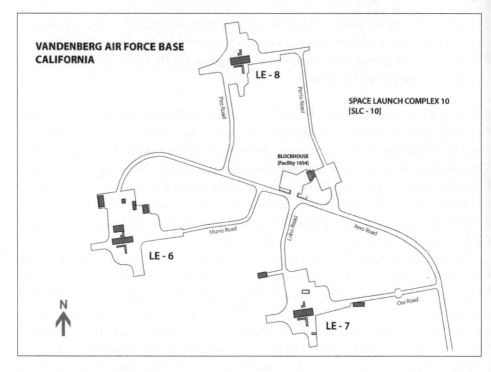

**VANDENBERG AIR FORCE BASE
CALIFORNIA**

LE - 8

SPACE LAUNCH COMPLEX 10
[SLC - 10]

BLOCKHOUSE
[Facility 1654]

LE - 6

Mona Road

Lobo Road

Aero Road

Oro Road

N

LE - 7

General David Wade assumed command of the 1st Missile Division, thus becoming the first officer to command an operational missile unit. However, as well as maintaining an operational capability, he was also tasked with training the crews that would man the missiles. On the same date the 672d Strategic Missile Squadron (SMS) was activated under the command of Colonel Harry H. Zink. On 3 January the Air Force publicly announced the formation of this unit along with a parallel Jupiter squadron, 864th SMS which would be activated on 15 January under the command of Colonel William (Bill) C. Erlenbusch. Both squadrons would be under the direct control of SAC, but their formation would allow plans to be made for the training of missile personnel. Of the two Zink had the easier appointment, as the decision to develop both missiles after the vicious conflict between the Army and Air Force was still an open wound for many of the Army missile personnel at the Redstone Arsenal. Fortuitously, when Erlenbusch arrived at Redstone he was able to confirm,

> […] the top people here like Wernher von Braun and Gen John Medaris, who is head of the Army Ballistic Missile Agency, are showing me utmost cooperation and support. They fully understand my position. But it's just some second level people who are a little antagonistic.[22]

Colonel Zink announced the plans for Thor at a meeting of the opening session of the Air Force Association's third Jet Age Conference on 26 February 1958. He unveiled details of the new automatic launching system and confirmed that the missiles could be launched at fifteen minutes' notice, and if special precautions were ordered during times of international crisis, or if circumstances dictated, this could be reduced to a two-minute countdown.[23]

Clearly it was going to be necessary to provide comprehensive training facilities for both USAF and RAF missile personnel, and to this end the 392d Strategic Missile Squadron (Training) was formed on 23 May 1957, assigned to the 704th Strategic Missile Wing. On 22 July both organisations were reassigned to the 1st Missile Division, ARDC. Reflecting a decision that strategic units should be directly involved in an operational role, the unit was renamed 392d Missile Training Squadron (IRBM-THOR) on 12 August. The unit was formally activated on 15 September under the command of Major Richard A. Plumley.[24] Command passed to Major Robert C. Owens on 25 October. Both these officers continued to serve with the AFBMD but a third change of command took place on 13 November, when Major Charles E. Bruck assumed permanent command. By the following month, five officers and six enlisted men had started an eight-week instructor training course at Sheppard AFB. On 5 March 1958, Major Bruck became Deputy Commander of the squadron when Colonel Robert W. Christy, a former B-47 pilot, took over command. On 1 April the 'Thor' nomenclature was dropped and the unit became 392d Missile Training Squadron (IRBM). By mid-year an RAF liaison office had been established at Vandenberg and Flying Officer Cyril D. Quinton became the first RAFLO. The squadron's directed mission was to:

—attain and maintain a training capability and train IRBM crews and units to meet programmed requirements.
—assist IRBM crews and units in preparation for deployment as directed by higher headquarters.
—establish requirements for and assure availability of IRBM technical training facilities.
—assure availability of equipment and material support peculiar to IRBM missile training.
—develop plans, procedures, and techniques for training of IRBM crews and units.
—develop and conduct a detailed evaluation programme for crews and units in training.

Christy, commented, 'we know the United States Air Force and the Royal Air Force, and the entire free world will benefit by the role we are playing in the world today.'[25]

The first Thor launch from Vandenberg was obviously a significant event both from the technical point of view, but also as a marker to the Soviets of growing US capability. In the spring of 1958 Lieutenant-General Wade therefore determined that the first launch would be an operational firing, defined as one conducted by service personnel—as opposed to missile engineers—success, or otherwise, would be judged by the level of target destruction the test caused or might have caused. The Air Force crew would be fully trained and qualified to undertake the launch, albeit with discreet contractor back-up. Rear Admiral Jack P. Monroe, Commander of the Pacific Missile Test Range at Point Mugu was in charge of telemetry and tracking. The missile allocated for this first launch was T151. It had been delivered to Vandenberg on 13 August and had thereafter been subjected to rigorous testing. There was at that time no missile-tracking capability other than that which was located at Vandenberg and nothing at all downrange in the impact area. Launch date was set for 16 December 1958 from Pad 75-1-1. A holiday was declared on the base so that all personnel could witness the launch, and a festive spirit prevailed during the countdown activities.[26] The *Santa Maria Times* had already alerted readers to the imminent launch:

> Intensified activity at the country's newest range at Vandenberg Air Force Base indicated today that the firing of a 1,500-mile Thor missile was imminent…. Firing of the mighty intermediate range ballistic missile will mean that it officially has moved from the test stage into the hands of the military as an operational device ready for use as a weapon. The Thor carries an atomic punch in its warhead. A tense expectancy filled the air in the city [of Santa Maria] which is brimming over with civilian missile technicians and reporters who have rented nearly all available motel and hotel room. When the Thor blasts off from the Pacific missile range at Vandenberg it will be the first missile launched by a strictly military crew comprised of Strategic Air Command men.[27]

Some 200 members of the press watched from a specially constructed stand 8,200 feet from the launch pad. The weather was ideal for the launch, warm and sunny with a slight breeze. Perhaps inevitably, delays to the countdown were caused by equipment problems. At one point Lieutenant-General Wade went to the press stand to assure them that all was well. The crew consisted of eleven men from the 392d Missile Training Squadron, commanded by seasoned combat pilot Captain John C. Bon Tempo,[28] who later confirmed, 'this was the first [launch] into the Pacific Range and was a complete success in every way.'[29] The *Toledo Blade* reported:

> The blastoff came only eleven minutes after the crew raised the Thor upright and began filling it with liquid fuel. Two and one half minutes after the first sign of fire in its tail, the missile was off and racing at a speed of 9,000 miles an hour. Seconds later the fuel tank section of the missile fell away and was burned up by friction as it re-entered the earth's atmosphere. The nose cone stage sped on, reaching its maximum speed of 10,000 miles an hour before plunging back through the earth's atmosphere to its impact area 1,500 miles away.[30]

Eight members of the launch team were awarded the Air Force Commendation Medal,

> [having] distinguished themselves in the performance of meritorious historic service while assigned as members of a missile launch crew […] during the period 18 August 1958 through 16 December 1958. As a result of their diligent and untiring efforts, coupled with the highest degree of initiative, they obtained the necessary skill to bring great credit upon the Strategic Air Command by participating in the successful launching of the first Intermediate Range Ballistic Missile ever to be launched by an all military crew.[31]

In addition to Captain Bon Tempo they were, Captain Bennie Castillo the Launch Officer who actually initiated the countdown sequence with the turn of a key. He was backed up by Senior Master Sergeant Charles E. Gifford Sr who manned a second launch console. There were five other enlisted men in the launch crew: Master Sergeants Thomas F. Addison,

Michael J. Auer and William L. Hodges, Technical Sergeant Otis J. Le Maire, and Staff Sergeant Max L. Meyer. Their duties covered the Launch Technician and his assistant who were responsible for placing the missile on the launch mount and connecting the umbilical for fuel and LOX; the Guidance Technician ensured that the guidance platform was aligned correctly. The remaining two supervised activities around the pad. The launch which had been preceded by a number of practice countdowns was supported by the ARDC's Ballistic Missile Division Field Officer and Douglas personnel. Nicknamed TUNE UP, the 15-minute, 1,460-mile flight was deemed a success landing 3 miles west and 6 miles north of the target. Today, a plaque in the SLC-2 blockhouse commemorates the event: 'FROM THIS SITE THE FIRST BAL. MISSILE WAS LAUNCHED FROM V.A.F.B. DEC.16 1958'.

The difficult task of launching the missile used new procedures and had been achieved with a weapon system that was, thanks to concurrency, constantly changing. The Air Force crew took over for the last fifteen minutes of the automated count-down with the launch taking place at 1544.45 PST. *The Los Angeles Times* headlined the event on its front page: 'Big Thor Missile Blasts Off to Open West Coast Base'. Correspondent Ralph Dighton reported from Vandenberg:

An Air Force crew lobbed a combat-type Thor missile 1,500 miles westward over the Pacific missile range yesterday. The deadly white dart rose slowly from its launch pad at this Strategic Air Command Base, then gathered speed swiftly. Three minutes later it was out of sight and racing towards its target area at speeds approaching 10,000 mph. The roar of its takeoff was heard for miles around. [...] The success of the shot was ammunition for the America's campaign to secure missile bases overseas.[32]

The *Santa Maria Times* further reported,

Tuesday's shot described as 'perfect' by all who saw it was the first of many that will be made from the launching-pads at Vandenberg. Many of the shots will be routine training shots—if any missile launch can ever be categorized as 'routine'. The Air Force is to be congratulated on making such an auspicious debut. And the men behind the crew—the Strategic Air Command officers who set up the training procedures and policies and the civilian contractor personnel who supervised the training—are deserving of a hearty pat on the back.[33]

The editorial ended on a sombre note—

The Thor launched Tuesday was fired as a weapon. It was designed to rain death and destruction on human beings. As the days and weeks and months pass and the fiery missiles flash across the western sky and out into the Pacific Ocean, let us pray that the day never arrives when the Thor, Atlas and all their counterparts will have to be armed with a nuclear warhead and launched 'in anger'.[34]

In many ways this was a remarkable achievement taking place just under three years since the contracts with Douglas were signed. While the missile was not yet truly operational, the launch had proved that the necessary components were in place to take the missiles to the UK and also most importantly for the Air Force, that the missile worked. US Senator Francis Case who was on an inspection tour of the base commented, 'it certainly should be reassuring for our British allies that the Thor is on the threshold of tactical readiness.'[35] To further reinforce the point, another IOC Thor (T146) was launched successfully from the ETR shortly before T151. Two successful launches on the same day. To the Soviets, it indicated that the US was serious about countering any threat from the Warsaw Pact. The next launch of an operational missile would be undertaken by an RAF crew.

Reporting the successful launch to General Thomas S. Power, Commander of SAC, Lieutenant-General Wade identified a number of 'firsts': the first ballistic missile launched westwards into the Pacific Missile Range; the first known operation in which new equipment, a new missile, new personnel, and a new organisation had been successfully integrated; the first fully automatic launch of a fully operational ballistic missile using normal launch procedures and the first ballistic missile to be launched by a SAC operational crew.[36] In fact this inaugural launch from Vandenberg was not the event originally planned to show that the base was 'open for business'. The debut launch was to have been T163, Thor-Agena A, 'DISCOVERER 1' launch, codenamed 'FLYING YANKEE'. Prior to the proposed launch date, the Douglas crew were unloading LOX from the Thor into the storage tank. At the same time, Lockheed engineers were conducting a simulated flight on the Agena. However, the retro-rockets had inadvertently not been safed. Their purpose was to separate the Agena second stage from the Thor first stage.

> During the simulated flight, [and] on cue, the retro rockets did what they were designed to do—they fired. [One] thing you don't want to hear during a propellant operation is the loud roar of rockets being fired. The Douglas Safety Engineer that was reversing the propellant operation was a middle-aged man named Al Benford. [He] surely set the land speed record for running about 200 yards up the steep incline in a heavy rubberised suit from Pad-4 to the blockhouse.[37]

The DISCOVERER mission was subsequently launched on 28 February 1959 but failed to reach orbit. Promoted to Major, Bon Tempo went on to serve as Operations Officer at Vandenberg.

RAF Training Begins

The Secretary of the Air Force of the United States authorizes and invites you to proceed from your present station in the United Kingdom to Tucson, Arizona, reporting to Mr B. G. Smith, Douglas Aircraft Company, Municipal Airport, Tucson.

The Thor Agreement had intimated that the RAF personnel involved in the programme would be trained on the missile systems and operations in the US. This was a significant undertaking which by the end of the programme would see some 1,254 RAF personnel, officers, and NCOs cross the Atlantic, while a roughly equal number were trained in the UK.[1] Fortunately, the need for adequate training had been identified from the start but the complexity of developing a suitable training programme was, perhaps quite understandably, underestimated. The training programme had, by its very nature, to anticipate a level of capability that was being defined day by day as work on the development of the missile progressed. As early as June 1956, meetings were taking place between the contractors and US Air Training Command. The main purpose at this stage was to identify which existing skills within the Air Force could be transferable and which new skills would have to be created. There was no existing experience of training missile crews, so a complex training programme had to be defined and implemented from scratch. This was the task allotted to S. E. Cowell, who was tasked with creating a Missile Training Division within DAC. It also had to run in parallel and be part of the overall concurrency programme. Cowell formed the Thor Training Group which by May 1957 employed fifteen personnel. The group had responsibility for all DAC missile programs so Cowell split the division into two. E. R. Hale would handle Nike, Sparrow and Genie missiles, while J. L. Hawkins would have responsibility for Thor. A separate project coordinator's office within the Thor Project Office was initially headed up by F. D. Ewing. It was this office that was responsible for developing the Qualitative Personnel Requirements Information Report (QPRI) on which early training was based. On 1 April, DAC had been issued with a contract[2] to 'establish, define, collate and correlate individual training and squadron training course technical information, procedures and techniques within each specific job speciality for Air Force Personnel.'[3] During the second half of 1957, the size of the training team progressively grew. Lack of sufficient information proved a particular problem, especially with reference to the Ground Support Equipment, much of which had still to be defined and required 'best guesses' to be made by those involved. Even the dates by which the training was expected to be started fluctuated between autumn 1958 and mid-1959. By December 1957 the fully sized simulated LE at Culver City had been completed, and this at least allowed everyone involved to see what the complete set-up looked like. However, by early 1958, the deployment schedule was accelerated and training had to begin with certain inevitable gaps in the programme. The training programme thus initiated failed to meet Air Force needs and was therefore termed 'interim training'. At this stage US involvement was still anticipated and the programme allowed for interim training for the first two squadrons—identified as the 672d and 673rd Strategic Missile Squadrons—while the 674th and 675th SM Squadrons would receive later, but formal, training corresponding to Air Force needs.[4] Lack of full equipment on which to train the first two squadrons raised the need for a training team to be available in the UK to complete training on site. In January 1958 five officers and ten airmen attended training at DAC Santa Monica and these US personnel were to form the initial training cadre at Vandenberg. By May personnel were in place to start the initial training of the RAF crews which had started arriving from the UK. However, the programme was still hampered by a lack of actual equipment on which to train. This led to frustration and much criticism by trainees on the early courses. Vandenberg was where crew training would take place using the actual launch facilities on the base. 'Crew Training' was by then considered an inadequate course description and the programme was renamed Integrated Weapon System Training (IWST).[5] Because by the time the crews reached Vandenberg they should be trained to a competent level to operate the missile, every effort was made to run the area as a quasi-operational environment.

It must be borne in mind that there had been no precursor to this type of training. Assumptions were inevitably made that proved to be misconceived when the actual training started to take place. IWST was initially divided into the following functions:

Static firings
Wet countdowns
Dry countdowns
Malfunction countdowns
Missile indexing
Pre-flight inspection
One live launch per class

Static firings were designed to give students a feel for the full fury, in sight and sound, of the engine. In practice, however, static firings proved difficult to integrate into the programme and could result in significant damage to the launch emplacement which caused delays when refurbishment had to be undertaken. The expected psychological benefits of experiencing live firings were also deemed to have been overestimated and static firings were therefore soon eliminated from the course. Specific countdown malfunctions were found to be unnecessary, as there were more than enough malfunctions happening under normal operating conditions! Pre-flight inspection was a heading found to be essentially

1. Douglas Thor production line at Santa Monica, California. (*Author's Collection*)

2. Major-General Bernard Schriever seen here with Senator (later President) Lyndon Johnson, Chairman of the Senate Missile Preparedness Sub-Committee. Between them is a model of Thor. (*Author's Collection*)

3. Donald Douglas Jr demonstrates a Thor model to Lieutenant-Colonel Sidney Greene, Deputy Director of the Thor Weapon System, Air Force Ballistic Missile Division. (*Author's Collection*)

4. A MATS Thor Haul C-124 prepares to unload at RAF Hemswell. (*Author's Collection*)

5. A Thor is unloaded at RAF Driffield. (*Author's Collection*)

6. Santa Monica in the Wolds. US trailer accommodation. (*Author's Collection*)

7. A 1957 Cadillac Series 62 brought across by its owner sits at the end of a launch emplacement. (*V. Laws*)

8. Leo Carter and Harvey Mathis pose for an informal photo with other Douglas staff. (*V. Laws*)

9. Brandon Park Great House as it is today, a residential care home—once accommodation for some of the US personnel. (*Author's Collection*)

10. *L to R*: Donald Douglas Jr, Andy Roman, and Peter Portanova during a visit by Douglas to the UK to review progress of Project Emily. (*V. Laws*)

11. The de Havilland Dragon Rapide used as an inter-site 'taxi'. (*Author's Collection*)

12. Nuclear Disarmament protesters at North Pickenham. (*Author's Collection*)

13. RAF Feltwell from the air. One of the Thors is erect. (*V. Laws*)

14. The Thor Transporter Erector Launcher (TEL) with a Leyland Hippo tractor unit. (*IWM*)

15. A shrouded Thor in transit, pulled by a GM M-52. (*Author's Collection*)

16. Missile convoy negotiating the village of Rothwell *en route* to RAF Harrington. (*Author's Collection*)

17. Two Thors being serviced in the RIM Building at North Luffenham. (*Author's Collection*)

18. Thor 47 is carefully reversed into its shelter. It was later launched during CTL-6, ACTON TOWN. (*Author's Collection*)

19. Thor launch emplacement at RAF Driffield. (*Author's Collection*)

20. Thor 08 on its launch emplacement. (*Author's Collection*)

21. Thor 08 complete with launch crew and RAF police contingent. (*Author's Collection*)

22. A warhead convoy prepares to leave. (*Author's Collection*)

23. A warhead is prepared for attaching to the nose of a Thor. (*Author's Collection*)

24. Close-up of the warhead in situ. (*Author's Collection*)

25. An RAF Policeman and his dog stand guard over one of the Thors at RAF Feltwell. (*Author's Collection*)

26. Personnel of No. 107(SM) Squadron, RAF Tuddenham. (*Author's Collection*)

27. The final RAF Thor is delivered to North Luffenham, 10 March 1960. (*Author's Collection*)

28. Vandenberg AFB, launch emplacement 75-1-2. (*L. Kasulka*)

29. Vandenberg AFB, launch emplacement LE-1. (*Author's Collection*)

30. The first Thor launch at Vandenberg AFB, Op TUNE UP, 16 December 1958. (*Author's Collection*)

31. The USAF launch crew for the first Thor launch at Vandenberg AFB, Op TUNE UP. (*Author's Collection*)

32. A mixed RAF/USAF training cadre. Chf Techs Richard Pratt (third from left back row) and Maurice Botley (back row right). (*Author's Collection*)

33. Construction of the 'Club Room' on top of the SLC-10 Blockhouse. (*J. Watters*)

34. SLC-10 Blockhouse, Bld 1654, in 2008. (*Author's Collection*)

35. Major John Bon Tempo (right) briefs visiting VIPs on the intricacies of the launch process. (*J. Watters*)

36. Chf Tech. Roy Carpenter reports to the launch control officer, Sqn Ldr Robert Coulson, that all is ready for the first RAF Thor launch, LIONS ROAR, on 16 April 1959. (*Author's Collection*)

37. IWST-1, the first RAF launch, LIONS ROAR, 16 April 1959. (*Author's Collection*)

38. IWST-5, GREASE GUN, Vandenberg AFB, 17 September 1959. (*Author's Collection*)

39. IWST-6, STAND FAST, LOX boils off prior to launch on 21 October 1959. (*Author's Collection*)

40. IWST-8, TALL GIRL, Vandenberg AFB, 15 December 1959. (*Author's Collection*)

41. CTL-8, WHITE BISHOP, Vandenberg AFB, 20 June 1961. (*Author's Collection*)

42. CTL-12, BLAZING CINDERS, the final RAF launch, Vandenberg AFB, 19 June 1962. (*Author's Collection*)

43. AVM Peter Dunn, AOC 1 Gp, Gp Capt. K. W. T. Pugh, Station Commander RAF Driffield, and personnel of CTL-11. (*Author's Collection*)

44. CTL-11 launch crew: F/S G. H. Thompson, Chf Tech. J. E. Parkinson, Cpl Tech. I. F. Stapley, Sqn Ldr P. I. Hart (OC No. 226(SM) Sqn), Flt Lt R. A. Whitcher, Cpl Tech. R. J. L. Berthiaume, Cpl Tech. J. M. Tinton. (*Author's Collection*)

45. Major-General David Wade, Commander 1 Missile Division, inspects a Thor launch emplacement at Vandenberg. (*Author's Collection*)

46. MRAF Sir John Salmond arrives as a VIP guest at No. 220(SM) Sqn and is greeted by AOC 3 Gp, AVM Michael Dwyer, and OC RAF Feltwell, Gp Capt. W. M. Dixon. (*Author's Collection*)

47. The long journey home: Thor No. 25 being loaded into a C-133 at the end of Project Emily. (*Author's Collection*)

48. The end of the project: the launch structure is removed from one of the Driffield LEs. (*TNA*)

49. Thors in storage in the RIM Building at Vandenberg AFB. (*Author's Collection*)

50. On 23 April 1962, Donald Douglas (left on stand) congratulates employees at Santa Monica on delivery of the 40,000th missile to the US Armed Forces since 1940. (*Author's Collection*)

51. Ex-RAF Thor T252, launched from Johnston Island on 29 November 1968. (*P. Hunter*)

Thor 304 (DMSP B5D1-05)   15 Jul 1980   WTR SLC-10W   01963

52. The last ex-RAF Thor to be launched: T304 ready for launch from SLC-10W on 17 July 1980. (*P. Hunter*)

53 A national historic landmark: the preserved SLC-10 LE at Vandenberg AFB. (*Author's Collection*)

redundant, the product of anticipating events based on theory which were deemed unnecessary in practice. However, all these problems paled into relative insignificance when it came to the live launches.

Launching missiles became the center point of all the effort that the Air Force and the contractors were capable of expending. It was under these conditions that the training of students became a secondary effort.[6]

The perception was that the missiles and the GSE being used were to an operational configuration which was not in itself untrue, however was erroneously taken as a standard against which to measure the performance of operational missiles being sent to the UK. Equipment being used repeatedly by semi-experienced crews for training purposes was subject to degradation, which should not have been translated as a comparison to operational missiles held on standby. The pressure exerted by the Air Force on the training schedule to succeed and the concern of the contractors' staff to demonstrate a reliable system led to sensible working hour limits being exceeded, in many cases by considerable amounts—some employees working in excess of a twenty-hour day. Their mistakes were born of exhaustion:

Conditions reached such a state of panic that many instructors were literally afraid to let students touch any equipment that had been placed in a readiness condition for fear that a launch schedule would be disrupted. This unhappy state of affairs existed almost from the beginning and followed the programme to its conclusion.[7]

A further problem was that most of the training took place at the launch complex, but the technical support was 7 miles away at the RIM Building. This inevitably caused delays when a piece of equipment was required and had to be located and delivered to the launch site. This early period of training was typified by a scenario where 'there was rarely a time when the right number of properly trained people were available for assignment where and when needed.'[8] Not until mid-1959 was the training programme adequately staffed with the properly qualified personnel. It was not a moment too soon, as by this time the delivery of missiles to the UK was in full swing and three of the four wings had either been declared operational or were reaching operational status.

Notwithstanding these problems, successful launches did take place and brought the initial RAF crews to a level of experience whereby they were able to return to the UK and fill operational posts on the nascent sites that were nearing completion. Once again Thor was at the cutting edge. This was an aspect of the programme that seemed to have caused a misunderstanding about the nature of command of the Thor squadrons. Some in Bomber Command saw the project as one requiring, above all, technical knowledge. This was potentially an attractive opportunity for technical officers' careers. It was not until early 1961 that Air Marshal Cross was to concede that the command of a Thor complex was a very rigorous task to which a risk factor no different from flying stations should apply. Cross cited the complexity of the weapon system, the high pressure on the crews during fuelling, and the potential for serious repercussions resulting from even the smallest mistake during routine countdown operations.[9] There is perhaps no better illustration of this last criteria than the major incident at Ludford Magna in December 1960, which may well have been the catalyst in altering Cross's perceptions.[10] Fortunately this vindicated the decision that general duties officers would form the majority of officer posts within the Thor squadrons.

It was a testament to the growing significance of the training programme that Wing Commander Peter J. S. Finlayson AFC, accompanied by his wife and two young children, should take over in May 1959 as the US-based liaison officer (RAFLO).[11] Leaving Southampton on 21 May aboard RMS *Queen Elizabeth*, the family arrived at New York followed by a three-day train journey to California. Based at Vandenberg and living in the ever expanding number of on-base housing, his role was to deal with any administrative problems arising that required RAF action. North Atlantic liners, too, took the first tranches of RAF personnel to the US. The SS *Île de France* left Portsmouth with the first group on 24 May 1958 with the Cunard-owned MV *Britannic* following a month later, leaving from Liverpool on 27 June. The first large intake of RAF personnel to undergo training started arriving at Vandenberg in August 1958 for the eight-week course, coincidentally the same month that the first operational Thor arrived there as well.[12] Launch teams selected from aircrew had to be trained on the launch operations of the missile. For the initial intake this was somewhat frustrating, as the launch complexes on which they were to train were not yet fully complete. Meanwhile, a further group of technical ground trades had to be trained on the complex systems for which there was little or no parallel experience within the RAF. This was emphasised when technicians began arriving at RAF Manby for initial familiarisation with the missile. Sergeant Doug Browne arrived there in November 1958;

> Naturally our teachers knew nothing about the rocket we were to operate; in fact, they did not even know what it was called! So they taught us some simple mathematics and how to get on with the Americans when we arrived in the USA for our training.[13]

Nonetheless, for many, particularly the technical trades, the opportunity to work on state-of-the-art equipment was an appealing prospect, especially when it became apparent that training would take place in the US. Missiles seemed to presage the future and it would be no bad thing to be in the queue when the door to this new technology first opened. Corporal Dave Humphrey had only recently completed apprenticeship training at RAF Halton when he saw that volunteers were needed to work with missiles. He chose to work as a refrigeration specialist technician, completing his training at the Radar and Wireless Training School at RAF Yatesbury before going to Davis-Monthan Air Force Base to complete his Thor qualification. For him, as for many others, the opportunity to volunteer for work on missiles was an exciting opportunity to which was added the prospect of visiting the US.[14] For some, working on the existing RAF equipment was hardly satisfying. Much of it was 'old, often of World War Two vintage and promotion was slow.'[15] The process started in early 1957, when

[...] an Air Ministry Order sought volunteers to work on new missile systems and computers as they became deployed. Their names would be added to a list for use on future undisclosed systems as the need became apparent.[16]

It may well have been that the thought behind this AMO was directed at the anticipated arrival of Blue Streak in the RAF inventory, but the direction soon changed to the need for expertise in Thor. Technical training was based at the Missile Training School at Tucson Airport where Douglas had set up the technical training facility and accommodation and other service facilities were available at the Davis-Monthan AFB some 14 miles to the east.[17] Training was the responsibility of Detachment 1, 3750th Technical Training Wing, who declared that they were there for one purpose only: 'to serve the WS-315A program in any way it could.' As the flags of Britain and America fluttered in the breeze and with the first RAF contingent lined up in the background, the training facility was formally opened on 27 May 1958. Local media reported:

An Air Force General snipped a blue ribbon today as British and American airmen stood at attention to formally open the Thor missile school here at the Douglas Aircraft Co. plant. The program is expected to be the largest joint activity since World War II with hundreds of Air Force and RAF men getting training in missile work. Military, civil and Douglas officials attended the ceremony held in front of the remodelled hangar which will be used for the school. A total of 141,000 square feet of training space has been provided for classrooms and offices in one of the airport's three hangars, a Douglas spokesman said. There will be 43 Douglas instructors with 12 Air Force and civilian instructors from Sheppard and Chanute Air Force Bases. More than 90 per cent of the students will be members of the British RAF. Heading the program for Douglas is Bryan Smith, supervisor of training. Major N. F. Crowder of the Air Training Command, USAF, and Flying Officer R. S. Mills, RAF, will maintain military liaison for the military students—both officers and enlisted men. Classes will be comprised of more than 100 students. Members of the first class were present today for the opening ceremony. [...] All trainees will operate, service, maintain, trouble-shoot and repair the Thor missile. None of the missiles will be fired, however. Work will also be done on ground support systems.[18]

In attendance at the ceremony were Brigadier-General Sam Maddox Jr (special assistant to the Vice Commander ATC), Brigadier-General Delmar E. Wilson (Commanding General 36 AD), Colonel Leslie J. Westbert, Base Commander Davis-Monthan, Flying Officer Mills (representing the RAF), and B. W. Clawson (manager of the Douglas plant) as well as a number of local dignitaries. Training was soon well under way.

While the Douglas personnel heading for the UK flew across the Atlantic in the relative comfort of chartered aircraft, the RAF personnel were often not quite so lucky. Many and varied were the ways used to travel to the US—a panoply of ships and aircraft as schedules permitted. Some transited via Canada, which involved a two-day rail journey. Chief Technician Richard Pratt was given only ten days' notice of his posting to the US. He crossed the Atlantic in, somewhat appropriately, a Douglas Super DC-7C. He worked at that time at RAF Lyneham servicing the Comet 2s and daily carried out test flights on almost silent jet power at 40,000 feet. The noise of the piston-engined Douglas aircraft came as a surprise to him at take-off. After eventually managing to climb to 11,000 feet, it struggled against a headwind and landed at New York's Idlewild Airport some thirteen hours later. He thereafter joined about thirty other RAF personnel and completed the journey to Tucson in an ex-USAF Curtis Wright C-46 Commando operated by Universal Airlines, with a worryingly smoking engine.[19] Twenty-two-year-old Corporal Brian Robertson was even less fortunate. One of a group of twelve NCOs, he embarked on the Holland-America Line's SS *Nieuw Amsterdam* in Southampton on 6 August, in civilian clothes and sworn to secrecy:

Since I was just a corporal technician among my group of senior NCOs I was berthed separately in (appalling) steerage while they enjoyed second-class comforts. We knew we were going to be trained as the top technicians—Missile System Analyst Technicians, crew chiefs as we saw it—for 'about four months' at undisclosed venues, which actually became eight, so sketchy was the training plan. I shared steerage with other junior NCOs, destined for shorter segments of our own course, who would eventually work for MSATs. I was quite pleased to be on such a superior team, I think the youngest trainee MSAT in the RAF and possibly a mistake. But my tiny, raucous, shared cabin above the propellers was uninhabitable, and our Atlantic passage very stormy. Arriving in New York was a great shock, the New World not nearly as familiar as today, but we began eagerly to adapt. We were unprepared for the claustrophobic, noisy and futuristic experience that was downtown Manhattan, but deeply impressed by the warmth and generous hospitality of our hosts. Time to visit some of the major sights before a USAF officer met us a couple of days later, at our skyscraper Governor Clinton hotel, with some cash and train tickets for Tucson, Arizona. We were sent on our way, fares paid of course, from venue to venue and became quite good US travellers. Our funding in the US came from the 'Mutual Defense Assistance Program'. The journey to Tucson took three days. After a penultimate stop at languid, semi-Mexican El Paso we got off at Tucson in 35-degree heat to find our luggage, last seen checked in at Grand Central Station, waiting for us in alphabetical order; Britain this was not. The custom of meeting consumers' needs was largely absent in the UK in 1958, yet was embedded in US culture. We loved it, despite being short of money.[20]

A 70-page introductory booklet gave everyone an introduction to the 'dos and don'ts', how not to upset Americans by ill-judged British humour, and where leisure time might be spent. There was a graphically illustrated warning about driving while intoxicated, which would automatically incur ten days in jail and a $100 fine. Also Tucson-bound and travelling by sea was Junior Technician John Thorndyke. An air-conditioning technician, he had 'volunteered' for Thor from RAF Watton and his voyage to the US was aboard the Cunard Line's RMS *Sylvania*, leaving from Liverpool on 23 January 1958 along with twenty-three other RAF personnel. It was not a good crossing but time on deck ameliorated the worst effects of the sea.[21]

The restrictions of US law limited the RAF personnel's access to nuclear-related technology.[22] Service ingenuity overcame this by inducting the British into the USAF:

We attended an Army base in Brooklyn to be sworn into the USAF and be issued with ID cards in the equivalent rank: staff sergeant etc. The greatest advantage of having membership of both services was that the USAF paid us the difference between our RAF rank and our USAF rank. We were told we should purchase USAF uniforms from the PX but our RAF minder told us we should retain RAF uniform. Later, everyone bought American uniforms and attached our RAF insignia. Their uniforms were infinitely smarter than our RAF KD and 'hairy blue' battledress. Purchase of USAF kit therefore became a first priority for many who bought USAF tropical uniform instead of the appalling, totally unsuitable and downright embarrassing tropical kit issued by the RAF. We could then look at our USAF colleagues on a more equal footing. There was a consensus about this, the resident RAF Officer turning a blind eye. Whoever designed other ranks tropical kit must have had a cruel sense of humour.[23]

The facilities at Davis-Monthan left much to be desired, although as a salute to the opening of the nuclear age the B-29 named 'Boxcar'—which dropped the second atom bomb on Nagasaki—was preserved there. Sergeant Maurice Botley recounts in his memoirs that most of the RAF technicians were senior NCOs,

[who were] used to single room billets or were in married quarters. Davis-Monthan provided [Neilson] two-storey barrack blocks with about 30 beds per room. While acceptable to the majority, the bathroom facilities were another story. Each block had one large open-plan bathroom which contained a urinal, together with a row of toilets and another of showers. This was very communal living and required friendliness when performing bodily functions! Many delayed such functions until use could be made of the more private facilities available at the base NCO club.[24]

Personnel were warned that 'shoes should not be left outside bedroom doors. They certainly will not be cleaned by the staff and it may even be assumed that the owners have deliberately thrown away the shoes. It is customary to have shoes polished in 'shoe shine parlours'.[25] Corporal Robertson found:

Open dormitory barracks with noisy air-conditioning. At night the chirping of cicadas and the racket of jet engine testing nearby was a trial. Toilets in the communal washrooms did not have doors at first; senior NCOs were mortified, but the messes were a thing apart as were the meals, cinemas, sports facilities, shops, and four swimming pools. The dry tropical climate I found invigorating. We were paid the grand [supplementary] sum of $1.50 *per diem* living on base and $7 living privately. Since most of my corporal-technician's pay was made to my new wife in the UK, I and some others struggled to make ends meet, but we survived, and had enough to enjoy weekends and recreation if we were careful and saved up.[26]

There was always the Bomb-Bay Club to relax in. It promised dances, free movies, Monte Carlo night, and quizzes for all. On Sundays there was 'coffee and doughnut hour', during which on average, 780 crullers were served. To replicate the tax-free shopping available to US servicemen in the UK, arrangements were made for a reciprocal arrangement at Vandenberg for the RAF personnel to purchase alcohol and cigarettes. Wing Commander Finlayson remembers that it was in fact 'not all that popular'. The RAF crews were all very well behaved, and by the time he left to return to the UK in late 1961 no one had been formally charged with misbehaviour.[27] By the end of February 1959, Vandenberg could report that thirty-five launch crews from the Feltwell and Hemswell wings had qualified in their training.[28] Numerically, however, they were outnumbered by the 255 US personnel who had also attended the training courses.

Seeing this as a 'once in a lifetime' opportunity, Corporal Humphrey remembers that most took the opportunity to see as much as possible of the surrounding countryside. The Americans generously provided transport at weekends to let the RAF personnel visit nearby Tucson, where some witnessed their first bullfight. He remembers that on arrival at Chicago's O'Hare Airport, a pay parade took place in the midst of the airport concourse when the 10 shillings a week kept back as savings from their pay of 17 shillings and sixpence was distributed to each of them. Alas it seems that it was not enough for them to purchase some of the bewildering array of transistor radios that were to be found in local shops, many set up by former serving USAF officers.[29]

For those whose training in the US was to last longer than six months, normal RAF rules would have allowed them to be accompanied by their families. Sadly this was not to be, allegedly because of the lack of suitable accommodation and schooling. This was a disappointment to the wives for whom, like their husbands, the prospect of time in America was an attractive proposition. In partial compensation they were promised that by the time their husbands returned from America, their families would be properly housed in accommodation at their bases. But by the time that the MT personnel and engineering staff who were already on site were accommodated, there was little left for the others. One officer is known to have resigned in protest at the poor handling of the situation.[30] Corporal Leon de Young was stationed at Carnaby, and his wife eventually found a hiring in nearby Bridlington. 'The advantage was that there were some lovely hirings available,' his wife commented.[31] William Taylor CBE, MP for Bradford and Parliamentary Under-Secretary of State for Air, took a keen interest in the catering and accommodation provisions within the service and visited the Feltwell Wing on 8 March 1960. Starting at Feltwell, he later in the day visited Tuddenham and displayed keenness to meet as many servicemen as possible during his visit, something that went down well with his RAF hosts. He appeared to be well satisfied by what he saw, which indicates that by the time Thor was becoming operational the major problems of accommodation had been overcome.[32]

The standard of training seems to have varied. Even a cursory look at the various training manuals is sufficient to emphasize the complexity of the Thor system. One flow chart, when extended, was some 20 feet long. Many of the Douglas instructors were from the company's aircraft sections and their knowledge of missile systems seemed to be little more than that of many of their RAF students. Indeed, the general level of technical knowledge and breadth of skills displayed by RAF personnel was far in excess of that anticipated by the Douglas training staff, who were accustomed to the more restricted nature of individual USAF competencies.[33] 'Much of the training consisted of self-study time in the library reading manuals produced by Douglas as courses progressed, dealing with specific sections of the missile system.'[34] Things did seem to improve after a visit by Minister of Defence Duncan Sandys, who spoke to the personnel in training. The training was also done to USAF protocols, which meant that skills were restricted to limited and specific areas, unlike RAF trade training, which was much more multi-skilled. But in spite of all the US's excitement, a Thor Hydraulic System expert returned to the UK to find that his skills were only being used infrequently.

Strong and lasting friendships flourished between many of the RAF personnel and Douglas staff. All the same, concern was voiced by AVM Wally Sheen CB, DSO, OBE, Commander RAF Staff at the British Joint Services Mission (BJSM) in Washington, who said conditions were 'more like Iraq than Hollywood.' Acknowledging that many of the RAF personnel were less than happy about being selected for Thor and had been badly briefed about the whole programme, he worried they would return to England to 'take up their duties with a pretty poor impression of both RAF and USAF organisation and training.' As the programme progressed, things did improve:

During our Douglas training we learned about the rather advanced, lightweight Thor airframe, the fearsome and impossibly-powerful Rocketdyne engine, whose thrust to weight ratio was about 70:1, a working life of about 3 minutes and dangerous fuels, the clever but troublesome autopilot and even a bit about the megaton warhead with its heavy copper heatshield. But we remained sceptical about automating a launch from storage to ignition of only 15 minutes, until we did it ourselves at Vandenberg.[35]

There was also a feeling that emphasis was, perhaps not unexpectedly, being placed on honing the skills of the crews designated to conduct an IWST launch to the detriment of the very necessary skills needed by the technical personnel. One event which is well remembered is being individually photographed and appearing to be operating next to a piece of test equipment which had the targeting sections papered over rather obviously.[36] Many of these photographs appeared in local papers in the UK. This was considered to be valuable publicity for the RAF, but was also a way of indicating to the Soviets that Thor was a serious intention. Perhaps in response to early criticisms about the poor standard of uniform compared with their American counterparts, khaki barathea uniforms were eventually issued. But problems with uniform continued to feature high on the complaints' list. When Corporal Robertson flew out of Tucson on a blazing 107-degrees-F November day aboard a silver Douglas DC-6 heading for Milwaukee (where the guidance training was to take place), he arrived at Wisconsin on the shore of Lake Michigan at 20 degrees F, deep in snow. There was one serious problem:

We had no winter uniform at all so our first freezing day was spent scurrying to clothing stores to buy thick blue parkas, gloves and boots. We rented furnished apartments, three of us sharing with Ed Kinder, a USAF tech-sergeant [also] on the Course.[37]

For those USAF personnel involved in the training programme, the experience was in many ways similar. Sergeant Buck Wise had been serving with the 28th Bombardment Wing, Heavy, which was taking delivery of its new state-of-the-art Boeing B-52D eight-engined bombers at Ellsworth AFB, Arizona. In May 1958 he had to make a decision to enlist or get discharged since his four years' service was up in August. Not wishing to be discharged and go back to his home in North Carolina where the textile mills offered one of the relatively few opportunities for work, he decide to re-enlist. He had read that the Air Force was getting involved in missile operations so, attracted by the idea of working in this new branch of technology, he went to the Base Personnel Section to find out more about the subject.

What I found out was that the first Thor IRBM Training Courses were due to start on the 28 May 1958 in Tucson, Arizona and if I elected to attend I would need to re-enlist as soon as possible. Further training was to follow at Camp Cooke AFB in California with later assignment to England.

Wise duly re-enlisted with the promise that he would be assigned to Thor. Within days he was on his way to Tucson. The twelve USAF students were assigned quarters on Davis-Monthan while attending school at the Douglas facility in Tucson. By then the first RAF students were arriving from England, although they attended different classes. The two groups got on well together and firm friendships were established. In June and July the temperature in Tucson reached 100-114 degrees F. Both groups of students would take their lunch break at a nearby bar which served cold beer—a novel experience for the RAF personnel more accustomed to drinking it at room temperature. Upon completing the training course some of the students were sent back to their home base because the training at Cooke AFB was delayed. Wise along with the other half of the class proceeded to Cape Canaveral, Florida, assigned to Patrick AFB.[38]

Sergeant Maurice Botley was one of those lucky enough to be selected to go to Vandenberg. As with all RAF personnel, he was issued with a special order stating that he was

[…] authorised and invited by the Secretary of the Air Force of the United States to proceed on or about 29 Oct '58 from Douglas Aircraft Company Tucson, Arizona, to Vandenberg Air Force Base, California, reporting to Director of Personnel, 704 Strategic Missile Wing, not earlier than 0800 hours 30 Oct '58 and not later than 1600, 31 Oct '58, to attend Missile Test Equipment Tech (Control) Interim IWST. Duration 8 weeks. Class starts 2 Nov '58.[39]

Sadly not all of the Thor personnel had the experience and enjoyment of training in America. By 1960 the Bomber Command Strategic Missile School had become fully operational at Feltwell and the later intakes of technicians were trained there. One such corporal technician was Harry Hitchcock, who was volunteered for working with Thor by the V-bomber OCU at RAF Gaydon. He was one of the RIM staff who undertook the servicing of missiles that had been brought in for major servicing, his specialisation being propulsion. He remembers,

> It was completely different to servicing jet engines. With jets you could test them afterwards to check them over. With rocket engines you did the servicing but there was no way of testing them so I never saw a Thor engine actually operating. I was due to go to the States for a live firing but this was cancelled when the Thor programme was terminated.[40]

Hitchcock remembers that along the wall of the RIM Building was an 80-foot-long chart which described the countdown from key-turn to lift-off. However, in true American style, it was graphically illustrated with Disney-type cartoons.

But the culmination of training of the RAF crews was by no means the end of 392d's involvement with the British. In April 1961 a combined team of personnel from 392d MTS, RAF, DAC, and Air Force Logistic Command took on the task of standardising the SM-75 operating and maintenance procedures. This involved a concentrated review of thirty volumes of RAF operating procedures and hundreds of maintenance work cards, along with operations specific to Vandenberg. Again demonstrating the commitment to the tasks in hand, a job that nominally would have taken three months was completed within three weeks and with only a number of minor changes required. The resulting document was heralded as a significant milestone in simplifying a complex weapon system to such a degree that relatively inexperienced personnel could operate the system safely and effectively.[41]

RAF Launches

All Thor crews were originally intended to be able to participate in an actual missile launch. In hindsight this was an ambitious idea, given the cost of such events. However, it was considered essential for at least some crews to have experience all the way through the countdown to a live launch. There was therefore a regular programme of such launches for the RAF crews lucky enough to be selected to conduct them. Initially these were termed 'Integrated Weapons System Training' (IWST) launches, with the emphasis on perfecting the training techniques.[1] While these courses were starting up, the programme of test launches from the AFMTC at Patrick Air Force Base continued. The missile's accuracy was improving, as the plot of missile impact points for Thors launched between March and October 1959 shows (see the figure on p. 107), albeit that the launch teams were all contractor personnel and there was no pressure to launch under quasi-operational conditions.

Of the thirteen successful launches during the period, seven fell within the 2-mile radius with a further three near misses. This was a sufficient accuracy to cause considerable destruction to the area targets to which Thor would be allocated.

It was up to the Vandenberg operations teams to see if the crews who would actually operate the missiles could match this sort of accuracy, which would be a more realistic assessment of what the Thors might achieve in operational use. The IWST courses each comprised ten officers and fifteen airmen who made up five launch teams. The first of these live launches, appropriately enough nicknamed 'LIONS ROAR', was conducted on 16 April 1959.[2] By April confidence in the US missile programme was increasing to the extent that three days earlier, on 13 April, the press had been invited to Vandenberg to watch the launch of a Thor/Agena A from Pad 75-3-4. This event was incorporated as part of a nineteen-day press tour for selected UK journalists of a number of Thor sites,[3] which gave the visitors as much background information as possible on the comprehensive development programme leading towards an operational Thor missile and at the same time letting them observe RAF students in training in the US and their participation in an actual launch.[4] It was clearly seen as a major publicity event as the group was accompanied by Brigadier Godfrey Hobbs CBE, Director of Public Relations for the MoD. In retrospect, this was a risky decision, for only four days before T178 had exploded on the launch pad during a static engine firing. However, the launch of the Thor/Agena (T170) was deemed successful and placed a DISCOVERER payload into orbit, although a subsequent and unpublicised problem with a faulty timing

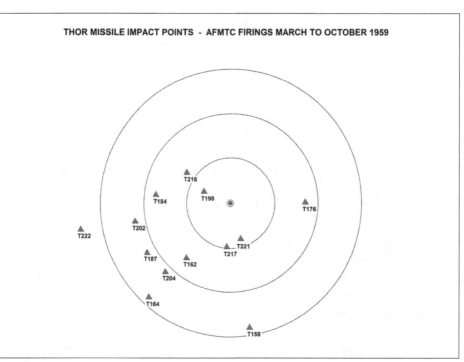

THOR MISSILE IMPACT POINTS - AFMTC FIRINGS MARCH TO OCTOBER 1959

device prevented the re-entry capsule from being ejected from the satellite as planned and it was lost.[5] Close by on Pad 75-2-8, Group Captain Robert T. Frogley OBE DFC, Chief Technician Roy M. Carpenter, Master Pilots Maurice H. Sloan and A. E. Cover, and Squadron Leader Peter G. Coulson were preparing to launch the first Thor (T161) by an all-RAF crew. The back-up crew consisted of Flight Lieutenant E. V. Ford, Master Pilot John Anderson, and Chief Technician Frederick A. E. Chivers. Eight weeks of preparation had preceded the launch and while USAF and contractor personnel were present, they were now there only in an advisory capacity.[6] Launch was scheduled for 14 April. Contemporary film footage shows the RAF officers inspecting the missile wearing hard hats suitably emblazoned with the RAF roundel. While subsequent footage shows the British team very much in charge of the launch, they are surrounded by USAF and civilian personnel, their faces clearly reflecting the tense atmosphere within the launch bunker. But dangers of an animal kind threatened the safety of the personnel. Flight Lieutenant Jack Docherty remembered that a degree of caution had to be exercised while on site, as a mountain lion had managed to

> [find] its way through the security fence and was feeding off the deer which were plentifully roaming the site. It was said to be fierce because it had been very aggressive with an airman on an adjacent missile site. We were not allowed firearms because of the numerous RP-1 and LOX tanks in the area.

Throughout the night the duty LCO, in this case Docherty, had to visit the launch pad to do hourly checks of temperature, pressures, voltages, and frequencies. He continues:

> [...] the door to the control room was like a manhole cover. At 4 a.m. one morning I emerged from the control room [...] just as the first light of dawn was breaking. Twenty yards in front of me was the mountain lion. It was huge and looked at me as if it was looking for breakfast. I shot back down the hole, slammed the lid shut and did not emerge again until the day shift arrived. I faked the readings.[7]

Adding further to this tension were adverse weather conditions and technical trouble which led to postponement of the launch until 11 a.m. the following day. Once again weather and technical problems intervened and at 4.45 p.m. an announcement was made that no launch would take place on that day. On the next day, 16 April, the countdown was once again initiated and, this time, all at last went well.

> At T minus 14 the missile was raised into the vertical position and its upper section could be seen over the sand dunes which surrounded the launch site. The final range safety check was made during a planned technical hold at T minus 4, and at the scheduled time of 12.46 (8.46 p.m. GMT) the Thor got away to a good launch, disappearing briefly into cloud before continuing almost vertically, chalking a white vapour trail against the upper blue sky.[8]

Thomas Cochrane, deputy chief of information for the Air Ministry enthused, 'it was a magnificent achievement.' Complementing the US Air Force he added, 'it was a tremendously complicated task you people accomplished with the Thor missile.'[9] Still perhaps reflecting the political concerns about the programme, Brig Hobbs cautioned that the launch did not mean that the RAF's Thors had reached operational status. 'It means the RAF can fire the missile, but the British Government still must make the decision as to when any of our RAF bases are operational.'[10]

Present as RAF VIPs at the launch were AVM Wally Sheen, Commander of RAF Staff at the BJSM, Washington, and AVM George 'Gus' Walker a celebrated one-armed wartime Lancaster pilot, who had appropriately enough been a wartime station commander of North Luffenham which was to become the last Thor base to be declared operational.[11] In a meeting with the press after the launch, Group Captain Frogley admitted:

> [...] the three days' operation involving the detection and rectification of malfunctions had been a time of strain on all concerned but had provided the best possible training [...] this was a great day for the Royal Air Force. The Thor has taken its place in the RAF's arsenal alongside our manned bombers.[12, 13]

As seemed to become common practice after a launch, the LCO, in this case Squadron Leader Coulson, was allowed to keep the launch key as a souvenir. Notwithstanding the successful launch, some of the journalists who had been waiting at Vandenberg were somewhat sceptical about the 'operational' label the US had awarded Thor after witnessing the frustration of the two-day postponement. 'Giving "technical" reasons for the delay means to the British public that the damn thing won't work,' commented one of them.[14]

Sandys, en route to a SEATO meeting in New Zealand had, to a degree, anticipated this possibility. On 1 April, he instructed Powell to write to Quarles on his behalf:

> You know how politically sensitive the whole subject of THOR deployment is in this country; no opportunity is missed of seeking to embarrass the Government by quoting, or quoting out of context, statements made from time to time in the United States about the present state of the missile and the progress being made in deploying it. [...] The line we have consistently maintained here is that the missiles are at present being deployed here for training purposes and we shall decide, after consultation with your Government in the light of the trials which are still being carried out in America, when the missiles can be regarded as operational. Duncan is very anxious that during the forthcoming tour of the British journalists all concerned on the American side shall be briefed not to say anything inconsistent with the line which we have been following here, and in particular not to say anything that might suggest a difference of opinion between the United States and British Governments over the present operational status of THOR. It would be very helpful to hear from your side expressions of confidence in the development of the missile to full operational status as a result of the continuing trials, and statements stressing how satisfactorily the trials are going; but it would cause difficulties for us if it were suggested that THOR has already achieved full operational status and that we are being awkward by refusing to recognise this.[15]

However, for those seeking to endorse the continuing progress of the trial launches, worse was to come. Missile T191 was originally scheduled to be launched on 18 May, the launch being nicknamed 'PUNCH PRESS'. It was to be plagued by problems typical of the early days of missile development. Onsite training had to be suspended for a time after a missile ground accident on 23 April. This apparently involved the slave missile used for launch pad training. Thereafter, various technical problems led to the launch being postponed with a completely new guidance system having to be installed on 20 May. The launch was then due to take place on 22 May, but this coincided with the scheduled launch of DISCOVERER III from Pad 75-3-4. It was considered inadvisable to attempt two launches on the same day. DISCOVERER itself was delayed—it was finally launched on 3 June—but meanwhile the RAF missile had suffered the failure of a launch pin to fully retract and of the fuel at Phase 5 to pressurise correctly. Colonel Robert W. Christy, Commanding Officer 392d Missile Training Squadron and in charge of the launch operations, summoned Squadron Leader E. R. Morris and his launch crew and recommended abandoning the launch attempt completely on the grounds of safety. However, he believed that despite the problems, valuable training had been achieved and that little more value would be added by an actual launch; the launch crew duly graduated on that day without undertaking a live launch.[16] It was a severe embarrassment for the RAF, quietly ignored at the time and subsequently written out of the list of RAF launches. Damage to launch pads after live launches, a problem compounded by the 23 April incident, was threatening to delay the whole training programme and the cancellation of the launch would reduce the burden of repair work. A pad-toughening programme was put in place which resulted in a significant reduction in pad damage. Pressure on the training programme was evident in an acerbic memo from RAFLO Group Captain E.

L. McMillan AFC, who advised Group Captain Rod Harman (DD Ops BM) that launch crew departure date should not determine the training schedule. For the small number involved, alternative return flights could surely be organised without too much of a problem or extra expense. He commented, 'you will agree that this episode scarcely demonstrates a 15 minute reaction time'.[17] Things were more positive at Cape Canaveral on that day, however, where T184, an IOC missile, was successfully launched. On 2 June Colonel Richard E. Barton took over command of 392MTS from Colonel Christy.[18] T191 was then quietly rescheduled to be launched as Operation RIFLE SHOT by a new No. 98(SM) Squadron crew. The missile had a Mk 1 engine and was fitted with a Mk2 Mod 3 RV. The launch eventually took place on 16 June from Pad 75-2-7, but did little to improve Thor's reputation.

After a successful launch, the missile continued straight upwards failing to enter its pitch programme. This did not present a safety problem as such as the rotation of the earth would take it over the Pacific so the flight continued. However, the vertical trajectory prevented the missile from achieving its planned velocity so Main Engine Cut Off did not occur. Concerned that the malfunction was clearly not going to rectify itself, the RSO had to destroy the missile 105 seconds into its flight. But at that altitude strong winds carried some of the debris from the explosion over the town of Orcutt, to the north-east of Vandenberg. There had been no prior notification of the launch, which was reported as being 'for training purposes' and it had not, therefore, been accompanied by the contingent of newsmen that had become a common feature of launches at Vandenberg.[19] This was the first missile fired from Vandenberg which had to be destroyed. 'RAF Thor Test Fizzles' headlined the *Salt Lake Tribune*.[20] The *Santa Maria Times* reported,

A Thor intermediate-range ballistic missile fired from Vandenberg Air Force base Tuesday afternoon was destroyed within minutes of the launching because of a malfunction. The Air Force said today that a team of missile contractors and Air Force personnel is investigating in an effort to determine exactly what caused the malfunction in the missile. From Santa Maria, the missile appeared to climb straight up into the sky and never veered off to the west out into the Pacific Missile Range. There was a puff of smoke at a high altitude and this may have been when the missile was destroyed.[21]

The LCO's key used to launch missile T 191

Subsequent investigation showed that a simple piece of wire in the Control Electronics Assembly was the culprit. The guidance system was programmed with a series of pre-set manoeuvres whereby, at lift off, a 35-mm plastic tape was run off a spool. Similar in concept to a punched tape, it ran across a sensor which activated the manoeuvre programme. The small piece of wire in question restrained movement of the tape until the Control Electronic Assembly (CEA) was placed in the missile. It should then have been cut. In the case of T191, it prevented any movement of the spool after lift-off. The range safety staff thereafter altered their procedures to take into account vertical as well as horizontal safety parameters. But the call of 'programme, programme' by an observer placed at a right angle to the flight path—who could thereby confirm that the pitch programme was operating—remained one of the most tense moments of launch process. The planned flight plan is shown in the figure below.

The third IWST launch at 2.41 p.m. on 3 August was a success which was reported on the front page of the *Santa Maria Times*, identifying the seven man crew as Flight Lieutenant Leon A. Roseveare, Chief Technician G. A. Purnell, Senior Technician W. H. Stenee, and Sergeants J. D. Rankin, M. Hodson, J. Docherty, and T. W. Cooper.[22]

No. 98(SM) Squadron provided the crew for the Welcome 5 launch, nicknamed 'GREASE GUN'. Flight Lieutenant Denis A. H. Mortimer, Flight Sergeant Allen J. Pye, Warrant Officer John L. Copelah, Master Signaller Charles L. Goldsmith, Chief Technician Bertram Forstad, Sergeant D. Hubery, Sergeant Albert E. Strawn, and Corporal Raymond Snow were assisted by Captain Sammy J. Hollis USAF who acted as the AO. The launch was originally scheduled for 16 September 1959 but technical difficulties—contaminated hydraulic fluid and telemetry readouts that were unsatisfactory—caused it to be delayed by

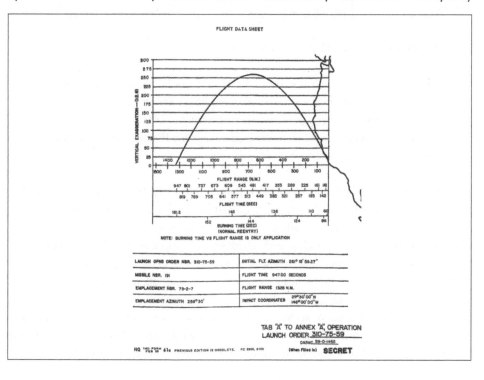

FLIGHT DATA SHEET

LAUNCH OPNS ORDER NBR. 310-75-59	INITIAL FLT. AZIMUTH 261° 15' 59.21"
MISSILE NBR. 191	FLIGHT TIME 947.00 SECONDS
EMPLACEMENT NBR. 75-2-7	FLIGHT RANGE 1326 N.M.
EMPLACEMENT AZIMUTH 269°30'	IMPACT COORDINATES 29°30'00"N 146°00'00"W

TAB "A" TO ANNEX "A", OPERATION
LAUNCH ORDER 310-75-59

DASMC 59-0-1465

HQ 140 FORM 61a PREVIOUS EDITION IS OBSOLETE. PC 2900, 6100   (When Filled In) SECRET a day. The launch of missile T228 without, on this occasion, apparently any RAF markings took place successfully at 14.09 PDST following short delays for weather and range clearance. The RV landed slightly outside the 2-nm radius target circle, 3 nm short and 3 nm right of the target area in the Pacific Missile Range (PMR). A SOFAR bomb, released at a depth 2,500 feet provided a reference for the Missile Impact Location System (MILS).[23] The Thor had been accepted directly from Douglas on 23 June and, apart from necessary Vandenberg range instrumentation, was a standard operationally configured missile. This was the first launch of a Thor fitted with Plan D remote alignment capability which allowed guidance alignment to take place from the blockhouse. In part this was considered a factor in the target inaccuracy, as it was the first time that the crew had experienced the Plan D modification. Colonel Virgil M. Cloyd, Director of Operations, was nevertheless satisfied with the conduct of the launch and the expertise of the crew. The Flight Data Sheet for the launch is shown here. The times of the five launch phases against nominal were as follows:

Phase	Actual	Nominal
Phase 1	4 min 20 sec	4 min 00 sec
Phase 2	3 min 01 sec	3 min 15 sec
Phase 3	4 min 45 sec	1 min 15 sec
Phase 4	5 min 27 sec	4 min 00 sec
Phase 5	2 min 27 sec	2 min 30 sec
TOTAL	20 min 00 sec	15 min 00 sec

This was a time of intense activity at Vandenberg.

[The base] was still being built at a furious pace [with] new buildings and roads appearing overnight. Thor was not alone with Titan silos and Atlas pads accounting for many of the increasingly regular launches. Apart from the CIA-managed DISCOVERER series, several civil satellites such as the Canadian Alouette mounted on a Thor-Agena took advantage of polar orbits for the first time.[24]

Nor was Thor the only strategic missile being launched from the WTR. Nine days before the IWST-3 launch, the Atlas 12D ICBM was launched for the first time from Launch Complex 576 A-2. It was a total success, travelling 4,480 nm downrange.

The next scheduled Thor launch in early October was the first of the CTLs. The purpose of the IWST launches was to demonstrate the tactical operation of the weapon system from T-15 readiness condition through to automatic countdown, missile lift-off, re-entry, vehicle separation, and impact of the RV in a pre-determined target area.[25] Thus, technical holds were allowed so that the crews could be fully trained on all aspects of an actual launch after their training period in America. The CTLs were designed to categorise the efficiency of operational crews who already had experience with their squadrons in the UK. But they also displayed and reinforced British capability to the US population. The outward appearance may have seemed convincing, but behind the scenes there were problems, perhaps inevitable given the multi-faceted nature of the launches. Wing Commander Peter Finlayson RAF Liaison Officer at Vandenberg reported,

> It is little wonder, then, on a two shift basis with the civilian instructor personnel and the USAF included, the total number of people attempting to carry out their various duties at and around one pad has been in the order of 120 individuals. The programming of training tasks in such an overloaded situation is not only extremely difficult but inevitably results in long delays and personal frustrations for those who cannot be kept fully employed.[26]

While the start of the CTLs represented a new phase in the programme, there were still four IWST launches planned as the final US-based training courses took place. IWST-6 codenamed 'STAND FAST' was undertaken by the North Luffenham Wing. By this time, too, successful launches were becoming the norm as confidence in the system improved. The launch crew were Flight Lieutenant David Scott, Flight Lieutenant Colin Reeve, Chief Technician Joseph Heath, Senior Technician Ronald Baldwin, and Sergeant George Freeman with AO Captain Fran I. Harvan. Thor T220 was delivered from DAC to the RIM at Vandenberg on 8 June 1959, and taken to LE8 22 days later. It was launched on 21 October. The missile's flight time was 15 minutes 47.1 seconds with a range of 1,326 nm.

In total there were nine IWST launches, the final one taking place on 21 January 1960, thereby completing the US-based training phase of the programme. Five of the launches were classed as successful, four of which were the last four IWST launches, which reinforced the increasing reliability of Thor. This was perhaps just as well, as by this time all the UK bases were fully up and running—the North Luffenham Wing being the last to be declared operational on 1 December 1959. The ninth and last IWST launch, RED CABOOSE, took place at 12.10PST on 21 January 1960, conducted by Crew 21 from the North Luffenham Wing. As this was to be the last US training course, a number of the candidates were destined to be posted to other sites to fill vacancies created by the change in status of the squadron leader LCOs upon their nomination to squadron command posts. Fortunately 392d Training Squadron was at its maximum establishment, which allowed the full IWST syllabus to be covered for each of the sixteen LCOs. Missile T272 was designated as the primary launch vehicle, with T215 as the back-up. Both were IOC missiles except for the addition of an instrumentation kit, a scoring kit, and a dual-command destruct system. This launch was conducted as a standard 'no notice' procedure. The initial attempt to launch the missile was stopped when the Phase V timer expired before propellant transfer was completed. The launch was then transferred to the backup missile and the ensuing countdown resulted in a successful launch: the warhead landed 1 nm short and 3 nm left of the target, so slightly outside the 2-nm CEP. This event marked the completion of the US training programme, and a graduation ceremony of the fifth increment of No. 144(SM) Squadron took place the following day. Because of the decision to link the launch with the graduation ceremony, advance warning of the date had to be given and this consequently required the advance nomination of the launch crew. Crew 21 were duly chosen: Flying Officer W. O. Hughes, who had obtained the best standardisation rating earlier in the course; Corporal Technician G. J. N. Milne; Chief Technician R. H. Gudgion; Corporal Technicians D. A. Clark and E. L. Daws; and Captain G. M. Tharp USAF. They had also undertaken four double-propellant countdowns. At the ceremony the RAF contingent presented Major-General David Wade, Commanding General of 1 MD,[27] with a trophy as a token of the 'esteem and appreciation for all the United States Air Force has done for us.'[28]

Since the programme began in July 1959, a total of 520 officers and 1,520 airmen had completed Thor training with SAC and at the various contractors' facilities. SoS(A) George Ward wrote to Lieutenant-General Wade:

> I am very disappointed not to be with you myself today to see the final firing of Thor by RAF trainees. [...] This occasion will mark the successful conclusion of the first stage of the Thor project. This is a remarkable example of practical co-operation between our two air forces. I am very glad to say that this firing does not mean the end of association between the Royal Air Force and Vandenberg. RAF Thor crews will continue to look forward to their return to this magnificent base.[29]

RAF VIPs at the ceremony included Air Marshal Sheen, Air Marshal Michael Dwyer, AOC 3 Group, Group Captain McMillan, and Wing Commander Finlayson. Air Marshal Sheen had also been a VIP at the first RAF Thor launch, and was later to describe the Thor programme as 'the most remarkable project between two countries to come to fruition since the war.'[30]

CERTIFICATE OF TRAINING
ON THE
THOR WEAPON SYSTEM

DOUGLAS

This is to certify that

FLT/LT. DONALD L. ROWELL

has satisfactorily completed a course of training as indicated below in the United States Air Force IRBM (Thor) Weapons System. This acknowledgement is presented as a record of his proficiency in the skills required to support this Air Frame and Ground Support Equipment.

PETROLEUM SYSTEM MAINTENANCE SPECIALIST – ACO 56850-1
COURSE NAME AND NUMBER

DOUGLAS AIRCRAFT CO., INC.　　3 Feb 59　　UNITED STATES AIR FORCE
　　　　　　　　　　　　　　　　　DATE

Department of the Air Force

CERTIFICATE OF TRAINING

This is to certify that

FLIGHT LIEUTENANT DONALD L ROWELL

has satisfactorily completed the

FORMAL INTEGRATED WEAPONS SYSTEM TRAINING   MAINTENANCE MANAGEMENT COURSE

Given by

392D MISSILE TRAINING SQUADRON   VANDENBERG AIR FORCE BASE   CALIFORNIA

ATTESTED   24 April 1959

C D Haynes
MR. C. D. HAYNES
Douglas Aircraft Company, Inc

ROBERT W. CHRISTY
Colonel, USAF
Commander

AF FORM 1258, 1 JAN 58　　　　　　　　　　　　　　　　　GPO:1955 O – 332252

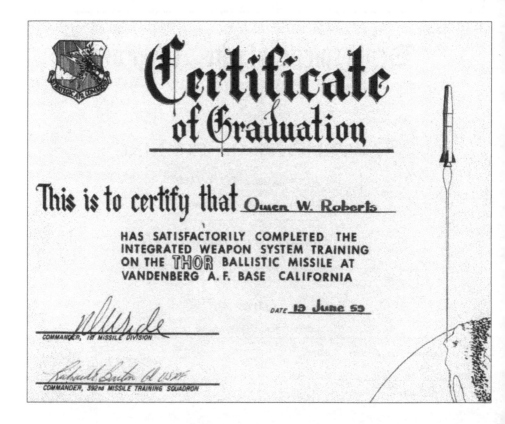

This is to certify that

Donald L Powell

HAS SATISFACTORILY COMPLETED THE INTERGRATED WEAPON SYSTEM TRAINING ON THE *thor* BALLISTIC MISSILE AT VANDENBERG AIR FORCE BASE

DATE : 24 APRIL 1959

COMMANDER, 1 st MISSILE DIV

COMMANDER, 392 MSL TRNG SQDN

Certificate
of Graduation

This is to certify that Owen W. Roberts

HAS SATISFACTORILY COMPLETED THE INTEGRATED WEAPON SYSTEM TRAINING ON THE THOR BALLISTIC MISSILE AT VANDENBERG A.F. BASE CALIFORNIA

DATE 19 June 59

COMMANDER, 1st MISSILE DIVISION

COMMANDER, 392nd MISSILE TRAINING SQUADRON

Combat Training Launches

After the conclusion of the US training programme, attention centred on Combat Training Launches.[1] Promulgated by an operations order from the 392MTS on 31 August, these were designed to duplicate an actual operational launch by a fully trained and operational crew selected from the squadrons and were undoubtedly the highlight of the crews' operational time with Thor.[2] These launches provided the only opportunity to assess the effectiveness of the Thor system, although they did not, and could not, assess the reliability of the Ground Support Equipment (GSE) which constituted about 80 per cent of the installation on each LE. Sadly, only a select few were able to participate in the CTLs. Working with such advanced technology gave some measure of job satisfaction, but never seeing an end result was not good for morale—neither was seeing more fortunate colleagues leave for America, for that matter.[3] Low spirits were exacerbated by the lengthened shifts that had to be worked to overcome the reduced numbers available for the launch crews while their colleagues were away.

There were twelve CTLs, starting on 6 October 1959 and ending on 18 June 1962. An additional one planned for 8 October 1962 was cancelled following the announcement of the pending withdrawal of Thor from service. It had originally been the idea of the USAF that the missiles used for the CTLs would be taken from Douglas production. This was to hold true for the first three CTLs. The first two missiles came straight from Douglas, as did the third, although this had already been used for a series of double-propellant loadings and an unsuccessful launch attempt at Vandenberg. There were concerns about the possible reliability of the operational missiles, which had been subject to some fairly harsh weather on their UK stations, and it was agreed retrospectively that CTL missiles would be randomly selected from the operational stocks in the UK and flown back to the US. These missiles had been routinely exposed to the elements, had been erected and filled with LOX on a regular basis, and although rigorously maintained and examined, it was hard to verify the integrity of the missiles without a live launch. Bob Condisine declared,

Stop shedding those tears over Britain's decline as a major military power. She can throw a much mightier punch than at any time in her long history. How do we know the RAF nows [sic] how to launch these complicated liquid-fuel jobs? Simple. Every so often the RAF selects a Thor at random, rounds up its crew, puts the missile and men aboard a big cargo plane and flies the lot to Vandenberg Air Force Base, Calif. There the crew fires the Thor and returns to its British pad. A new Thor is there by the time it returns. We built quite a few of them.[4]

Specifically, the launches were designed to

—establish confidence in RAF missiles exposed for a long period in the field (this applied from CTL-4 onwards).
—establish confidence in the combat readiness of the launch crews.
—establish confidence in the maintenance procedures used by the RAF.
—help the morale of the crews which have not had the opportunity to launch a missile or see one launched.
—derive training benefits.

CTL-1, nicknamed 'FOREIGN TRAVEL', was undertaken by a crew from the Feltwell Wing, of which Squadron Leader R. P. Flood, OC of No. 107 (SM) Squadron, was in overall charge.[5] It was a composite launch crew. Flight Lieutenant Richard Cowling from Feltwell acted as the LCO and Chief Technician Milburn, also from Feltwell, acting as pad controller. Flight Lieutenant Cowling had also been instrumental in the full commissioning of the LEs at Hemswell. MSAT Brian Robertson was one of the lucky ones from the Feltwell Wing chosen to return to Vandenberg to take part:

> I don't remember anything of the flight there, but we had six weeks to prepare and launch a brand new Thor waiting for us, destined for Pad 75-2-8 [the same pad from which the first RAF launch had taken place]. Half the team set about checking every component of it, the rest stripping down and refurbishing the pad. A previous launch left a lot of damage, cables to be replaced and insulated, and endless wiring checks. We got used to regular earth tremors in that part of California, a rather large one overnight had us rushing to the pad to check for damage, check the survey points and re-swing the theodolites. For most of us the trial wet countdowns were scary but interesting, returning LOX to the storage tanks was a new experience. We lost about 1,000 gallons of LOX in boiloff; it is interesting to see puddles of this pale blue liquid boiling away to nothing. We knew of the tragic experience of two contractors at the Cape some time earlier; a wet countdown and decanting of LOX took place on a cool misty evening. These men were wearing woollen pullovers, eventually returning to the hangar for a smoke. They immediately burst into flames from their super-saturated clothing, and desperate efforts to douse the flames were unsuccessful until their clothes were ripped off and they were rolled on the ground; they suffered serious burns. We were under no illusions that this first CTL was an important milestone in demonstrating that the UK was up to scratch in this Thor business, and resolved to make it as good as possible.[6]

Preparations were therefore intense to ensure that nothing went wrong. On the one hand it was important to demonstrate that Thor was a fully operational system, thereby signalling a strong hand to the Soviets. On the other hand, the RAF was also keen to show its American collaborators that it was fully up to the job. By coincidence, in respect of the former, Soviet Premier Nikita Khrushchev was paying an official and, as it turned out, eventful two-week tour of the United States, and was in California during the preparations for CTL-1. Travelling north from Los Angeles to San Francisco by train after a somewhat strained visit to Hollywood—where he had taken strong exception to some ill-judged comments by the Twentieth Century Fox Studio chief—his journey was to take him through Vandenberg, as the Southern Pacific Railroad ran through the base close to the shoreline. An Atlas launch was due to take place. The RSO wisely postponed the launch rather than hold up the train, but the Soviet leader no doubt saw the large sign adjacent to the railroad line: 'Home of the First Missile Division'. Brian Robertson continues:

> Our guidance system, on which many hours had been lavished, failed a few days before launch, so a replacement was obtained for round-the-clock calibration and targeting. Range Safety engineers installed a command destruct system on our bird a couple of days before launch, making extensive end-to-end checks of the telemetry installation. A friend and I toyed with putting a field mouse in a box on board too, in the now-crowded equipment section, but thought better of it.[7]

The CTL launches were meant to be an 'instant order to launch' with no advance warning given as to the time of the command order. In practice, it was impossible to disguise what was happening as the tempo of events increased and a number of range safety precautions had to be initiated.

> A small technical team, operated out of the blockhouse on launch day, was quietly confident that we would have a model countdown. When the last pad tasks were complete, a bit nervously, we all retreated behind the 6-inch-thick steel blockhouse door, which was locked and manned by an armed guard. We now relied on a number of black and white television monitors, and countdown indicators on the Launch Control console. We were given clearance by Range Safety and NORAD, shipping, aircraft and trains being warned off some time before, guidance needles staying in band, then ignition at about 16 minutes from key turn, the fastest by far of any Thor launch to date, with the erector still lowering. Our modified dash 9 main engine thrust developed with a large bang, too early we thought—the pad obscured by flames—but she quickly flew off the tops of the TV screens, with battering noise and vibration as if the 8-foot-thick concrete was tissue paper. We scrambled to get outside to see her, but an aching minute went by before the door was finally opened, by which time she was far aloft, leaving an arching smoke trail behind her glowing engine. The pad was burning fiercely, water drench turned on full. Propellant transfer system was made safe, residual fuel and LOX allowed to burn off.

The day before the launch, Chief of the Defence Staff Earl Louis Mountbatten flew into Vandenberg aboard a gleaming de Havilland Comet CMk2. Due to his impeccable connections to the British royal family he was accorded celebrity status, as was his aircraft, for the Americans had nothing comparable at that time. He was later joined by Lady Mountbatten, who had been visiting friends in Los Angeles, and the couple witnessed the successful launch,[8]

> [...] with the rest of our team at a safe distance. [He] came into the blockhouse to congratulate the [four-man] launch crew, us technical types at the back given barely a glance. Of course we celebrated well, especially after being informed the missile had landed on target; we never did find out how accurately.[9]

In fact, the warhead landed some distance south-east of the target, but still close enough to be designated a success. Initiation to lift-off went without incident. The countdown had taken 21 minutes 10 seconds, but this included a planned 2-minute-55-second hold at the end of Phase II to acquire the LRT. So in fact the RV had failed to separate properly from the missile because of a malfunction in the separation circuitry, however insufficient instrumentation was carried to positively identify the cause.[10] The balance of evidence suggested the inertial switch as a similar problem had occurred on an earlier R&D flight. The separation circuitry was modified on all subsequent missiles to eliminate the problem. Specifically mentioned in the No. 77 Squadron ORB were Flight Lieutenant Richard Cowling, who acted as LCO for the launch, and Chief Technician Milburn.[11, 12] *The Oregon Register-Guard* reported,

> The missile was one of three which streaked away from American Bases Tuesday. Another Thor and an Atlas were at Cape Canaveral, FLA. [...] The Air Force said the firing, by a four-man Royal Air Force crew, was completely successful.[13]

The *Miami News* joined in the chorus:

> Three brilliant successes by two of America's most powerful ballistic missiles have given US space scientists something other than Russian luniks to think about.[14]

At that time, the Soviet Luna 3 spacecraft was en route to the moon where, completing a space spectacular, it was to send back photos of the—until then—hidden far side.

> To space experts the engine performances and accuracy successes meant another degree of reliability for the two missiles they are counting heavily on to break Russia's monopoly on moon exploration.[15]

So the RAF crew could also take some credit, albeit small, for raising morale in what was to become President John F. Kennedy's 'Race for the Moon'. As well as visiting the Thor personnel, Lord Mountbatten was shown an early Titan missile in its silo. Perhaps surprisingly, he appeared to have little knowledge of American missile capability, but what he saw both impressed and appalled him and was seminal in crystallising his views on nuclear warfare and deterrence. He noted in his diary, 'The whole thing has a gruesome and horrific effect which makes one really fear for the sanity of mankind.'[16] The Mountbattens were but two of an ever increasing number of VIP visitors both British and American, including 'senators by the dozen', keen to witness the progress of America's missile programmes.[17] VIP accommodation was at the Marshallia Ranch House to the north-east of the launch complexes. Built in 1837, this was the oldest building in the Vandenberg base area.[18]

Behind the scenes, however, CTL-1 had been something of a 'hash-up'. By the time that the next CTL was ready, Squadron Leader Broad had compiled a proper all-embracing Operations Order, based largely on that used for V-bomber detachments to the US. While this had worked well, it would have been a cumbersome procedure for every individual launch. It covered all subsequent launches and was, in essence, a calendar detailing what should happen before and after a launch; it specified nominal roles and reports, among other details. This led BJSM in Washington to complement the Thor programme, commenting that its training launches were the only detachments where they knew where everyone was at any one time.[19]

CTL-2, nicknamed 'HARD RIGHT', took place on 2 December 1959. It was the first night-time launch from Vandenberg. Once again, a success was declared but the critical analysis was somewhat different. This time a failure in the X-accelerometer loop of the Inertial Guidance Equipment caused the warhead to overshoot by some 92 miles. Because of this substantial error the Operational Flight Safety System did not allow the pre-arm signal to be sent to the RV. A secondary failure occurred in the roll programme, too.[19] The amount of activity now taking place on the overworked LEs was threatening the overall continuity of the training. However, on 15 December the penultimate IWST, nicknamed 'TALL GIRL', was successfully launched from LE 75-1-2. Missile T185 had been delivered from DAC on 2 March. The launch crew came from No. 144(SM) Squadron and were Flight Lieutenant John Waiting, US Captain Emanuel Hellenbreck, Corporal Irvin Keen, Sergeant Victor Cook, and Corporal Morris Lynch. The countdown was the fastest recorded at Vandenberg so far—17 minutes 56 seconds.[20] At launch the missile weighed 110,298 lb, of which just under 90 per cent was accounted for by fuel and LOX. Fitted with a Mk II Mod III RV, the missile was to all intents and purposes an operationally configured vehicle, with the addition of an SXK-3 scoring kit and SOFAR bomb designed to detonate at a depth of 2,500 feet. Lift-off appeared normal but the consensus of observers was that after about 80 seconds the brilliance of the exhaust flame began to fade, and flaring at 3 to 4 second intervals occurred. The missile appeared to be spiralling until after VECO a brilliant blue-white light was seen at which point the vehicle broke up. The subsequent report on the launch was delayed some two months because of 'difficulty in translating the record of IWST training maintained by the Electronic Data Processing system, and by the transfer to other tasks of 392d Missile Training Squadron personnel familiar with the EDP', to which DD(Ops) (BM) added the cryptic handwritten note, 'Machine masters Man!!!'[21] Regardless, the *Fairbanks Daily News—Alaska* had already reported on the day after the launch, 'RAF Fired Thor Missile Blown Up.'[22] On Christmas Day, Lieutenant-Colonel John F. Watters took over command of 392MTS. Colonel Watters had served with the USAAF's Eighth Air Force during the

Second World War, and was again in England prior to his appointment at Vandenberg. He therefore knew well the ethos of the RAF and this was to stand him in good stead during his time at Vandenberg, of which he said he 'loved every minute.'[23]

CTL-3, nicknamed 'CENTER BOARD',[24] was launched at the first attempt on 2 March 1960. By this date the missiles installed in the UK were soon to be declared operational, so it was particularly important that the launch was successful to give the necessary reassurances to all parties concerned. The missile used, T272, had previously acted as the back-up missile for IWST-8. The plan had been to hold T272 in a launch-ready state and transfer the countdown in the event that the prime missile T185 failed in any way during the countdown. However, it was T272 that presented the problems as two countdown attempts failed at the 'Engine Centered' stage. T185 went on to a successful launch. Subsequently, a series of dual flow exercises took place between 15 and 28 December. T272 was then allocated to IWST-9 and installed on LE1. But once again problems intervened, and the launch was cancelled at T-8 minutes 28 seconds, when the missile failed to reach the 'Propellant Transfer Complete' mark. Launch was transferred to the back-up missile, T-215. Not until 29 February was the missile declared ready and, twice the bridesmaid, it at long last lifted-off at 1814.30PST. The total launch time was just over an hour, but this incorporated three holds during the count-down to rectify problems. These holds amounted to 44 minutes 21 seconds, but some 40 minutes of this total was for range safety matters. Excluding these delays, the countdown was performed in 21 minutes 4 seconds. CTL-3 had not been without its problems and the subsequent RAF report on the launch mentioned a 40 minutes 33 second hold—

> At this stage some misgivings were felt as to whether the launch would be achieved; it was possible that the engine-sequencing valves might be frozen solid after such a prolonged hold with Lox in the missile.[25]

After this CTL, 392d Missile Training Squadron wrote and published an evaluation report covering all facets of the CTL operation.[26] This report became an invaluable asset for the RAF and to all the agencies involved in the Thor programme. Its format was later adopted by the 1 Strategic Aerospace Division for other weapon systems.[27]

TIMELINE OF THOR T272. 'CENTER BOARD' PACIFIC MISSILE RANGE.
DATE: 2 MARCH 1960
COMPLEX/STAND: 75-2/LE8

Event	Expected Seconds after Lift-off	Actual Seconds after Lift-off
Lift-off	-	1205.55 PST
RV Baro-Switch Lockout Closure	73.10	71.97
Guidance Initiation	108.5	108.7
MECO	155.9	155.9

Guidance Pre-arm	156.1	156.3
VECO	163.1	162.6
RV Unlatch	170.9	N/A
Missile/RV Separation	171.9	169.1
RV Re-entry Time	817.0	N/A
RV Airburst Altitude	N/A	N/A
Total Flight Time	946.0	N/A

MISSILE DATA	EXPECTED	ACTUAL
LOX at Lift-off	67,712 lb	67,392 lb
Fuel at Lift-off	30,004 lb	30,648 lb
Total Lift-off Thrust	152,000 lb	153,000 lb
MECO Impulse	34,000 lb/sec	35,000 lb/sec
Total Lift-off Weight	109,870 lb	109,739 lb
Range	1,326 nm	1,326 nm
Cross Range Miss	-	0.1nm Left
Range Miss	-	1.4 nm Short
Total Miss	-	1.4 nm
RV Separation Rate	7.4 feet/sec	Small

The quickest countdown was that of CTL-4, but this was in part as a result of the missile being in the vertical position from the start of the countdown. The launch, codenamed 'CLAN CHATTAN', was also significant in that it was the first missile taken back from an operational site in England. Missile 31 (T233) had been subjected to the full effects of English weather on its pad at Driffield. Under the overall command of Squadron Leader P. G. Coulson, the veteran of the 'LIONS ROAR' launch, its launch crew was led by Flight Lieutenant L. S. Naile from No. 102(SM) Squadron.[28] An RAF spokesman confirmed that the launch had been a success.[29]

On the conclusion of the first four CTLs, Bomber Command commissioned a report on the launches from its Operational Research Branch. Rather more critical than the officially declared results, it noted that, 'Although none of the missiles fired in the CTL programme to date have suffered a catastrophic failure, only one of the launches (Welcome IV) can be considered a success.'[30] Success was defined as delivery of the warhead within a 2-mile CEP of the target and, as far as was known, the arming and fusing of the warhead had taken place satisfactorily. In CTL-1 and -3 separation had not taken place properly. In the case of CTL-4, the dummy warhead had been changed three times before launch. The report continued, 'The experience of the limited number of CTL firings carried out does not inspire a high degree of confidence that the missile system can be counted down, launched, reach its target and detonate satisfactorily'.[31] The report accepted that CTL-1 and -3 were launched at the first attempt, and that CTL-4 could technically be included as well because the problems it experienced would not occur in an operational system. CTL-2 had failed because of a gross guidance error which resulted in the warhead overshooting by some 90 miles. However, with such a small sample size it was difficult to predict a likely success rate, but the report concluded that, 'there is a 90-per-cent confidence that the probability of success is greater than 0.1 but less than [0].80.'[32] Two further factors made the CTLs unrepresentative: firstly, the intensive exercise of the missile and GSE, and secondly, the inadequate maintenance of the Vandenberg GSE between launches, which gave rise to a number of problems during the countdowns. The length of the countdown was a key factor in Thor's credibility, but the report found it difficult to establish a realistic figure because of the necessary holds imposed on the process by range safety factors ensuring that the range was clear of shipping and rail traffic. However, these were still early specification missiles and it was known that a 'fast countdown' modification (codenamed 'KATHLEEN GUIDE') was in the pipeline. In mid-1960, Pad-6 was home to the In-Service Engineering programme (ISE). This programme was an engineering effort to reduce the 15-minute countdown period. In order to reduce this time period a number of short cuts were evaluated. The main changes were: stopping the retraction of the shelter short of full retraction, not fully lowering the missile erector, and increasing the flow rates of the propellants. Many other small changes were incorporated, along with considerable redesign of the electrical circuitry and the net result, after many trial countdowns, was a reduction of the countdown time in perfect conditions to about 8 minutes.[33] These changes were first tested 'live' in CTL-7 and thereafter progressively incorporated in the UK missile stock. The overall assessment of the British Thors was that 'The results of the CTL programme are likely to be fairly representative of the United Kingdom missiles as far as in-flight success is concerned and somewhat optimistic as far as count-down and launch is concerned.'[34] In summary the success rate demonstrated by the first four CTL firings was 20 per cent, with the majority of failures resulting from in-flight malfunctions and a recommendation to modify the instrumentation was requested.

The North Luffenham Wing was chosen for CTL-6 nicknamed 'ACTON TOWN'. Missile T267 had been allocated to No. 144(SM) Squadron at North Luffenham. It had originally arrived in the UK on 6 November 1959, been mated to LE47 on 28 December, and subsequently been declared operational on 4 February 1960. It had been erected no less than 164 times, subjected to thirty-one Dry Countdowns, and eight times filled with LOX. Before leaving the UK for Vandenberg, it had twenty-eight modifications installed with a further two on arrival, before it was launched. Such was the dynamic nature of Project Emily, which continued to implement a relentless programme of improvements. The launch was witnessed by AOCinC Bomber Command Air Marshal Cross who, despite what he may have thought personally about the Thors, was always quick to praise the system. He was accompanied by his AOA HQ Bomber Command Air Vice-Marshal Brian Burnett, who remarked, '[the launch] was, of course of very great interest and gave one enormous confidence in the likely effectiveness of the weapon.'[35] Prior to arriving at Vandenberg, Cross and his party—which included E. Perkins from the Air Ministry—had visited Norton Air Base to see elements of the logistic support that kept Thor fully operational. He congratulated those involved in Thor on their excellent service, commenting that the RAF and USAF were working together as if in one team. Air Marshal Cross referred to rumours that the US missile programme was faltering, stemming from, among others, President Elect John F. Kennedy himself. He said that bringing the Thor missile into operational being within a period of four years and three months was no less than a miracle. The lead time for a new weapon system was more likely to be in the order of eight to twelve years. The rush job by Douglas and the Air Force proceeded, and all major schedules were met and Thor was made ready to operate in England much sooner than anyone would ordinarily have the right to expect. He added that 'sometimes people had to hear from an authority outside of the United States that certain of the accomplishments in the missile field are tremendous, carping critics notwithstanding.'[36]

The WELCOME VII course for personnel from the Driffield Wing which led to CTL-7 may be taken as a typical example of how a CTL was undertaken. Nicknamed 'SHEPHERDS BUSH' and under the command of Squadron Leader David 'Dicky' Downs, it was significant in that it was the first launch to employ the revised 'fast countdown' which sought to reduce the time from key-turn to lift-off from a nominal 19 minutes to below 15 minutes.[37] This modification had been initiated in December 1960, and during the subsequent three months called for many hundreds of man hours to make the necessary modifications. It was originally planned to involve depot-level assistance, but 392d MTS achieved the programme using only their own technicians. There was an additional feature which gave a recovery capability from any hold prior to engine start sequence, this being controlled by a recycle switch fitted to the LCO's console. RAF crews at their UK bases were by then routinely achieving a 15-minute nominal countdown, and this figure was usually taken as the time it took to launch, so the fast countdown was expected to initially achieve a time of between 13 and 14 minutes. The reduced countdown was achieved by incorporating the following changes:

Phase 1: Gravity chill-down of the LOX transfer lines eliminated.
Phase 2: LOX pressure increased from 88 to 115 psi. Engine slew check completed at the start of the phase as the shelter was being retracted. The shelter was then retracted fully in one operation.
Phase 3: By now virtually eliminated and merged with Phase 4 to create a new Phase 3. Rapid and fine load valves were both opened at the start of the phase. Fuel fine-loading started at the beginning of the phase and incorporating increased fuel storage tank pressure. The erector-transporter lowered on completion of fuel loading.
Phase 4: Transfer to internal power. Inverter warm-up time reduced from 30 to 15 seconds.
Phase 5: LOX transfer resumed and continued to lift-off.

The missile chosen for the CTL was T243. It was removed from its LE and thereafter taken by road to Mildenhall, where it was loaded onto a Globemaster. This needed considerable care, as there was minimum clearance between the missile and the forward cargo-loading doors of the aircraft. A small team of RAF technicians accompanied the missile to ensure power was provided to the gyroscopes of the Inertial Guidance System at all times. The power heated the fluid in which the gyroscope gimbals were suspended to prevent the mechanism seizing up. A small petrol-driven generator was mounted in the vacant nose cone space and used if no power was available from the aircraft or when transporting the missile by road.

The journey to T243's first transit stop at the Lajes Field Air Base in the Azores was not without incident. On starting the descent after an eight-hour flight at 8,000 feet, a loud bang was heard by USAF and RAF personnel seated near to the centre of the missile. The pilot stopped the descent at 6,000 feet while an examination of the missile took place. It was found that negative pressure within the LOX tank had caused the bulkhead to depress by around 8 inches. Removal of a polyurethane disc in the desiccant assembly had been overlooked in the pre-flight missile checkout, and although this had allowed pressure to escape from the LOX tank it had formed a seal against air flowing back into the tank. After landing at Lajes, the assembly was removed and reassembled. The onward flight to Vandenberg via Dover AFB, Delaware, was without further incident or any apparent damage to the missile.

On arrival at Vandenberg the missile was transferred to the RIM Building, where a programme of rigorous testing took place. This verified and calibrated where appropriate all sub-systems, the guidance unit, and CEA. These tests were all performed by the RAF CTL detachment. At this stage, DAC staff also installed the telemetry package to monitor the missile's progress after launch. This telemetry tended to prove troublesome. Thereafter, the missile was moved to the LE and would typically be on the launch pad for up to four weeks before launch, during which time the following tests would take place:

—one complete functional test
—one dry countdown
—one single-propellant flow countdown
—one double-propellant countdown

The target launch date for CTL-7 was 28 March 1961, but the launch was scrubbed after a 95-per-cent LOX malfunction occurred which could not be corrected. Although the launch team considered simulating the required signal, the 1MD Command Post overruled this course of action as it was not a standard procedure. The launch was re-scheduled for the following day when, despite a hold of 75 minutes due to problems with the impact radar, a successful launch took place late in the evening after a countdown of 13 minutes 43 seconds. This was also the second flight of the Mk 2 RV fitted with two small chaff ejectors placed diametrically opposite each other on the afterbody of the RV. The launch weight of the missile was 109,851 lb, made up as follows (all weights in ounces):

DM-18 missile structure	8,110
RV	2,928
Pressurised gas	117
Lubricating oils	127
Transfer propellants	460

RP-1	30,436
LOX	67,673

The official report on the launch advised that:

> Operation 'SHEPHERDS BUSH' was a completely successful operation. Again it demonstrated in a highly satisfactory manner the ability of Royal Air Force personnel to launch one of their Thor missiles which had been exposed to field conditions in the United Kingdom for an extended period. It was the finest example seen thus far during the Combat Launch Training program of what the weapon system is capable of, when prepared and operated by skilled, professional personnel. For the first time in either the IWST or CTL program, each of the major preparatory checks of the system during the MOS to Standby Phase was successfully completed on the first attempt [...] It is also noteworthy that this accomplishment took place immediately following the 'RAF Consolidate' major modification program.[38]

Sadly, the quality of film footage of the launch provided by 1352d Motion Picture Squadron was of unacceptable quality for public release. Phase times measured against the original nominal 15 minutes countdown were:

Phase	Actual	Nominal
Phase 1	3 min 57 sec	4 min 00 sec
Phase 2	2 min 41 sec	3 min 15 sec
Phase 3	5 min 39 sec	1 min 15 sec
Phase 4	0 min 39 sec	4 min 00 sec
Phase 5	0 min 47 sec	2 min 30 sec
TOTAL	13 min 43 sec	15 min 00 sec

From this it can be seen how much time was saved during the last two phases, with the bulk of activity taking place during the revised Phase 3. The official report also contained a paragraph which noted,

> The Commander, 392MTS, wishes to take official note of the cordial working relationship which existed during the entire period of the Welcome VII operation. It [was] his considered opinion that the highly effective performance of the Driffield CTL group [was] attributable in no small way to the manner in which Squadron Leader Downs exercised his command function during this operation. His entire approach to his mission at Vandenberg invited a co-operative attitude from his USAF counterparts.[39]

CTL-9, nicknamed 'SKYE BOAT', was undertaken by the Feltwell Wing in September 1961. The missile selected was T165, from No. 77(SM) Squadron. Pilot Officer John Moles, in charge of the Engineering Wing at Feltwell, headed up the five-man installation party that flew out with the missile.[40] The missile was taken from LE2 to the RIM Building for a complete pre-flight check-out. It then travelled the usual route to Mildenhall and was flown on a C-124 to America via the Azores (Bermuda), Donaldson Air Force Base (North Carolina), and thence to Vandenberg.[41] At every stop the forward doors of the aircraft were opened and a ground power supply immediately connected to keep the gyro temperature stable. On arrival at Vandenberg, the missile was subject to the most meticulous checks to ascertain its fitness for flight and also to provide valuable information on any components that had deteriorated due to the British climate. While the engineering team were erecting and checking out the missile on LE-7, the forty-six-man main party arrived separately,

> [...] one day late on 3rd August after a chaotic transit through McGuire AFB and an apprehensive flight across the United States to Bakersfield. The final 200 miles of the journey was completed in two Greyhound coaches.[42]

A USAF missile was as usual available for pre-launch training and installed on LE-8. However, use of this missile was hampered by a leaking main erector cylinder. This was only rectified on the day prior to the launch and the launch crew could only undertake a single flow RP1 countdown before 'the real thing'. By this time the live missile had already been brought to Standby on 3 September. All the CTLs were no-notice exercises, and the missile would be on full stand-by for three to four days before the 15-minute order to launch was given. In the run-up to the launch it was discovered that the LOX, although well over 99 per cent pure, was contaminated. This required the decanting of all the LOX in the storage tank—a time-consuming operation that required four tankers. To make matters worse, it was the weekend. The USAF pad controller had the wisdom to be 'required elsewhere' and during his absence sufficient LOX was released from the tank into the surrounding scrubland to reduce the requirement to three tankers, thereby making an otherwise unpleasant task that bit easier. It was an operation also much enjoyed by the resident rattle snakes, who could be heard enjoying this sudden release of oxygen![43]

The Americans were very sensitive to the need for flawless launches and would double- and triple-check all the systems on the missile before sanitising it and sealing all servicing apertures. Any broken seals had to be reported and explained. Despite this attention to detail, the Feltwell missile did carry a payload in the nosecone, a pretzel sealed in a plastic bag which had been discreetly inserted prior to launch despite the security precautions and with the full knowledge (or even involvement?) of the wing commander in charge of the launch team![44] How the perpetrator managed this without breaking even one seal was never explained. The countdown was achieved 14 seconds earlier than the nominal countdown time of 15 minutes 30 seconds. The 'pretzel into space' was revealed at the post-launch party, the US team entering into the spirit of a prank which, admittedly, would have provided some relief in the high-pressure environment that surrounded a launch. The launch crew consisted of Flight Lieutenant Colin Reeve, who had been the Acting Launch Control Officer on IWST-6, Master Signaller M. W. Willis, Chief Technicians K. S. Ware, E. M. Beresford, R. Cooper, and J. D. McIntyre. They were situated in the launch blockhouse, a mere 250 m from the LE, well protected by concrete but perhaps a little close if anything went wrong. To add further to the stress of the launch procedures, a target change was ordered during Phase 3 of the countdown. The engineering team who had effectively completed their job prior to the stand-by period were not on site but were alerted to the launch order being given. However, Vandenberg was a very big place and they were 5 miles from the LE. By the time they neared the pad the missile was already on its way, rising vertically through the clear blue sky before arcing out over the Pacific.[45] 'Old reliable does it again; 19th Shot Good,' headlined the *MESA Missileer*:

> An RAF crew fired its 18th Thor missile on a successful journey into the Pacific Wednesday at 3.30 p.m. from Vandenberg AFB. RAF training launches are conducted under the auspices of the 392nd Missile Training Squadron commanded by Lieutenant-Colonel John F. Watters.[46,47]

On 4 November 1961, newly appointed and promoted RAF Liaison Officer Wing Commander David Downs awaited the arrival of Thor T214 accompanied by the 'WELCOME 10' launch crews.[48] The launch of CTL-10 on 5 December 1961 by a crew from the Hemswell Wing proved to be very spectacular. Codenamed 'PIPERS DELIGHT', the launch was delayed by technical problems until late afternoon. The rising missile's vapour trail reflected the setting sun. The *Santa Maria Times* reported:

> A Thor missile streaking upwards from Vandenberg Air Force Base combined with unusual atmospheric conditions Tuesday caused a bright vapor trail in the evening sky.

Public sightings of the launch were widespread:

> At twilight yesterday, for the first time in their lives, hundreds of Redlands area people saw a sky show created by the launching of a ballistic missile. Today the sight continued to be the talk of the town. Observers were mystified by the sudden appearance of the luminous cloud in the otherwise clear western sky. They were fascinated by the way it spread, changed shape, shifted color and persisted for about eight minutes. Some thought it was an airplane exploding in flight.[49]

Amazingly the airframe was visible 1,000 miles downrange due to the reflection of the sun on its skin until it disappeared into the gathering darkness.[50]

The next launch was the only CTL not classed as a success. The penultimate RAF launch, CTL-11, nicknamed 'BLACK KNIFE', took place on 19 March 1962. Thor T229 was removed from LE35 at RAF Catfoss on 11 December 1961 and taken to the RIM Building at Driffield two days later. It was then airlifted from RAF Leconfield to Mildenhall on 25 January 1962, fully serviced and checked out prior to its transatlantic journey to Vandenberg, where it accompanied by the advance party it arrived on 28 January. Pre-launch training was undertaken using missile T226, a standardisation missile retained at Vandenberg which was updated with the latest modifications.[51] This allowed the CTL missile to be thoroughly checked out and readied for its launch, during which the missile failed a tank pressure test—caused, it transpired, by faulty workmanship during the consolidation modifications. As this had not been logged by the servicing team at RAF Driffield, urgent steps were taken to check all missiles in the wing. By then the Thor deployment was a mature programme and T229, the 35th Thor to be delivered, had been in service long enough to have experienced 237 erections, 56 dry countdowns, 5 single LOX flows, 6 single fuel flows, 8 dual fuel/LOX flows, and 1 warhead mate/de-mate, as well as to have undergone 23 modifications and 28 Time Compliance Technical Orders (TCTOs) and Engineering Change Proposals (ECP). During the training phase, the crews were visited by AVM Patrick 'Paddy' Dunn, AOC 1 Group.[52] The launch crew consisted of Detachment Commander, Squadron Leader P. I. Hart (OC No. 226(SM) Squadron), Flight Sergeant G. H. Thompson, Chief Technician J. E. Parkinson, Corporal Technician I. F. Stapley, Flight Lieutenant R. A. Whitcher, Corporal Technician R. J. L. Berthiaume, and Corporal Technician J. M. Tinton. AVM Dunn stayed on as a VIP to witness what appeared to be a normal launch. However, the pitch programme on-board the missile failed, possibly as a result of an obstruction in one of the gyros, and the RSO was forced to destroy the missile at T+26 seconds. The event was also witnessed by Douglas engineers who were working on Pad-2, modifying it from a weapons system training pad to a Thor-Agena launch facility. Dick Parker was one of them.

> Surprisingly we were not required to evacuate Pad-2 for the launch we all eagerly awaited, we had a front row seat. This was the closest that any of us had been to a launch. As the launch approached, some of the braver souls got on top of a one story tall revetment to get a better view of lift-off. In case something went wrong I was told to get them down with the forklift parked next to the revetment. At the instant of lift off it became apparent that something was badly wrong. The missile lifted off at a 45-degree angle, pointed in a westerly direction. It just happened that there was an overcast cloud layer with a ceiling of about 500 feet. Just as the missile disappeared into the cloud layer it started to straighten up and suddenly blew up just as it reached the ocean. When the guys on the revetment saw what was happening they raced towards the forklift but I was nowhere to be found. I was no dummy. The instant I saw the thing pitch over I ran for cover![53]

To No. 218(SM) Squadron of the North Luffenham Wing fell the honour of being the last RAF crew to launch a missile from Vandenberg. Missile T269 originally delivered to Pad 50 at RAF Harrington was selected for the launch. This missile had been wrongly filled with fuel on 17 August 1961 following the inadvertent opening of the fuel storage pressurising valve. It had been returned to Douglas for refurbishing and was understandably a sensible choice for the CTL, so this time it was not necessary to fly a missile back from the UK. Nicknamed 'BLAZING CINDERS', the successful launch took place on 19 June 1962 under control of the squadron's OC Wing Commander Colin Burch. The warhead landed within 1 nm of the target, making this the most accurate launch thus far.

The original training programme allowed for each Thor Wing to be allocated two firings per annum for the five-year duration of the agreement. After CTL-1, however, it was suggested that the CTL programme would likely be severely curtailed unless money could be found in the US budget to support the launches. On being informed of this unwelcome development by General Blanchard, DCAS, Air Marshal Sir Geoffrey Tuttle, replied protesting the situation and pointing out that the provision of missiles for these launches was an obligation under the agreement. As Mountbatten was in the US, it was indicated that he wished to discuss the situation with General Twining, Chairman of the US Joint Chiefs of Staff, after ascertaining the Air Ministry viewpoint. It became clear that the USAF was sympathetic to the Air Ministry attitude, but the problem lay within Washington.

Harold Watkinson wrote a letter to Deputy Secretary for Defense, James H. Douglas Jr, advising him that although the preliminary agreement allowed for eight annual launches, this was subject to the normal Military Assistance Program review and approval. Douglas Jr replied,

> The principal element which necessitates our position to limit the annual launches to four was the increased cost of the THOR program related to the funds available and anticipated to be available for worldwide military assistance programs.[54]

Douglas suggested that there was some misunderstanding between the two countries of the purpose of CTLs.

> The requirement is operational and the primary objective is to establish confidence and reliability factors for targeting purposes. A secondary objective, which is a by-product of the primary objective, is crew proficiency and product improvement. I do not mean to minimise the contribution to morale and proficiency of a live launch. However, I am sure you will agree that there are other methods which can and must be used to provide these essential elements in missile squadrons.[55]

The RAF view was that there was no real substitute for a live launch and the promise of participation had been an accepted and no doubt attractive recruiting feature of the programme. It was at this point that Douglas did concede to the argument to use Thors from the UK stock and allowed this to be implemented, as we have seen, from CTL-4 onwards. The Thor launches were also attractive from a VIP point of view. For each launch eighteen places were allocated on a commercial flight to Los Angeles for 'Observer Tours' of the Vandenberg facilities, which culminated in viewing the launch. Nine places were allocated by the Air Ministry and nine by the CinC Bomber Command. Squadron Leader Broad anonymously filled the latter nine places and tried very hard to reward deserving officers, although his decisions were attributed by stations to the CinC. He did himself go out once a year. [56]

Although a CTL-13 was planned and a missile, T211, selected with a launch date of 8 October 1962, this was cancelled—not this time the victim of financial constraints but a casualty of the early termination of the Thor Agreement. The following chart shows the impact point of the CTL warheads with reference to the target point. It shows that 66 per cent fell within 3 nm of the target, while 42 per cent fell within 2 nm. Excluding CTL-11, which was destroyed by the RSO, 78 per cent of the missiles taken from RAF stocks fell within 3 nm of the target. This degree of accuracy would undoubtedly have inflicted adequate attrition on the selected Soviet targets.

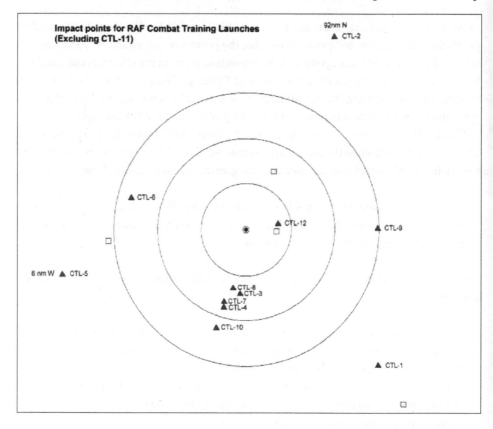

This last launch brought to an end the relationship between the RAF and the various teams, both service and civilian, at Vandenberg. Recognition and praise had come from AVM Stewart Menaul CBE, DFC, AFC, SASO HQ Bomber Command who offered a formal commendation of Colonel Watters's services in directing the training of RAF Thor launch crews.[57] He commented that the 'evaluation reports of combat training launches, initiated of your own volition and accomplished at considerable expense of personal endeavour, were invaluable to this headquarters in assessing the efficiency of RAF launch crew training.' He also cited Colonel Watters's ability to yoke US and RAF personnel into a completely harmonious, consolidated operation, and finally for the initiative and devotion to duty in providing maximum training benefits to the RAF launch crews. In writing to Colonel Watters, Lieutenant-General John P. McConnell, Vice Commander in Chief Strategic Air Command, further commented,

> I am pleased that your work with RAF personnel has produced these favourable comments from their commander. Your direction of the training program for RAF THOR launch crews, since its inception in 1958 has been a source of pride to this command.[58]

Yet more recognition came from Major-General Joseph J. Preston, Commander of the 1st Strategic Aerospace Division, who added,

It is noteworthy that you have been working with the Royal Air Force Thor Launch Crews over an extended period of time. During this period your efforts and performance of duty have been outstanding. This is evident by the comments of crews which visit Vandenberg on TDY and the operational success of the entire combat training and launch program.[59]

In September 1963, for their services in training the crews, the 392d Missile Training Squadron (IRBM) was awarded 'The Air Force Outstanding Unit Award' and its Commander, Colonel Watters, was entitled to permanently wear the ribbon representing this award. The awarding certificate was signed by Major-General Selmon W. Wells, Commander of the 1st Strategic Aerospace Division who had succeeded General Preston. In recommending the award, Lieutenant-General Hunter Harris Jr, who had in turn succeeded General McConnell, remarked,

The unit's training of British Royal Air Force ballistic missile crews was a major contribution to the improvement and development of international relations and resulted in the Free World's first operational deterrent ballistic missile force.[60]

The 392d MTS was also the recipient of one of the first USAF Missile Safety Awards for its outstanding safety efforts while establishing and implementing the training programme for the RAF in the operation of Thor. The unit's 'policies, procedures, and safety techniques resulted in a large number of successful operations and launches, with a zero accident rate.'[61]

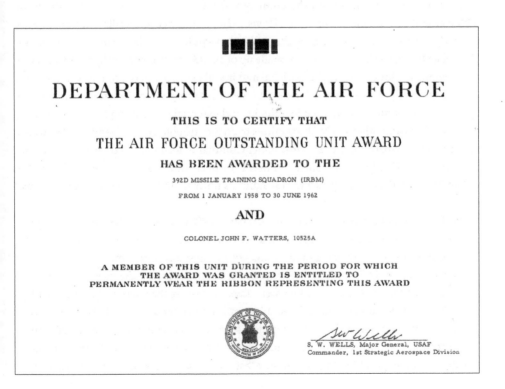

The UK Bases

Daily life at the twenty Thor bases consisted mainly of practice countdowns for the crews handling the regular 'top-ups' of LOX and of the routine maintenance of the missiles, which mostly lay horizontal in their shelters accompanied only by the background hum of electrical equipment. Corporal Technician Harry Hitchcock remembers the rush of adrenalin when the Master Bomber's tannoy announcement was broadcast at Feltwell: 'Bring all missiles to ready position.' The two 'live' missiles were duly activated, but the third missile used for training was without warhead or pyrotechnics. All the sites had an ongoing programme of VIP visits which for many provided some relief from the daily routines.[1] Others welcomed the more regular life that the three-shift day offered, and certainly this was a bonus to those who had families. To keep everyone on their toes, regular and unannounced incursions by the RAF Police teams to test the security system were conducted, often at the most inconvenient time, such as during a VIP visit. The police became skilled in unorthodox methods of gaining access and scored a 'hit' if they could reach the launch emplacement. The police traffic section (each section made up of six RAF policemen led by a sergeant) was also responsible for escorting the warhead and missile convoys between bases, sometimes up to four times per week, which would take about a day each to complete. When not thus employed, the section maintained its vehicles and essential contents and did route checks for road works and other likely obstructions to ensure trouble-free movement.[2] All twenty squadrons participated in the regular Bomber Command no-notice readiness and dispersal exercises, MICKY FINN. In reality, and in this respect similar to the situation during the Cuban Missile Crisis, this represented life much as normal other than heightened tensions.[3]

By the time this affair took place in October 1962 I had been at North Luffenham about eighteen months. Although it took the world to the brink of nuclear war, I have no recollection of there being massive anxiety amongst any of my immediate circle of acquaintances at RAF North Luffenham. I can certainly remember the incident—I think most people can remember what they were doing and where they were at the time—but I think we all felt that wiser counsels would prevail and that the crisis would be defused as the alternative was too awful to contemplate. I suppose as a twenty-year-old at the time, in common with youth everywhere we tended to think that we were immortal—these things happen to other people, not to us. I am sure that there must have been many at the camp at the time, those who would have to fire the missiles if ever the time had come for example, who were very much more anxious about the situation than we were. There was certainly a lot more urgency about making sure spares for unserviceable Thors were obtained with speed, but I think this was only to have been expected anyway and was not far removed from the priority it was always given as a matter of routine. The Cold War was always in the background of anything and everything in those days and I think we had become used to the sort of sabre-rattling that went on incessantly it seemed.[4]

Service humour also helped to relieve the long hours of doing very little except monitoring the health of the missiles:

One of the corporals at North Luffenham when I arrived had been a Flight Sergeant Air Gunner in the Pathfinder Force during World War Two. Quite why he was then only a corporal I do not know but he was an accomplished scrounger. He knew everybody and could obtain almost anything—within reason! One day, one of our officers told him to take everyone from the office, go with them on the squadron's delivery vehicle to a building on the airfield, pick up a piano and deliver it to a certain ante-room in the Officers Mess. Cpl 'S' protested that it would be unfortunate if a missile component was urgently needed with the accounts office empty but his protest was overruled—the Mess function was obviously more important. Said piano was found and lifted onto the lorry, but not secured in any way. As the vehicle turned the first bend on the way to its destination the piano fell onto its back with a noise which I can only describe as the 'lost chord'! It was nevertheless delivered to the Mess, manhandled along a long series of corridors and deposited in the ante-room. As to whether it was ever able to play a tune thereafter I do not know. In any event I personally heard no more about it. Only a few months ago during a programme on family history, 'Who Do You Think You Are', a few short clips were shown of a Lancaster bomber which had landed in Northern Germany in order to pick up some former British prisoners of war who had been marched from the camp in which they had been held back deep in to Germany as the Germans retreated at the end of WWII. Lo and behold, there was none other than Flight Sergeant 'S' helping the ex-prisoners of war onto the aircraft. Cpl 'S' was an inveterate practical joker and neither rank nor age nor sex was a protection from his practical joking.[5]

But if the moment had come for Thor to play its part, what would have happened? Command and Control of the weapon was the subject of much concern. The UK Chiefs of Staff were sceptical about the missiles and their capability right from the start. They believed that the missiles, being immovable and above ground and unhardened, were vulnerable, which indeed they were. *Flight* reported:

Doubts have been expressed about the value of a missile on 'soft' sites so close to the Soviet Union. Obviously what value there is in the Thors has been multiplied five-fold by the decision to spread them out in parcels of three. This would impose a large number of targets on the Russians if they proposed to launch a surprise attack: indeed, if it is assumed that they must fire three times to be sure of each target, it would take 60 missiles to destroy 60 missiles. This would be 'counter force' warfare in its purest and most futile form. But the Russians must surely ask themselves whether these 15 bases (which they can have had no difficulty in charting) are the only possible ones [and then perhaps a deliberate piece of disinformation aimed at the Soviets]. Are there some hidden Thors somewhere? Has someone buried the occasional one or two in an ancient coal working or in some isolated part of an old artillery range? Even in Britain there is plenty of room for concealment. Whether or not these are the only 60, at least 45 of them are on their sites in the hands of men who understand them. In the 24 development firings of the Thor up to January 1959, 10 were successful. In the following year, 22 were fired of which 20 were successful, one partially successful and one a failure. At regular intervals a British squadron will take one of its missiles to Vandenberg Air Force Base and fire it to see that it is still fully operational. The West, in short, has its first vulnerable batch of ballistic missiles. They are showing the way to what may be the hundreds or even thousands which come after.[6]

Intelligence sources believed that a Soviet 650-nm-range ballistic missile would become operational by the end of 1958 and, if based in East Germany, be capable of hitting the Thor bases in less time than the countdown would take. In terms of defending the Thor sites, the whole question of how the SAGW shield would protect both Thor and Blue Streak had been considered in terms of the siting of the Bloodhound SAGW squadrons. Until 1962–63, only SAGW Stage 1 would be available and a decision had to be made on whether to protect either the V-bomber bases or cities. The thirty-two projected sites for SAGW Stage 1½, coming into service from 1963, would be able to cover both. The Blue Streak underground sites were considered too small a target to be destroyed by a missile and, like the Thor sites, would possibly be targeted by manned bombers, so wherever possible the Blue Streak sites would be located within the SAGW Stage 1½ defensive area. It would be more difficult to provide defence for Thor, which, it was noted, ACAS (Ops) and ACAS (OR) staff considered operationally unacceptable unless it too could be housed underground.[7] While intelligence was largely correct in assuming Soviet missiles were based in East Germany, they underestimated the deployment date. The 650-nm-range SS-3 Shyster missiles became operational from May 1956.[8]

The estimated capital expenditure on Thor was about £10 million and some 4,000 personnel had to be diverted from other duties and trained. There was also the early inherent doubt about the reliability of the weapon which as a result would require costly modification to bring it to an acceptable standard of readiness. Bomber Command was sceptical about the ability to hold the missiles at fifteen minutes' readiness. 'Everything is possible,' ACM Sir Harry Broadhurst had written to DCAS, Air Marshal Sir Geoffrey Tuttle, 'but I would remind you that we are not yet beginning to solve the problem of holding the "V" Bombers at any state of readiness.' This was perhaps a rather alarming admission when the whole *raison d'être* of the RAF's deterrent was to be off the ground by the time the Soviet bombs arrived. However, a further factor was the ability to recall the V-Force when airborne, for a window of over an hour existed, whereas Thor, once launched, could not be aborted. Clearly a destruct system could have been installed, but if the nature of this command destruct were compromised by a Soviet radio signal, the integrity of Thor would be void. ACM Broadhurst therefore commented that the Thors, unlike the V-Force, could not be launched on first warning. Launch orders could only be initiated when the radar plots were positively identified as hostile, by which time they would be perilously close to the UK. This presented the Thors with an entirely different problem, because the military readiness and the political decision to launch had to coincide if the missiles were not to end up being destroyed on their launch emplacements.[9] Since Thors were armed with American warheads, they would never be under full British control, and this predicament was to pervade discussions on the role of the UK deterrent well after the Thors had been removed. Joint control inevitably produced a complex Command Structure (outlined in the figure below), starting as it did with the UK Prime Minister and the US President and filtering down to the twenty squadrons.

Fears over reliability were not unfounded. The reports from Cape Canaveral in the early days of the project were not optimistic, although things did improve once the Vandenberg launchings began. General consensus seems to have been, 'if the Americans want Thor over here, then let them bear the responsibility and the cost.' From this standpoint the issue of USAF crews manning the first operational missiles in the UK was not unduly contentious, but for others it was a downright stumbling block. DCODS Lieutenant-General Roderick W. McLeod accordingly advised Sandys of the Chiefs of Staff's views, making special note of the fact that they were very concerned that Britain may find itself committed to an unsatisfactory weapon system.[10] They were further concerned by a communiqué from the Atlantic Council issued in December, which advised: 'In view of the present Soviet policies

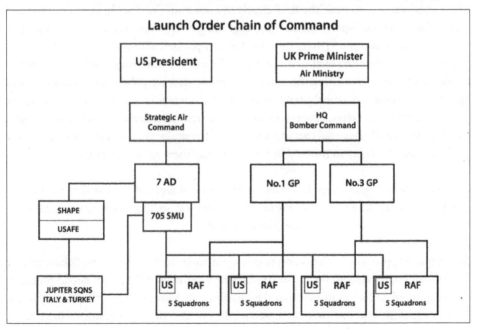

in the field of new weapons, the Council has decided that IRBMs will have to be out at the disposal of SACEUR.'[11] As we have seen, Field Marshal Montgomery had indicated that SHAPE was now considered the authority for deployment and role of the missiles and that SACEUR saw them as adjuncts to his forces and they would be used with that in mind. Yet the Chiefs of Staff saw the UK-based missiles as a strategic component of the British deterrent force, which should be used in accordance with SAC and Bomber Command's wishes, notwithstanding the views of the victor of El Alamein. They were therefore more than a little concerned to learn from a NATO communiqué issued in December that IRBMs—including, by implication, both the UK Thors and the Jupiters destined for Turkey and Italy—would be put at the disposal of SACEUR. This was a step too far. Thor was deemed a strategic weapon and should therefore be treated in the same way as the other elements of the nuclear reprisal forces represented by SAC and the medium bombers of the RAF. If they came under SACEUR's control, he might conceivably be tempted to use the IRBMs as tactical weapons. Furthermore, seeking the agreement of NATO's fifteen nations to launch the missiles presented significant political problems; conversely, host nations should always be able to veto the launch of the weapons if it was deemed contrary to their national interests. It seems clear from the start that the only UK perspective was that Thor was to be operated by the RAF under the joint control of the UK Prime Minister and the US President. This was, of course, the path that was followed.

Then there was the question of Thor's operational status. The US was keen to report that the missiles were 'ready to go' if only to be seen to be countering the Soviet threat, but the RAF was much more reticent. They had accepted delivery of the missiles initially 'for training purposes'. This was in major part linked to the five-year period of US support that had been an element of the undisclosed secondary Thor Agreement. The five years started when Thor was operational. The RAF clearly did not want the clock to start until the first missile base was fully operational. At the beginning of 1959 this was clearly not the case, even to casual observers. Matters were further complicated after a visit by Senator Stuart Symington to Britain to see at first hand how the project was progressing. Symington, a former SecAF, was a staunch critic of the Eisenhower defence policies and had a personal agenda to pursue as a potential presidential candidate—a matter of little consequence to the RAF, however. Nonetheless, he was critical of the security arrangements at the Feltwell base, which he visited. He reported that the dispersal of the sites was insufficient, that they were so close to public areas that it would be hard to protect them against sabotage;[12]

> The people of England were lulled into a false sense of security because they were not given the facts. There was nothing ready to go. There was nothing which met operational standards. There was nothing adequately dispersed.[13]

Symington had previously taken exception to a statement made to the House Subcommittee on Defense Appropriations on 23 January 1959 by Chairman of the JCS, General Nathan F. Twining, when he had indicated that the missiles were indeed 'sitting there ready to go.' Technically, if the warheads were mounted on the missiles, this was not untrue *in extremis*, but the missiles were certainly not at 15 minutes' stand-by, and would have required a considerable element of civilian technical support for them to leave the launch pads (though granted, this was on-hand). Following Symington's less than helpful intervention, the Air Force decided to 'clam up' in the hope that the story would quieten down, but Murray Snyder, Assistant Secretary of Defense for Public Affairs, persuaded SecDef McElroy to issue a public statement on the matter:

> Some questions have been raised as to whether the Thor intermediate-range ballistic missiles on English bases are operational. There has been no problem in delivering the committed number of missiles to the British bases. There has, however, been somewhat longer time required to prepare the bases and to install ground equipment than was originally anticipated. Moreover, the British Royal Air Force which is the receiving agency has determined the best way to use the first missiles delivered and set up at the British bases is for training purposes. Missiles in training condition can be fired, but only after the passage of a number of hours. Thus, none of these missiles are ready for immediate count-down and firing. It is not intended that we in this country will announce when Thor missiles are operational in England, because the determination of this will naturally be made by the deploying service—the Royal Air Force.[14]

But Symington was not the only American politician to seek to make political capital of Thor. Congressman Charles O. Porter from Oregon visited Feltwell in June 1959 and witnessed a practice countdown. First Lieutenant Robert Mazik was the duty US Authentication Officer responsible for arming the warhead, but Porter was equally aware that RAF officer, Flight Lieutenant Kenneth Hunter, could veto the launch if he did not receive the launch instruction from HQ Bomber Command. Porter contained his concerns until he addressed Congress in March 1960. Unfortunately, he had seen the RAF officer in possession of both keys:

> There is no danger that the British will suddenly decide to launch the missiles; the danger is probably the other way round. But the arrangement I saw introduced an element which belied the contention that an accidental or deliberate nuclear explosion was impossible.

He went on to say that the US Defense Department had blue-pencilled a mention of this in a magazine article he wrote after his visit. However, a USAF officer had since confirmed that the arrangement he had seen had subsequently been changed, and the RAF no longer held both keys. In any case, at the time of Porter's visit, the whole system was being checked out and was not yet operational. *Daily Express* Air Reporter Peter Woon visited Feltwell in April 1960 and, for his part,

> [had] seen the two keys side by side in a glass-fronted box beside the missile control panel with one of the American Team on a round-the-clock detachment and it would not be possible for an RAF man to arm the nuclear [war]head on a Thor missile without the Americans' consent.

Furthermore, he reassured the readers,

> [the warheads were] kept under permanent American control in a concrete building surrounded by barbed wire where the RAF [had] no authority.[15]

In fact, at that stage there was little to worry about as it was to be a full year after the Congressman's visit until the first live warhead was mated to one of the Feltwell missiles on 3 June 1960. That this represented a significant delay from the time that the first missiles were declared to be operational was indicative of the serious disharmony between the two countries. Although much of the reason for the differences is still shrouded in classified files, certain evidence can be cited. Since the UK possessed its own nuclear weapons, certain safety standards had been agreed for their safeguard to ensure against accidental detonation of a warhead. It was almost inevitable that there would be differences in the rules that the RAF operated under *vis-à-vis* the USAF. One fundamental problem was the warhead design. Spurred on by the needs of concurrency, the warhead was a sealed unit. Everything needed to arm and detonate the warhead was sealed inside at the time of manufacture, albeit that a number of safety features were incorporated to ensure against accidental arming. The worst that could have theoretically happened would have been a conventional explosion which scattered radioactive materials over the surrounding area, but a full nuclear explosion would have in theory been impossible. British practice was to ensure that the warhead was inert until it was armed during the flight to its target. British concerns surrounded the basic safety of the warheads not only in storage, but also in their transit by road from site to site. Thor now faced operational impotency. The missiles would be in place but without warheads. In August 1959 Major-General Blanchard wrote, somewhat acerbically, to DCAS, Sir Geoffrey Tuttle:

> In the recent discussions on Thor warhead safety between certain USAF and RAF officers it appears that our military officers, not being scientists, and because of security restrictions are not able to cope with the scientific aspects of safety which might be required by British Government determinations. As far as I am concerned, I am perfectly happy with all the Thor warhead safety features and the back-up information I have been provided [with] by the various military and scientific agencies of the United States. We think it is as safe as modern technology will permit from every possible contingency. [...] If safety assurances cannot be rendered by British scientists as a result of the disclosures made to date, I would appreciate an early reply so that I may inform those concerned in the United States.[16]

The exact nature of British concerns is opaque but these concerns were not without foundation although the reality of their concerns was not known at the time. Nuclear weapon security was far from perfect and there was a fundamental difference of opinion between the AEC, who sought custody and locks placed on weapons, and SAC, who wanted the freedom to use them in times of crisis or when those vested with the authority to use the weapons may have already have been eliminated by a pre-emptive Soviet strike. The W-49 warhead was not as tamper-proof as it seemed, but the knowledge of this was not fully appreciated at the time. A Sandia report was to comment that on the W-49 warhead, 'a saboteur, with knowledge of the warhead can, through warhead connectors, operate any arm/safe switch with improvised equipment.'[17] Notwithstanding all this, Thor warheads were in Britain from December 1959. Indeed, DCAS, AVM Charles Elworthy, who had succeeded Sir Geoffrey Tuttle, had reported on the movement of nine warheads from Lakenheath to Feltwell between 17 December and 8 January. But he warned that there would be times 'when fairly large numbers of warheads will arrive by air in USAF aircraft.'[18] Their subsequent onward movement risked becoming a lengthy procedure without the use of multiple warhead convoys. ACAS (Ops) AVM John Grandy had also noted a further constraint on warhead arrival. Only a small number of US aircraft had been modified to carry the warheads, and the ability to turn these aircraft around in the shortest possible time was a priority. The plan called for an early morning arrival with departure later the same day. Each aircraft would deliver six or possibly eight warheads at a time and the lack of storage for this quantity at the Wing HQs predicated their onward movement as quickly as possible. AVM Grandy, seeking authority for multiple warhead convoys, noted that:

[No] criticality is involved, even if a number of warheads [are] placed next to each other. [But] as this would increase the HE risk, and hence other ensuing risks, we would not carry them in this way but spread them out at such a distance in a convoy that an accident involving any one warhead in an accident or a fire would not lead to a similar accident in any other warhead. The total number to be carried in one convoy would be limited to three. This proposal has also been discussed with Group Captain [John] Rowlands, our representative at AWRE, who states there are no technical objections to such a plan.[19]

AVM Elworthy subsequently approved this proposal with the proviso that each warhead carrier would be separated by a distance in line with existing safety parameters. The first such multiple warhead convoys took place on 9 February 1960 with the movement of six warheads from Scampton to Hemswell in two convoys of three each. Although the road movement had to be closely coordinated with the movement of a USAF aircraft from Lakenheath to Scampton, the transfer took place without any problems.[20]

Parliamentary concerns about Thor's safety had been raised as early as June 1958, when Manchester MP Mr Konni Zilliacus asked the Minister of Defence whether,

[…] in view of the accidental chain-explosion of eight United States rockets, resulting in the loss of several lives and much damage, and the consequent danger to life and property in this country through the establishment of rocket bases in the United Kingdom, he will now reconsider his decision to allow United States missile bases to be stationed in this country.[21]

In response, Sandys no doubt took some satisfaction in telling the Rt Hon. MP that the missile in question was not Thor, but the surface-to-air Nike missile.

Had the unthinkable happened and the Thors been launched in anger, the order to launch would have been given by the Prime Minister to HQ Bomber Command via the

Air Ministry. The order would then have been disseminated to the four Thor wings and thence onwards to the twenty squadrons. HQBC would also have confirmed the order with the 7AD and would receive in reciprocation confirmation of the US authority to launch. Concurrently the US President would have informed SAC of his agreement to launch which would have been sent down the chain of command via 7AD and 705 SMW and then onwards to the twenty authentication officers who were then authorised to initiate the arming of the warheads. 7AD would also have alerted SHAPE and HQ USAFE of the decision and the latter would alert the Jupiter squadrons in Italy and Turkey.

There were, however, two incidents during Thor's deployment that could have resulted in a nuclear incident. The first was at Ludford Magna (affectionately known, because of the amount of water that accumulated on the site, as 'Mudford Magna', or 'Ludford Magma', and noted as a heavy clay site in the original survey), on 7 December 1960. A double propellant flow countdown was taking place on Pad 28, standard practice following a routine periodic maintenance. The warhead and igniters had been removed from the missile but the other two missiles on site had warheads fitted. The countdown would see the missile filled with LOX. The delivery of fuel would also be tested, but the RP-1 would be by-passed into the F6 fuel tanker parked adjacent to the fuel tank, rather than actually being loaded into the missile. This was a standard procedure. A missile would therefore never be loaded with fuel and oxidant concurrently. This was in part a safety precaution, but the RP-1 was also a contaminant. On the few occasions that a missile was fuelled in error it had to be returned to DAC for cleansing. As was often the case, particularly with the early countdowns, there were a number of onlookers of senior rank also present in the LCT. The incident occurred owing to uncertainty regarding the status switch on the LCO's console which had three positions: 'Maintenance', 'Checkout Exercise', and 'Ready'. Wet countdowns required the switch to be in the 'Ready' position. On the day in question, the countdown progressed normally until the LCO noticed that the status switch (seen circled in the opposite figure) was in the 'Maintenance' position, not a configuration that he was accustomed to during such a countdown. He therefore stopped the count and sought clarification. No one offered any worthwhile suggestions, however, so he consulted the overseeing authority, a Douglas civilian engineer, whose advice was to resume the countdown.

Wet countdowns normally ended when the systems checks detected that the vernier engines had not ignited. This inhibited main engine ignition and automatically terminated the countdown. However, in this instance at 1650(Z), with the launch switch set to 'Maintenance', three relays were activated, thus indicating to the system—*for maintenance purposes only*— that ignition had taken place. The main LOX valve therefore immediately opened and discharged 7,000 gallons of LOX onto the pad. The LOX first changed from a light blue liquid into a gel which filled the trenches around the LE before forming a dense white cloud as the super-chilled LOX boiled off and vaporised. The danger lay in the possibility of the LOX mixing with any hydrocarbons, oils, or grease for instance, which was a distinct possibility around the LE, whereupon it would spontaneously combust with potentially devastating results. A further problem lay in the possibility that the super-chilled liquid cascading over the pad had crystallised the metal launch structure presenting problems in lowering the missile.

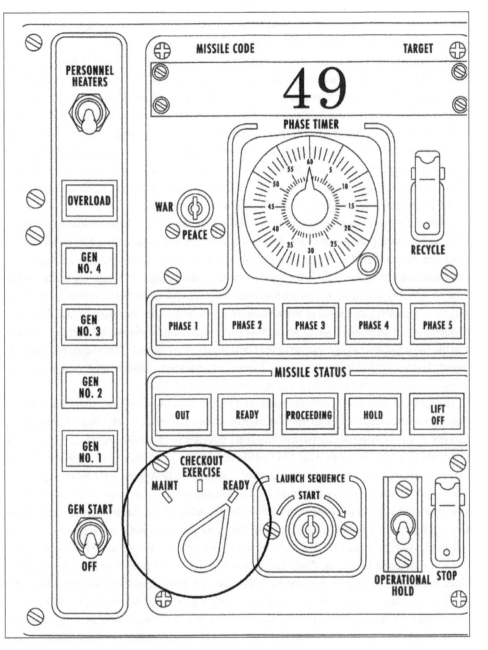

The concrete pad had cracked, there was the possibility of a significant fire, and the other two missiles—although their tanks were empty—had their warheads in place.

Civilian firefighters were summoned from Louth, Grimsby, Market Rasen, Brigg, and Grainsby. An RAF fire team from Scampton was also summoned but, somewhat surprisingly, and a matter that was questioned at the subsequent enquiry, the RAF Special Safety Team from Hemswell was not deployed. Three RAF fire tenders suffered damage from the LOX, one having to be abandoned as a matter of urgency, leaving its engine running. The USAF was reportedly 'aghast' at what had happened. Fortunately, the threat of nuclear contamination was avoided because, as a safety measure, wet countdowns did not take place with a nuclear warhead in place. There was little the fire services could do until the LOX had dispersed, whereupon the missile was recovered.

A Board of Inquiry was convened and a number of personnel were redeployed after the incident, a not uncommon practice in those days when mistakes were made. The Hemswell Station Commander was posted to Singapore at very short notice.[22] He was followed into oblivion by the Squadron Commander and the OCs of the Operations and Technical Wings. The replacements were all accorded 'acting' rank—substantive rank being dependent on their ability to get things in order—so something of a reign of terror ensued for a while. Perhaps strangely, unlike V-bomber accidents which generated copious amounts of paperwork, all that was needed after this incident was the writing of a two-page minute to the CinC Bomber Command.[23] Thereafter, No. 104(SM) Squadron's fortunes improved. It won the Quarterly Inter-Squadron Efficiency Award three times in the subsequent years, as well as providing a launch crew for CTL-11.

The Ludford Magna accident is almost certainly the incident referred to by Secretary of State for Defence Geoff Hoon in the Commons written answers on 17 July 2001.[24] Interestingly, this event was not one of the twenty incidents referred to in a 1992 report on UK nuclear incidents by Lord Oxburgh, Chief Scientific Advisor to the Ministry of Defence.[25] What *was* referred to, however, was an incident at Carnaby on 17 August 1962 involving one of No. 150(SM) Squadron's missiles on LE38. The missile, armed with a Mk-49 Y2 Mod 3 (War Reserve) warhead was undergoing an OFSS check during which the pre-arm indicator light in the RV simulator failed to light. During the subsequent re-check of the missile, the two retrorockets and all three RV latch squibs fired. The pad was immediately evacuated. After it was deemed safe to return, it was found that the latch safety pins were holding the RV in place and that no damage had occurred to the warhead. It was classified as a DULL SWORD incident and blame was attributed to a failure to follow prescribed safety rules for Thor.[26]

Considerable time was spent by the squadrons on practice countdown, leading eventually to the Triplox countdowns when all three missiles were counted down simultaneously. Flight Lieutenant Frank Nancarrow DFC was the first officer to conduct a Triplox in the Feltwell Wing, and directed No. 107(SM) Squadron's second such event at Tuddenham in April 1961 as part of Bomber Command's spring exercise. Present on that occasion was CO of 392d Training Squadron, Colonel Watters, who during the Thor deployment made a number of visits to the UK, where he remembers that an Avro Anson was put at his disposal to allow him to visit all the twenty Thor sites. In recognition of the welcome that the No. 107(SM) Squadron CTL crews had received at Vandenberg, Colonel Watters was made an honorary member of the squadron.[27]

Logistics

It was one thing to declare the sixty Thor missiles operational, but quite another to keep them that way, vital as it was for the sake of credibility for them to be held at the highest state of readiness twenty-four hours a day. Servicing and downtime, therefore, had to be kept to a minimum. This required that a satisfactory level of stock be maintained; but it was impractical for a full inventory of parts to be kept in the UK, so a sophisticated re-supply chain had to be set up linking the suppliers in California with the twenty bases in the UK. Nothing of this nature or complexity had previously existed, and this at a time when computerised stock control and resupply was in its infancy.[1]

The Thor logistic plan was part of a larger programme from as early as November 1956. It recognised the need for an accurate stock control system to identify the location of every part. The aim was to create a fully integrated inventory system for all the proposed US missile programmes. Reflecting the concurrency of the Thor programme, the logistic developments were run in parallel to the ongoing development programme of the missile itself and necessary changes incorporated in an almost real-time scenario. Difficult enough perhaps if supplier and user had both been in the UK, but in this case most of the parts supply would have to come from California. Clearly, from the start heavy reliance was going to be placed on MATS aircraft, the whole operation being based at SBAMA at Norton AFB, some 50 miles east of Los Angeles. Right from the beginning it was vital that a secure and direct link between the UK Thor sites and SBAMA was established. The system had also to be able to respond proactively to the unexpected. The Commander of SBAMA from 1 February 1960 was Major-General Ben I. Funk. He had previously been the first commander of the AMC Ballistic Missile Center at the AFBMC, so was in a most favourable position to take over the Thor programme when executive management responsibility transferred from the BMD on 1 January 1960. A stock of the most frequently requested operational items would be held in the UK, but initially this stock had to be based on anticipated usage. This would be automatically replenished and stock levels adjusted based on historic usage. Levels would be calculated on the basis of all sixty missiles being serviceable, although in practice a 90-per-cent readiness target was adopted. In total, there were about 35,000 separate components that had to be accounted for. These were all held on the Weapon System Stock List (WSSL). When the even larger parts list for Atlas and Titan were added to the system, it can be appreciated how immense the logistic problems were. The system was designed to minimise complex accounting work at individual squadron locations, the bulk of the work being handled by a central data processing centre. The experience of the early launches was closely monitored to predict likely demand for spares and the whole system was designed so that maximum servicing could be done on location within the missile shelters without the expensive and time-consuming need to return missiles to the Wing HQs for comparatively minor servicing. Inevitably, many of the components would be sourced directly from the contractors in California, so reliance was placed on an air bridge provided by MATS to transport the components. This was on occasion further reinforced by using civilian freight aircraft from civilian operators, such as Pan Am and TWA. The usual path for parts was via MATS to Mildenhall and thereafter taken to site by British Road Services. Urgent parts were often flown in on civilian flights when 'an RAF MT detachment at Booker, near Heathrow, would deliver the item [as soon as possible to the relevant Wing HQ].'[2] The not much loved but ubiquitous Morris J2 vans or Bedford RL 3-tonners, depending on the size of the load, operated on a twenty-four-hour basis to deliver the parts. Unstable and basic by modern standards, the J2s were universally unpopular but were the standard issue of the day and over the life of the programme travelled many hundreds of thousands of miles in support duties. On more than one occasion, a disgruntled duty driver was raised from his slumbers in the early hours to take an MOCP item to another base.[3] The Thor hauls would continue, albeit to a revised schedule. The system became live on 1 July 1958 when the Feltwell Wing communicated its first supply request.

Seventeen-year-old LAC Chris Webb arrived fresh from RAF Kirton-on-Lindsey in May 1960 for his first posting to Feltwell, with the illustrious title of 'AC1, Clerk, Equipment, Accounting'. He was assigned to the Electronic Data Processing Flight (EDPF), part of the Supply Squadron which was attached to No. 2 Hangar, between the MT section and the RIM Building. The flight was initially run by Corporal Eddie Bowers, later promoted to Sergeant and transferred to North Luffenham. A further office was provided for USAF Sergeant Ernie Bish, most remembered for the maniacal way in which he drove his hired Vauxhall VX4/90.

> The whole building was devoted to Thor and had its own packing department for [return] shipments to the USA. The squadron commander and his Flt Lieutenant had offices above our section and the hangar was overseen by a Warrant Officer. Our section comprised a Flt Sgt or Warrant Officer, a corporal and about eight airmen—a Junior Technician some SACs, LACs and ex-boy entrants as well as myself and two other AC1s.[4]

To familiarise themselves with Thor and its operational deployment the group were given a quick lecture which ended with the instruction, 'forget RAF procedure, we do it the USAF way here.'[5] Ronald Muggleton received the same message when he arrived at North Luffenham in April 1961 as a Junior Supply Technician. Fresh from nineteen months as an apprentice at RAF Bircham Newton, he found his training in RAF accounting systems and equipment was largely irrelevant in the face of the new complexities of a USAF stock control system.

The basics were essentially similar but the detail was very different and it took a while to become accustomed, not only to working under the pressures imposed by the requirements of an operational unit, but also to adapt to these differing working methods. Thus the consolidation which would normally have taken place on posting from training to operations on a normal RAF unit did not take place, something which happened again on the majority of my postings over the next 12 years.[5]

Two 'J' Type hangars existed at North Luffenham and the easterly one had been designated as the RIM Building, the other being used by the MT section. Adjacent to the RIM Building in the technical area was a 'B1'-Type hangar which housed the Supply Squadron.

The majority of the floor space within the hanger was given over the standard RAF storage racking and steel pallets. This storage contained the bulk of the spares requirement to support the fifteen Thor missiles for which North Luffenham was responsible. At the end of the hanger opposite the RIM Building was located the Receipts and Despatch Section. [This area] received and recorded all receipts of incoming material before passing [these] on to the Technical Stores for either placing into stock or issuing [immediately to satisfy] an outstanding demand. Despatch operated in reverse but there would have been nothing like the quantity of material going out as coming in. Along the airfield side of the hangar were located the offices for the OC Supply Squadron and his subordinate officers, the General Office and two accounting offices plus a Transceiver Room. The section which dealt with Petrols, Oils and Lubricants (POL) was located on the opposite wall—away from the airfield. I found myself in the larger of the two accounting offices in which the stock records were kept manually of the fairly large stockholding of missile spares and a very small section which dealt with the requirements of [other] sections such as the MT Section. This section used RAF accounting procedures. All requests for parts, locally from the RIM Building or from the other sites, were received by a senior aircraftsman and processed accordingly.[6]

At RAF Feltwell, LAC Webb remembers that all transactions—receipts, issues, exchanges, shipments, etc.—were initiated on

[…] four IBM 80-Column punched card machines and an IBM card transmitter plus our own teleprinter room at the end of the section run by the Communications Flight. Although officially 'out of bounds' it soon proved to be a comfortable area to relax in during quiet hours. The cards were coded according to the type of transaction, after which they were batched and verified by another machine before being sent by the teleprinter section to South Ruislip and onwards to SBAMA. In return the department would be advised, again by punched cards, of the confirmation of the items shipped, a code for the aircraft owner and an ETA in the UK. The relevant site could therefore be kept fully updated on the status of the parts they had requested. All stock held was on an automatic resupply basis. Thus it was hoped to eliminate 'panic' orders. While some requests were for noncritical parts, there were inevitably some parts that jeopardised the operational status of the missile or its associated launch equipment. In these instances a 'next higher assembly' (NHA) check was undertaken to confirm if the failed part might be a sub-component of a unit that might already be in stock. If this did not produce a result the parts were the subject of a 'missile out of commission awaiting parts' (MOCP) demand. This was essentially the highest level of parts request and had to be authorised by a Chief Tech or above. Nearly all Thor parts were held at SBAMA, although some specialist [items] would come direct from the contractor. Expensive or 'hi-valu' parts such as short- and long-range theodolites, vernier engines and guidance gimbals were transported in specially built packing cases.

LAC Webb often accompanied the MT driver in a Leyland Hippo and trailer from Feltwell to Mildenhall with these items.

We got access to the airfield via a back entrance guarded by huge—and I mean huge—armed USAF police who led us to the storage hangar. The paperwork was checked by USAF personnel and taped to the cases. A quick coffee and away under guard again to the gate.[8]

Parts were identified by a unique eleven-digit part number of which the last seven digits identified the specific part.[9]

Our 'Bible' was the Weapons System Equipment Component List (WSECL). It contained all the Thor stock and would convert part numbers into the accepted format for accounting.[10]

Everything was coded including a code for each Thor major location:

5A—Vandenberg
5B—North Luffenham
6A—Feltwell
7A—Hemswell
8A—Driffield
WA—SBAMA

This coding was the basis of the inter-site shipments such that 6A7A identified a shipment from Feltwell to Hemswell. Stocktaking took place on an annual basis (very much in terms of the standard commercial accounting procedures of the day). Done on a 'four hours on, four hours off basis,' LAC Webb remembers it as being 'hard work'.

Existing part numbers could not be recorded on punched cards so the format had to be changed to a compatible format.[11] The WSECL also gave the value of each item and repair and disposal instructions.

Some items could be repaired locally and some even scrapped, but [those] over a certain value would be packed and shipped back to the US for repair. [This was known as

Repairable Progression and] could be a real pain, sometimes sending signals requesting disposal instructions for an item that couldn't be identified.[12]

When an item was required but was not in local stock it was first

[…] stock-checked against all stock in the UK, in geographical order, so as far as Feltwell was concerned the first Thor base to be contacted was North Luffenham, then Hemswell and finally Driffield. If the item was available, special transport was laid on and the item dispatched to the requesting base. If it was not available in the UK then an MOCP request would be raised on a punched card, backed up by a signal to HQBC and SBAMA, and processed in the normal way. We would get a reply, almost immediately, of the shipment details.

Because of the permanent readiness of the Thors, the supply squadrons too had to operate on a twenty-four-hour basis, unlike many other sections of the Air Force, which enjoyed more conventional working hours. Out of hours responsibility rested with the Duty Storekeeper, a less than popular duty which was undertaken in turn by all supply squadron personnel of the rank of corporal and below and covered the out-of-hours times from 5.00 p.m. to 8.00 the next morning on weekdays and for the full two days over a weekend. Ronald Muggleton was familiar with the routine.

Accommodation was provided in a small room adjacent to one of the accounting sections and consisted of a small room containing a single bed, small locker and a telephone! It was a remote spot during the night-time hours and a very tedious job especially when, if as we all hoped it would be, things were quiet. However, there was usually some activity involving a spares requirement at some point during the night and this helped to relieve the boredom. It goes without saying that out of normal hours needs meant that the Duty Storekeeper had to be conversant with all aspects of the supply chain operation and meant that those normally based in the office would need to be able to find their way around the Tech Stores and Receipts and Despatches and also be able to operate the IBM punch card machines when necessary. Similarly, those based in Tech Stores or R&D would need to be able to use both the stock records and prepare the relevant paperwork and use the IBM machines. This was by no means easy for any of the supply personnel and meant that we had to keep ourselves up to date on how the rest of the squadron worked. Delays in getting a spares demand away using the IBM machines to prepare and send a set of punch cards to the United States via the Transceiver Room when a Thor was out of commission for parts was liable to result in a 'carpeting' for the errant airman.[13]

At about the same time as Chris Webb was coming to terms with his job at Feltwell, General Funk, accompanied by Colonel C. W. Hahn, Captain W. P. Reaver, and civilians Jack A. Posey and Jack E. Schmid, visited the UK to review operations at the receiving end of the system.[14] Arriving at Mildenhall at around noon on 23 May they were met by representatives of the RAF, 7AD and the London Logistics Office of the Air Materiel Force European Area (AMFEA). On the following days the party toured the four Thor wings, starting with Feltwell. Visits were interspersed with a meeting with General Charles B. Westover, Commander 7AD and his staff and at Bomber Command Headquarters in High Wycombe. This enabled a full discussion to take place on existing problems within the supply chain and for technical problems to be aired and solutions agreed. Of particular significance was confirmation that the target date for delivery of the modification kits for the updated short countdown was 15 August. On 26 May the final meeting of the Joint USAF/RAF Co-ordinating Team took place and was attended by some of the visitors. On completion of the installation programme around 25,000 items had been taken into the RAF inventory and were being identified with the help of AMFEA staff. The report concluded,

> [...] overall evaluation of the weapon system status was determined to be very satisfactory. [...] Enthusiasm and confidence on the part of the RAF for the weapon system seemed to be much improved.[15]

In early December 1960, Air Marshal Cross accompanied by AVM Brian Burnett, AOA HQ Bomber Command and AVM Maxwell Perkins, Senior Technical Staff Officer Bomber Command, visited the San Bernadino facility as part of a tour of various US air bases. Much impressed by what he saw and seated beside General Funk he addressed the press, commenting, 'we get simply splendid service from Norton. I wish it were as good in every other field.' He also took time to speak to the RAF representatives at Norton, Wing Commander George Weston and Squadron Leader John Wilson.[16]

But the reliable and timely resupply of components was not the only duty undertaken by the Supply Squadron. Because the unit had a reasonable number of personnel, the bulk of the Special Safety Team (SST) was made up of members of this group along with some SHQ staff. At fairly regular intervals the SST was brought to readiness by a tannoy message, this being followed in fairly short order by a further tannoy message ordering the SST to report for duty.

> We never knew whether these were to service a real event or whether, as was fortunately always the case where our SST was concerned, it was simply a drill. For the most part these exercises invariably began in the early to mid-afternoon on a Friday, which meant that any notions those of us had who were able to go home over the weekend were dashed, especially if the exercise took place at one of the outlying satellite stations, usually RAF Harrington. After picking up the kit needed, we would board the transport, usually a Bedford lorry with a canvas tilt, and be taken to the exercise point. If we were lucky it would be the airfield at North Luffenham, otherwise it was invariably Harrington. The exercise usually involved deploying tape around an imaginary accident area, using a geiger counter to locate a radioactive source and then pack everything up and returning [to base]. It was never explained to us what this exercise was designed for and so we tended to assume it was likely to have something to do with hostilities. Clearly this cannot have been

the case since, if the UK had been on the receiving end [of a Soviet attack] it would have been the end of the UK. It was obviously more likely to have been [related to a probably] non-nuclear accident.

On 8 October 1962, Air Marshal Cross, aware by then that the phasing out of Thor had begun, visited Norton AFB. He reserved his highest praise for Colonel Lynn DeWitt Sifford Jr, Commander of the SM-75 System Support Management Division who he described as a friend and adviser of great value.

Without you here at the San Bernadino Air Materiel Area at Norton we could have done nothing. Your support has been tremendous and enthusiastic. Figures tell the story. In all the years we have had the Thor, serviceability has never dropped below 90 per cent—and this in a 6,000 mile supply line.[17]

The *Redland Daily Facts* in pre-announcing Cross's visit reported,

The SM-75 System Support Management Division [...] has had the responsibility of keeping the Thors in ready posture. Together with other supply, maintenance, engineering and transportation specialists at Norton they have maintained this missile shield protecting Western Europe.[18]

Materiel support had throughout been the responsibility of SBAMA, under the overall command of Colonel Johnnie R. Dyer, Head of SBAMA's Directorate of Materiel Management. Colonel Sifford had handled the Thor aspect of operations but was in June 1963 leaving SBAMA to attend the Industrial College of the Armed Forces at Fort McNair, Washington DC. Before leaving he outlined the Thor story to visiting press:

The Thors in England represent a $300 million investment including installation and back-up equipment in the United States. We have an outstanding working relationship with the Royal Air Force which has operational control of the Thors in England. Automatic resupply has given us about 100-per-cent supply effectiveness in support of the Thors there and at the same time we have been able to reduce inventory supplies. The Thor is as close to a round of ammunition as we have been able to achieve in missiles. It is very reliable and is seldom out of action.[19]

What Happened to
the RAF's Thors?

Millions of pounds of American rocket equipment was sold yesterday at Stamford, Lincolnshire, for a total of £37,832. The material lying at RAF stations at North Luffenham, Feltwell, Tuddenham, Hemswell and Driffield had become surplus by the closing of the Thor rocket stations.[1]

The Thors weren't included in the sale! They were urgently needed elsewhere. Despite the number of round trips that had been made by MATS during Project Emily, things could still go wrong. The former RAF Cottam, which had closed in 1954, received a surprise visit. John Fletcher, who farmed Avenue Farm at Sledmere, was also an air enthusiast. He was out in his fields one day in 1963 when a C-124 hove into view and landed. A door opened and a crewman alighted. He looked around, took in the fact that he was not seeing that which he expected to see, then climbed back in. The aircraft took off for the short hop to its intended destination, nearby Driffield.[2] The RAF Police were busily occupied in coordinating the decommissioning of the missiles and accompanying the convoys as they were taken from their bases to suitable airheads for the return flight to the US.[3]

On return to the US the missiles were initially placed in storage and then taken to the Douglas plant at Tulsa, Oklahoma, where they were subsequently refurbished by Douglas for a series of launches from ETR, WTR, and Johnston Island in the Pacific. In December 1963, California Governor Pat Brown paid a visit to SBAMA. He was escorted on a tour of the Base by Major-General W. Austin Davis, Commanding Officer of the Ballistic Systems Division (BSD), and came face to face with some elements of the Air Force's missile arsenal. He saw some of the Thors recently returned from the UK laid out in a warehouse were awaiting conversion, but still showing their RAF roundels. Keen to know the cost of the missile arsenal, he was told that the BSD annual budget very nearly equated to the budget for the whole of the state of California.[4] It would not be long before these missiles finally got their opportunity to actually take to the skies.

The Tulsa plant was chosen as it already had experience of refurbishing aircraft. New guidance systems, telemetry, and command-destruct systems were installed. Engines were removed and refurbished by Rocketdyne. These vehicles were re-designated LV-2D (Launch Vehicle 2D), but this designation was subsequently changed depending on the mission they were used for. Although Thor was, fortunately, never launched in anger, launches with live nuclear warheads and subsequent detonations did take place and former Project Emily hardware and missiles were used in these roles. Project FISHBOWL, part of the Operation Dominic series of nuclear tests, was a series of Thor high-altitude (30-248 miles) nuclear tests conducted at Johnston Island an atoll some 780 nm south-west of Hawaii. The purpose was to evaluate the destructive effects of these nuclear explosions on RVs by 'carrying nuclear payloads to a prescribed point in space, detonating the payloads and then measuring the effects with three instrument pods placed in close proximity.'[5] Logistic support for the missiles remained with SBAMA now under the command of Major-General Clyde H. Mitchell. His spokesman commented, 'instead of relegating [the missiles] to the scrap heap, the Air Force has assigned "Old Reliable" to a bigger and more important mission as a booster for space shots.'[6] Fifty-five of the ex-RAF missiles were subsequently launched on a series of military related missions between 18 September 1963—11 days before the last Thor left the UK—and 15 July 1980.

A number of the missiles were used for a purpose much more closely related to their original design. These launches were undertaken by the USAF on Johnston Island, which may have been remote but was a vital communication link between the continental US and US interests in the Far East at a time when Vietnam was increasingly a focus of attention. It also monitored Soviet missile launches into the central Pacific. As was commonplace at the time, the programme operated under a cover story—namely, research into high-altitude nuclear explosions. The reality was, as always, somewhat different. While in part it did indeed test the effects of nuclear explosions in the atmosphere, it was also a sabre-rattling exercise designed to show the Soviet Union that Thor was a viable weapon still capable of delivering its nuclear payload. The initial operation was to disassemble the launch structure and its associated equipment from Vandenberg's Pad-6 and transport it all by sea and air to Johnston Island, where it was reassembled as LE-1 on the north-west corner of the island. This was undertaken by the construction company Holmes and Narver Inc. David Prebish was part of the team,

[...] working an eighty-four hour week at Vandenberg to move [the] launch pad over to the island, and check out Thor missiles to be launched from the island. [Project FISHBOWL] was an all-out US effort to complete as much atmospheric testing as possible before an international atmospheric test ban treaty came into effect. The Soviets were doing likewise. The Air Force dug up some of the oldest 'tiredest' Thors I knew of because they were available immediately for refurbishment and launch. These were unenlightened times, when world governments didn't yet realise how dangerous it was to release massive amounts of radiation into the atmosphere.[7]

If it was designed to make the Soviets think about US nuclear capability, it could not have suffered a more ignominious start. The first launch in the series was that of Thor T177 on 2 May 1962. Codenamed 'TIGERFISH', its purpose was to determine if instrument pods attached to the base of the Thor would work. Each missile would carry three pods which would be jettisoned before the nuclear explosion and would gather data as they parachuted back to earth for recovery. All three pods were recovered, although two had suffered handling damage. BLUEGILL, launched on 4 June, was the first live launch of a nuclear-tipped Thor. Although it appeared to have followed a correct course, the tracking system, which had been giving problems in the run up to the launch, lost contact. This gave the Commander of Joint Task Force 8 which was controlling the tests little option but to order the destruction of the missile before detonation took place. A third launch took place on 20 June. Codenamed 'STARFISH', two of the three pods were replaced by experimental re-entry vehicles. A normal initial flightpath was achieved until, after fifty-nine seconds at a height of 30,000 feet, the rocket motor stopped and the RSO ordered the missile's destruction. Parts of the missile, one RV, and the instrument pod fell back onto Johnston Island and there was some localised contamination. The next launch was STARFISH PRIME on 9 July, using a refurbished Thor T195 which had been part of the RAF's allocation, although actual delivery to the UK cannot be confirmed, and indeed seems unlikely. This proved successful: all systems operated correctly. A 1.44MT explosion took place at 248 miles altitude. Unforeseen was the effect of the resulting electromagnetic pulse (EMP), which left a large number of electrons trapped in the earth's magnetic field, supercharging the Van Allen radiation belts and causing degradation in the solar arrays of a number of satellites.

> The EMP [...] sent massive electrical currents surging through power lines in the Honolulu area, 800 miles from air zero. Hundreds of burglar alarms were set off and thirty strings of streets lights at various locations on Oahu Island were knocked out. The sudden surge of current burned out fuses and opened circuit breakers over a wide area.[8]

This was typical of the uncertainties and unknowns associated with high-altitude nuclear detonations. The next launch was a repeat of the BLUEGILL device codenamed 'BLUEGILL PRIME', this proved to be the low point of an already troubled programme. T180, also a missile allocated to the RAF but whose actual delivery to the UK cannot be confirmed, now reconfigured as a DSV-2E, malfunctioned just after ignition on 26 July. The LOX valve failed to open properly and the RSO instantly destroyed the warhead by radio command, after which the missile blew up, causing extensive damage to the launch emplacement and the surrounding equipment, and further exacerbated by alpha particle contamination from the warhead. Burning rocket fuel flowed down the cable trenches, destroying yet more equipment. This catastrophe halted the programme in it tracks as major decontamination of the plutonium on the launch pad area and the surrounding coral had to be undertaken. It was a reminder that, however well prepared the missiles were, accidents could and did still happen. Radioactive debris also covered the runway and pilots could not fly off their aircraft for two to three days after the explosion. 'An Air Force official issued a public statement on 27 July stating that the Thor failures should not be equated with the state of US military preparedness', pointing out that several of the Thor failures were related to pod and exhaust flame interactions and other causes not related to Thor's military use.[9]

Pad refurbishment took three months and required another launch emplacement to be deconstructed at Vandenberg and reconstructed on Johnston Island. On 16 October, yet another attempt to launch a successful warhead was made using T156, this time not a missile from the RAF inventory. Eighty-six seconds into the flight of BLUEGILL DOUBLE PRIME a control failure occurred and after the main engine had been driven to maximum deflection, the missile tumbled earthwards out of control. Again, a small amount of localised contamination was registered. Ten days later, after a number of technical delays, the refurbished LE-1 saw the successful launch of BLUEGILL TRIPLE PRIME carrying a Mk-4 RV containing a W-50 warhead with a submegaton yield.[10] The commander of the JTF had by this time little faith in Thor's ability to carry out a successful mission, but on this occasion was proved wrong when the planned detonation took place at an altitude of 31 miles and was visible from as far away as Hawaii. A similar payload was carried on the KINGFISH TRIPLE PRIME shot, which was launched successfully on 1 November. The detonation took place at a height of 61 miles and caused massive disruption to communications over the entire central Pacific for a period of about three hours. This concluded Thor's part in Operation FISHBOWL. Of seven attempts at using Thor to test a nuclear warhead, only three had succeeded. While this may be seen as a disappointing record, it was not atypical of the launch success rate experienced during the early days of missiles. Of the first twenty Thor launches, nine had failed. Even von Braun's team had eight failures in the initial twenty Jupiter launches. What the RAF's success rate might have been had the Thors been launched in anger is, of course, purely speculative.

Vehicle (ex-RAF in bold)	Codename	Date	Pad	Description
Thor DSV-2E T177	TIGERFISH	2 May 1962	LE1	Suborbital test carrying three instrumented packages. Success.
Thor DSV-2E T199	BLUEGILL	4 Jun 1962	LE1	W-50 warhead in a Mk-4 RV. Success.
Thor DSV-2E T193	STARFISH	20 Jun 1962	LE1	W-49 warhead in a Mk-4 RV. Failure after turbulence caused damage to the boat tail. RSO Destruct at T+65.
Thor DSV-2E T195 **RAF Allocation**	STARFISH PRIME	9 Jul 1962	LE1	W-49 warhead in a Mk-4 RV. Success. 1.4MT warhead detonated at 248 miles altitude.
Thor DSV-2E T180 **RAF Allocation**	BLUEGILL PRIME	26 Jul 1962	LE1	Failure. RSO destructed on the pad after LOX valve failed to open properly. Warhead ruptured scattering radioactive material over the launch emplacement.
Thor DSV-2E T156	BLUEGILL DOUBLE PRIME	16 Oct 1962	LE2	Failure. Main engine control failed after a gyro fault in the CEA. RSO destruct at T+156.
Thor DSV-2E T141	BLUEGILL TRIPLE PRIME	26 Oct 1962	LE1	W-50 warhead in a Mk-4 RV. Success.
Thor DSV-2E T226	KINGFISH TRIPLE PRIME	1 Nov 1962	LE2	Success.

During the early years the main programmes for which the refurbished Thors were used were the ASSET (Aerothermodynamic/Elastic Structural Systems Environmental Test) programme and Project 437. ASSET was used to test the concept of a lifting body and was a scaled-down version of the USAF's proposed multi-mission capable hypersonic X-20 Dyna-Soar Programme. Six ASSET launches took place, all from LC-17B at the ETR, all using ex-RAF Thors, three designated DSV-2F and three DSV-2G.

Thor's next mission was USAF Program 437, the first US anti-satellite system (ASAT) designed to counter Soviet military satellites or orbital bombs. Employing direct ascent and tipped with a nuclear warhead, it was a programme not without its critics, who were alarmed at its nuclear element. In competition, the US Army was keen to put forward its Nike Zeus anti-ballistic missile (ABM) system. Project 437 cited in its favour the use of already proven missiles and the proposed location using launch facilities previously used for Project FISHBOWL as both cost saving benefits. The location on Johnston Island would allow interception of targets well before they neared the US coastline. Antagonistic of the project, the CIA maintained the position that there were no satellites which might represent a hostile threat and the corollary to this was that the US was at risk of initiating the militarisation of space with unknown implications. However, the fear that if the Soviets placed a bomb in orbit to which the US had no remedy, the political fallout could be significant, proved an even more unacceptable scenario. General Schriever proposed the project to SecAF Eugene B. Zuckert on 12 September 1962. The ground had been prepared the previous February by Zuckert and General Le May, who sought a budget appropriation for an ASAT system. Secretary of Defense McNamara approved the programme on 20 November 1962 and Zuckert put Colonel Quentin A. Riepe in charge of a five-man team to study the proposal. On 28 March 1963 the programme was given highest priority status. Its Primary Mission Objective was:

> To achieve optimum operational effectiveness to negate, by means of a non-orbital [nuclear] payload, an earth satellite within the area of influence of the system. This is accomplished by launching the vehicle within a bounded time window, guiding the vehicle through MECO, and delivering the payload to a preselected time-space intercept point (IP). The bounded time window may be defined as the maximum variation in lift-off time that will allow successful completion of the mission.[11]

Zuckert was confident in the viability of the project, but a limiting factor was the two to three days that the tracking element of the system took to plot the orbits of potential targets. The Johnston Island base would support two operational launch pads with storage of missiles and logistic and training support located at Vandenberg. Initially, a highly classified programme, fourteen development launches took place using refurbished Thors from the former stocks of the RAF, designated DSV-2J vehicles.[12]

The following is a full list of the Thors allocated to the Royal Air Force and their use in allocated programs:

Column 1: Douglas Serial and RAF Serial where known
Column 2: USAF Serial. These were allocated via the Military Assistance Program. Those in italics not delivered to the UK.
Column 3: Launch location
Column 4: Launch Emplacement
Column 5: Launch date
Column 6: Program/Event

l. 1	Col. 2	Col. 3	Col. 4	Col. 5	Col. 6
10	56-6760				Facilities Test Vehicle
39 [01]	56-2647				First to be delivered to the UK
43	58-2254	WTR	SLC-10W	1 May 1978	DMSP B5D1
44	58-2255	ETR	LC-17A	13 May 1960	Echo A10
47	58-2258	WTR	B-6	31 Mar 1966	Burner 1. Program 417
48	58-2259	ETR	LC-17A	1 Apr 1960	TIROS 1
50	58-2261	N/A	N/A	N/A	On display at NMUSAF.
52 [03]	58-2263	JI	LE-1	27 Mar 1970	ASAT Test, Program 437, CTL
53	58-2264	WTR	SLC-10W	24 Mar 1972	Thor-Burner IIA
55	58-2266	JI	LE-2	05 April 1965	Program 437
57	58-2268	N/A	N/A	N/A	Unknown
59	58-2270	WTR	SLC-10W	14 Oct 1971	Thor-Burner IIA
61	58-2272	WTR	75-2-8	16 Apr 1959	IWST-1
65 [10]	58-2276	WTR	LE-7	6 Sep 1961	CTL-9
66	58-2277	N/A	N/A	N/A	Allocated to Program 437
67	58-2278	WTR	B-6	16 Sep 1966	Thor-Burner II
68 [15]	58-2279	JI	LE-1	31 Mar 1966	Sim Mk 49 warhead.
69	58-2280	WTR	B-6	8 Feb 1967	Thor-Burner II
71	58-2282	WTR	LE-6	29 Jun 1967	Thor-Burner II
72	58-2283	WTR	SLC-10W	11 Sep 1976	Thor-Burner IIA
73	58-2284	WTR	SLC-10W	23 Oct 1968	Thor-Burner II
75	58-2286	WTR	75-1-1	3 Aug 1959	IWST-3
80	58-2291	JI	LE-1	26 Jul 1962	BLUEGILL PRIME
81	58-2292	WTR	75-1-2	12 Nov 1959	IWST-7
82	58-2293	WTR	SLC-10W	19 Feb 1976	Thor-Burner IIA
83	58-2294	WTR	SLC-10W	5 Jun 1977	Thor-Burner IIA
85	58-2296	WTR	75-1-2	15 Dec 1959	IWST-8
86	58-2297	WTR	75-2-8	11 Oct 1960	CTL-5
88	58-2299	JI	LE-2	7 Dec 1965	H-30A RV
90	58-2301	WTR	75-2-6	14 Aug 1959	IWST-4

T-191	58-2302	WTR	75-2-7	16 Jun 1959	IWST-2
T-195	58-2306	JI	LE-1	9 Jul 1962	STARFISH PRIME
T-196	58-2307	JI	LE-2	12 Mar 1966	H-30A RV
T-197	58-2308	WTR	SLC-10W	24 May 1975	Thor-Burner IIA
T-201	58-2312	JI	LE-2	19 Sep 1975	BMDTTP
T-205	58-2316	JI	LE-1	14 May 1968	Sim Mk49 Warhead
T-207	58-2318	WTR	SLC-10W	16 Mar 1974	Thor-Burner IIA
T-209	58-2320	JI	LE-1	2 Mar 1964	Program 437
T-210	58-2321	WTR	SLC-10W	8 Jun 1971	Thor-Burner IIA
T-211	58-2322	N/A	N/A	N/A	Allocated to cancelled CTL-
T-213	58-2324	WTR	B-6	11 Sep 1965	Thor-Burner I FW/4
T-214 [214]	58-2325	WTR	LE-8	6 Dec 1961	CTL-10
T-215	58-2326	WTR	75-1-2	21 Jan 1960	IWST-9
T-220	59-2341	WTR	75-1-1	21 Oct 1959	IWST-6
T-224	59-2345	WTR	B-6	19 Jan 1965	DMSP 4
T-225	59-2346	JI	LE-2	24 Apr 1970	Sim Mk49 Warhead
T-227	59-2348	JI	LE-2	28 May 1964	Program 437
T-228	59-2349	WTR	75-1-2	17 Sep 1959	IWST-5
T-229 [35]	59-2350	WTR	LE-7	19 Mar 1962	CTL-11
T-232	59-2353	ETR	LC-17B	18 Sep 1963	ASSET ASV-1
T-233 [31]	59-2354	WTR	75-2-7	22 Jun 1960	CTL-4
T-236	59-2357	JI	LE-1	16 Nov 1964	ASAT Test, Program 437, CTL
T-239	59-2360	WTR	75-2-8	6 Oct 1959	CTL-1
T-240	59-2361	ETR	LC-17B	24 Mar 1964	ASSET ASV-2
T-242	59-2362	JI	LE-2	18 Jan 1966	Sim Mk49 Warhead
T-243 [39]	59-2364	WTR	75-2-7	30 Mar 1961	CTL-7
T-247	59-2368	ETR	LC-17B	9 Dec 1964	ASSET AEV-2
T-248	59-2369	ETR	LC-17B	22 Feb 1965	ASSET ASV-4
T-249	59-2370	WTR	SLC-10W	17 Feb 1971	Thor-Burner II
T-250	59-2371	ETR	LC-17B	22 July 1964	ASSET ASV-3
T-251	59-2372	WTR	B-6	8 Jan 1966	Thor-Burner I FW/4
T-252	59-2373	JI	LE-1	29 Nov 1968	Program 437
T-260	59-2381	ETR	LC-17B	28 Oct 1964	ASSET AEV-1
T-264	59-2385	WTR	SLC-10W	6 Jun 1979	Thor-Burner IIA
T-265	59-2386	WTR	75-1-1	2 Dec 1959	CTL-2
T-266 [49]	59-2387	WTR	LE-6	23 Aug 1967	DMSP B4A
T-267 [47]	59-2388	WTR	LE-8	13 Dec 1961	CTL-6
T-268 [48]	59-2389	WTR	LE-6	11 Oct 1967	DMSP B4A

69 [50]	59-2390	WTR	LE-8	19 Jun 1962	CTL-12
71	59-2392	JI	LE-2	24 Sep 1970	High Altitude Program (HAP)
72	59-2393	WTR	75-2-8	2 Mar 1960	CTL-3
73 [51]	59-2394	N/A	N/A	N/A	
74	59-2395	JI	LE-2	6 Nov 1975	BMDTTP
75	59-2396	WTR	SLC-10W	6 Aug 1974	DMSP B5C
76 [54]	59-2397	WTR	75-2-7	20 Jun 1961	CTL-8
77	59-2398	WTR	SLC-10W	23 May 1968	DMSP B4B
78	59-2399	N/A	N/A	N/A	Program 437
79	59-2400	WTR	SLC-10W	23 Jul 1969	DMSP B4B
80	59-2401	N/A	N/A	N/A	
82 [06]	59-2403	WTR	B-6	20 May 1965	DMSP 4
84	59-2405	N/A	N/A	N/A	Ex-Program 437. Now at VDB
85	59-2406	N/A	N/A	N/A	
87	59-2408	WTR	SLC-10W	11 Feb 1970	DMSP B5A
88	59-2409	WTR	SLC-10W	3 Sep 1970	DMSP B5A
89	59-2410	JI	LE-2	2 Jul 1966	Program 437AP
90	59-2411	JI	LE-2	21 Apr 1964	Program 437
91	59-2412	WTR	SLC-10W	17 Aug 1973	DMSP B5B
92	59-2413	N/A	N/A	N/A	Used as high power laser target
94	59-2415	WTR	SLC-10W	9 Nov 1972	DMSP B5B
99	59-2420	JI	LE-1	14 Feb 1964	Program 437
04	59-2425	WTR	SLC-10W	15 Jul 1980	Sat S-4
06	59-2427	WTR	B-6	18 Mar 1965	DMSP 4 - Program 417

Sadly, T304, the last ever firing of an RAF Thor ended in failure when the vehicle failed to reach orbit. Three ex-RAF Thors and parts of a fourth are known to remain:

Serial	Location	Reference
T110	RAF Museum, Cosford	RAF Facilities Test Vehicle
T150	National Museum of the USAF	Identified to LE38 at RAF Carnaby
T284	Vandenberg AFB	Allocated to Project 437
T292	Vandenberg AFB	Used in a test of a high-power laser weapon and destroyed in the test

And so was Thor's duty done.

Epilogue

Fortunately Thor was never ultimately put to the test, and so the reality of the command and control of the weapon and its reliability were never proven. It is certainly true that the later live launches at Vandenberg demonstrated that the accuracy of Thor was improving. But military training in general will struggle to duplicate all aspects of actual war conditions, and although the CTLs were ostensibly 'no-notice launches' and were as close to operational launches as could be achieved, they were still interrupted by problems during the countdown. It could be argued that there was an overriding need to demonstrate a successful launch, which was also true. There would almost certainly have been a percentage of failures if all sixty missiles had been launched in anger, and it is reasonable to suppose that a further percentage would have failed to some extent after launch. However, it is equally reasonable to suppose that some would have achieved a range and accuracy sufficient to cause major destruction on the target if the target was indeed where the targeters thought it was. It must be remembered that there was a distinct paucity of accurate mapping information on the Soviet Union. There had been some spy flights over Soviet territory, but these were restricted to only certain areas. Mainly conducted under cover of darkness, these tended to be radar mapping operations. So the actual location of some of the targets may have been somewhat distant from the believed location, although how big or widespread the errors were will possibly never be fully evaluated. Nonetheless, it should be remembered that fifty-nine of the missiles, and for a short period of time all sixty, were operationally available during the Cuban Missile Crisis. This was no mean achievement and far in excess of the percentage of the V-force that was generated, the other main component of Bomber Command—a fact duly noted by Air Marshal Cross in his post-Crisis analysis.

The control of Thor was encompassed within an exchange of letters which was updated during the Thor deployment as the US President changed. The Kennedy presidency such an update with an exchange of letters which duly took place on 6 February 1961. When Lyndon B. Johnson took over after Kennedy's assassination, a further exchange of letters took place to update the understanding. These letters had previously been an object of discussion between US Secretary of State Dean Rusk and British Foreign Minister Sir Alec Douglas-Home. They identified two general types of commitment, the first of which covered Thor. It provided for 'the President and Prime Minister [reaching] a joint decision by speaking personally with each other before certain forces equipped with US nuclear weapons and operating from bases within the UK will use nuclear weapons.' These forces now specifically noted and excluded 'the IRBM (Thor) force set up under the Anglo-United States Agreement of February 22, 1958 [which] is no longer operational.' The paper was substantially the same as the one upheld by Kennedy and Macmillan except that the Thor's 'technical flaws made it easy for both London and Washington to agree to end the deployment during 1963.'[1] Perhaps these were technical flaws of convenience to both sides.

In analysis, Thor was principally a political weapon. Indeed, if Sputnik 1 had been launched a year later, with the imminence of Atlas and the proposed fielding of Blue Streak by the RAF, the IRBM programme would most likely have been cancelled. What the programme did demonstrate, however, was the achievement of a complex weapon system developed over an extraordinarily short space of time and deployed operationally by the efficiency and joint understanding of two air forces. And that is Thor's historical legacy.

For the Douglas staff, Project Emily was both exciting and rewarding. The rewards for the Douglas Company were measurable in millions. They had designed a missile from scratch to first launch in thirteen months and saw it operationally deployed within four years. This was a period of time unheard of for any major weapons system before or since and undermined, to some extent at least, those who were critical of the company's management—the son supposedly not being up to the father. The company's investment in missile technology was significant. On 23 April 1962, Douglas Jr congratulated the work force on the production of the 40,000th missile for the US armed forces. However, it was Thor's legacy in real scientific terms, its contribution to future US military and civilian space programmes, which bore the most valuable fruit. Project Emily had produced a group of people who knew how systems developed and were made to work. This knowledge was later disseminated though the company in developing the Saturn S-IVB boosters and the later Thor and Thor-derived Delta rockets.[2]

By mid-1962, the USAF's first generation of ICBMs were fully operational. President Kennedy was keen to limit defence expenditure, and US bases on foreign soil were an area where significant savings could be made. The world of missiles was fast evolving. Britain's Blue Streak had been left behind as technology advanced apace and vulnerably exposed Thor was by many seen to be obsolescent as a strategic deterrent. But as orbiting satellites started to make significant inroads as intelligence gathering assets, demand for launch vehicles increased and the USAF saw potential in the Thors in England as filling a new role—bearing satellites into space. By October, only a few weeks before the Cuban Missile Crisis, the first of the RAF's stock of back-up Thors was being quietly stood down and being made ready to be taken back to the US. On 23 August 1963, the final Thor wing, North Luffenham, was closed, and by the end of the year there was little left as evidence of where the missiles had stood other than the buildings and concrete structures that had serviced them. All the ex-RAF Thors were to start a new life with many new functions, and they continued in USAF service for some years to come. Launches also took place from Johnston Island, where hardware used for the RAF launch emplacements at Vandenberg was taken to form new launch pads.

For the RAF, the legacy of Thor was perhaps less significant. From the British perspective, Thor was from the start a political rather than a military weapon, and so it continued to be. The view of the RAF's High Command was, at best, ambivalent, and it may be argued that the Chiefs of Staff never really came to terms with the programme. At a meeting of the US Joint Chiefs of Staff in Washington in March 1962, General LeMay commented, 'the Thor program in the UK was entirely political; there was no military requirement for it and the RAF had never wanted the program.'[3] Nonetheless, Air Marshal Cross on his visit to Norton AFB in October 1962 expressed a rather more generous opinion: that although the Thors were being phased out, they had played a great part in maintaining world peace and deterring aggression during the four years of their deployment.

> The Thors [have] not only been a military success, but perhaps even more important, it has demonstrated how two nations with similar beliefs can work together. British and American people are not war-like. They believe in justice and in peace. The Thor has been the guardian and the symbol of our intention to defend that peace.[4]

He even quipped,

> The operation was so successful little has been said about it. Only when things go badly are they reported.[5]

Only three weeks later the Western Bloc faced the Cuban Missile Crisis. Despite the noteworthy performance of Thor during the Cuban Missile Crisis, the RAF preferred to concentrate on its V-force. It had seen two major weapon projects, Blue Streak and Skybolt, cancelled. The latter had been considered essential to maintaining the V-bombers' credibility until the end of the decade. It now had to revert to a complicated and essentially unreliable Blue Steel with the demoralising knowledge that the Royal Navy's brand new Polaris fleet would in due course be taking over responsibility for Britain's deterrent. After the phasing out of Thor, the number of weapons Bomber Command held at fifteen minutes' readiness was reduced by 79 per cent, from 68-54 Thors and 14 aircraft to just 14 QRA aircraft. Trade expertise developed during the Thor era could be carried over to the Blue Steel squadrons, but this transfer was short-lived. Still, in its own way Thor was part of the story of Britain's path to largely self-sufficiency in nuclear warheads, reliant on the US only for the delivery systems. Whether the dual-key system would have worked in the heat of a pre-emptive attack on the UK was fortunately never tested.

In summary, the final paragraph of the Operations Record Book of No. 113(SM) Squadron recorded the following thoughts as a final testimony to the Thor programme—similar, no doubt, to those expressed by the other nineteen squadrons.

> The Squadron was reformed on 22nd July 1959 for the purpose of maintaining three Thor Intermediate Range Ballistic Missiles in a state of constant readiness. This task the Squadron performed with great success until 23.59 hours on 30th June 1963. As far as men were concerned the Thor Force had the cream from the top of all the engineering trade groups. As far as Operational Equipment was concerned the spares were always

forthcoming and the technical backing was always first class. The ancillary backing in the shape of domestic equipment, welfare services and accommodation were not so good and the Thor Force personnel always thought of themselves as the Cinderella of the RAF. But they have always been conscious of the fact that they were the spearhead of the Deterrent and acted with a loyalty and devotion to duty that has been a joy to behold. They will leave Thor having put it together, operated it through all its trials and tribulations in every sort of weather and taken it apart and packed it up for return to the USA. The relief felt on leaving the Thor Force and its permanent shift work will be tinged with sadness at the passing of a wonderful weapon and a unique experience shared with a very fine bunch of men.

From the USAF perspective, Major-General Charles M. Eisenhart, Commander 7AD, wrote to Group Captain W. M. Dixon DSO, DFC, AFC, OC RAF Feltwell:

1. The current phase out of the Thor IRBM weapon system will terminate a reliable missile capability which has provided an extremely essential contribution to our force posture during a critical period of advanced weapon development. It will also bring to an end a highly successful joint military operation.

2. I attribute the success of the SM-75 program primarily to the professional performance and technical excellence demonstrated by the Royal Air Force personnel and to the exemplary 'host-tenant' relationship which has prevailed among all elements of the Royal Air Force and the United States Air Force. Although the association of our two services in a united military enterprise is not new, the outstanding cohesive spirit evidenced in the joint operation at RAF Feltwell has conclusively served to enrich and enhance the effectiveness of our forces.

3. It is a privilege and a genuine pleasure to congratulate you, your officers and your airmen for having accomplished this unique and vital mission in an exemplary manner. I am confident your future contribution to the mission of the Royal Air Force will prove to be equally distinctive.

4. I extend my personal good wishes to all personnel of your command.

For four years the RAF had operated with great professionalism the first ballistic missile system fielded by the Western Allies. It was an exercise never to be repeated.

Appendix 1
Memories of Project Fishbowl-Jay Simmons

Jay Simmons had been one of the five Senior Operations Engineers on Project Emily and was the Douglas project manager for the programme. His role was to oversee the checkout and launch the Thor vehicles from Johnston Island for the USAF.

I was leaving for Christmas vacation on the Friday before Christmas 1961, when my boss, Starr Colby, the Manager of Advance Design, caught me and told me he had airline tickets for me to go to Albuquerque, New Mexico the next day to brief some Army people about the Thor launch vehicle and its capability.[1] He said I was chosen because I was the youngest in the group and I knew about the Thor.

When I arrived at Kirkland AFB the next afternoon I was expected at the gate and was escorted to a conference room where I was the only person there for about 30 minutes. Then people started arriving, first was a Navy admiral, then a few Army captains and majors, followed by two or three civilians. The only Air Force person there was a captain from headquarters. What was really strange was that not one person said a word to me or to each other, they just sat there in silence.

This all changed when a very tall, 6-foot-2 star Army general came in and introduced himself as Starbird and said that he was the commander of Task Force Eight and all the other people of which I now only remember two names, Major Roger Ray, the general's aide (who, when Starbird found out that I had not eaten all day, went out and brought me a sandwich) and Dr Bill Ogle from Los Alamos.[2] Ogle was the scientific manager for this project and later in 1962 was on the cover of Time magazine. Another one of the civilians was the Managing Director of Holmes and Narver, a construction contractor. Later we were told that the codename for the Thor part of [Joint] Task Force Eight was Project FISHBOWL.

Starbird's opening remarks were brief; he said, 'Tell us about the Thor's performance capability, reliability and availability.'

After about six or seven hours, and having missed my plane to Los Angeles, Major Ray took me to the BOQ for the night and I came home the next day after I agreed to meet the General and his party on the day after Christmas at Santa Monica airport to go with him to the Pacific to select a launch site for Project FISHBOWL. The General's plane was a very nicely outfitted DC-6, it got us to Hickham Field in Hawaii. From there we went to

Christmas Island, Washington Island (by boat from Christmas) and finally Johnston Island, where we decided what to do to the island to get in position for the project.

Holmes and Narver Inc., the construction engineers for the project, did a fantastic job in a very short time. They doubled the size of the island by dredging and extended the runway up to a mile so that Douglas C-133s could land and take off. They built quarters for about three hundred people and mess halls and kitchens, built wharfs and docks for supply ships and a dock for a range safety ship. And of course launch pads for the Thor and numerous other smaller instrumentation rockets.

Holmes and Narver also did an amazing job in moving two of launch pads that had been used for RAF training at Vandenberg AFB to Johnston Island in less than two months. Douglas gave them launch site drawings used in the construction of Project Emily and they divided the drawing into areas which were color-coded red, green, blue, etc. and then drew these lines on the existing launch pads at VAFB and went in and painted every item in those areas the same colors as on the drawings. They then disassembled the launch sites and after shipping the equipment to JI they reassembled the launch pads on the new dredged up sites. The only piece they built new was the huge metal structure [grillage] that was buried in concrete under the launch mount that held the fuelled Thor and kept it level. [A significant visual difference to the UK launch emplacements was that the two 'L'-shaped blast walls were extended and roofed in providing an enclosed area for the trailer mounted GSE, the compressed gas semi-trailer, and the air conditioning unit.]

We got the eight Thor vehicles from storage at San Bernardino, AFB California. Some had been returned from Project Emily, but most had been used as training vehicles for the RAF at VAFB. Several mission modifications were made to the missiles. The major mod was made on the boat-tail, where we were to carry three instrumentation pods which were to be released from the Thor. These pods were cylindrical and were spin-stabilized after release. We mounted them on each of the vertical main structural beams in the boat tail. We also had to provide a tripod structure above each pod to protect the pods during the early part of the flight. Three additional small rockets were mounted in a line up the side of the Thor at right angles to the flight centre line. These rockets were fired after burn out and prior to reaching apogee to move the Thor out of the ground instrumentation line of sight with the payload.

Once the construction of the two launch pads, designated LE1 and LE2, had been completed, the missile was mated and checked out by a Douglas crew from Cape Canaveral, headed up by Harold Burkett. The launch equipment was essentially the standard IOC configuration, with the launch control and electrical trailers installed in semi-hardened buildings.

All in all this was an amazing accomplishment; moving two launch pads to a remote island, finding and modifying nine Thor vehicles, building payloads and mating them with the Thor and performing eight launches in nine months from getting the go-ahead. The Air Force project team had only three people, Colonel Mike Myers, Lieutenant-Colonel Sid Greene for technical support and Lieutenant-Colonel Sam Wilson, contracting officer.

After Project FISHBOWL Johnston Island was used for a Blue Suit Launch called 'Program 437' Weapon System.

Appendix 2
The Epistle of St Bernadino

Here beginneth the first lesson, which is taken from the manual according to Douglas, beginning at the 77th Squadron.

And it came to pass, that on the day set aside for firing, the mighty god Thor lay stricken of the guidance. And in the camp of Sac and the tribe of Dac there was much alarm and despondency. And the followers of Sac and Dac did run around in circles, among them were those that rotated violently: these were known as wheels.

But in the great army of Raf, encamped on the plains of the Le, were sages and wise men who did minister unto the lord Thor. And these sages in their wisdom did gather together bowing their heads into the task and thus did accomplish the miracles of diagnosis.

And after two days of sojourning betwixt the seat of Thor and the House of Rim, these apothecaries didst work wonders. And Thor didst then arise from his reclining position and didst survey his subjects from a majestic height. And in the camps of Sac and Dac there was great rejoicing for the lord Thor was now made whole.

But among the army of Raf there was anger against Clot, the son of Oaf, who was a tribesman of Sac and Dac, for it came to pass that Clot had had his finger well inserted.
And thus the great army of Raf did give life to the god Thor. And then they did minister unto him with much wine and victuals, whereby he grew strong and powerful. And the great god Thor was well pleased and did issue forth much vapours.

And at the appointed hour for the great god to rise into the heavens, he did utter roaring noises and ascended mightily, casting a great shadow amid smoke and flame upon the multitude beneath. And the sound of his passage did echo like thunder upon the multitude who uttered his praises loud and long. And the followers of Raf were exceeding glad.

(Anon)

Appendix 3
RAF Thor* Launches at Vandenberg AFB

Serial N	Pad	Date	Codename	Comments
	75-1-1	16 Dec 1958	TUNE UP	First Operational Thor Launch—Success USAF Crew launch
	75-2-8	16 Apr 1959	LIONS ROAR Welcome 1	IWST-1. First RAF launch—Success The operator set an excessive 'velocity to be gained' in the x direction into the guidance set, resulting in an impact 93 nm beyond the target.
302	75-2-7	18–22 May 1959	PUNCH PRESS	Operation abandoned after technical problems and conflicting with DISCOVERER III launch. Replaced by 'Rifle Shot'.
302	75-2-7	16 Jun 1959	RIFLE SHOT	IWST-2. The lift-off pin was not extracted at lift-off, thereby failing to start the programmer tape in the CEA, causing the missile to climb vertically. RSO destruct at T+105 secs.
	75-1-1	3 Aug 1959	BEAN BALL	IWST-3. Success The main LOX valve did not close at MECO, extending the range approximately 63 nm beyond the target.
301	75-2-6	14 Aug 1959	SHORT SKIP	IWST-4. Failure due to inadvertent fuel depletion.
349	75-1-2	17 Sep 1959	GREASE GUN	IWST-5. Partial success—Warhead off target.
	75-2-8	6 Oct 1959	FOREIGN TRAVEL Welcome I	CTL-1. Feltwell Wing. Success

T220	75-1-1	21 Oct 1959	STAND FAST	IWST-6. Success
T181	75-1-2	12 Nov 1959	BEACH BUGGY	IWST-7. Success
T265	75-1-1	2 Dec 1959	HARD RIGHT Welcome II	CTL-2. Hemswell Wing. Succes The missile did not roll to the pitch plane azimuth, and instead programmed downrang approximately along the launch azimuth. At guidance initiation. however, the guidance set gener control signals to correct the trajectory. Component failure suspected.
T185	75-1-2	15 Dec 1959	TALL GIRL	IWST-8. Success The engine position feedback voltage began to change at T+6; secs and the voltage deviation increased until T+83 secs, wher missile became unstable and br up.
T215 58-2326	75-1-2	21 Jan 1960	RED CABOOSE	IWST-9. Success—Last IWST. N Luffenham Wing
T272	75-2-8	2 Mar 1960	CENTER BOARD Welcome III	CTL-3. Feltwell Wing. Success
T233 RAF Serial 31	75-2-7	22 Jun 1960	CLAN CHATTAN Welcome IV	CTL-4. Driffield Wing. Success First missile from UK Stock. Nc 102(SM) Sqn
T186 RAF Serial 14	75-2-8	11 Oct 1960	LEFT RUDDER	CTL-5. Hemswell Wing. Succes
T267 59-2388	LE-8	13 Dec 1960	ATON TOWN Welcome VI	CTL-6. North Luffenham Wing. Success [†] No. 144(SM) Sqn. RAF Missile Pad 47
T243 59-2364 RAF Serial 39	75-2-7	30 Mar 1961	SHEPHERDS BUSH Welcome VII	CTL-7. Driffield Wing. Success First FAST countdown. No. 98(9 Sqn
T276	75-2-7	20 Jun 1961[††]	WHITE BISHOP	CTL-8. North Luffenham Wing. Success Missile from RAF Polebrook
T165 RAF Serial 10	LE-7	6 Sep 1961	SKYE BOAT Welcome IX	CTL-9. Feltwell Wing. Success

4	LE-8	6 Dec 1961	PIPERS DELIGHT	CTL-10. Hemswell Wing. Success No. 97(SM) Sqn
9 350 Serial	LE-7	19 Mar 1962	BLACK KNIFE Welcome XI	CTL-11. Driffield Wing. Failure The pitch position gyro did not spin up until 12 seconds after lift-off. During lift-off, the missile hit the mast and the impact caused a penetration of the LOX tank. At T+13 secs the gyro became free and the controller issued a nose-up pitch command. RSO destruct at T+26 secs. No. 102(SM) Sqn
9	LE-8	19 Jun 1962	BLAZING CINDERS	CTL-12. North Luffenham Wing. Success
1		8 Oct 1962		Cancelled following announcement of draw-down of Thor programme

* All the Thors were designated DM-18 (Douglas Model-18). They were single-stage launch vehicles. Anomalous launch data under 'Comments' was extracted from Douglas Aircraft Company Report SM-44832. Launch dates can sometimes vary by a day depending on whether UK or US time is used.

† The Thor used for this launch was an RAF missile that had been inadvertently fuelled in the horizontal position and could not therefore be used as a live round.

†† From this date all CTLs were undertaken solely by RAF personnel.

Appendix 4
Thor Bases and Squadrons

No. 3 GROUP	MILDENHALL			
SITE	SQUADRON	FROM	TO	NGR
FELTWELL	No. 77(SM) Sqn	1 Sep 1958	10 Jul 1963	TL7189
Shepherds Grove	No. 82(SM) Sqn	22 Jul 1959	10 Jul 1963	TL9972
Tuddenham	No. 107(SM) Sqn	22 Jul 1959	10 Jul 1963	TL7671
Mepal	No. 113(SM) Sqn	22 Jul 1959	10 Jul 1963	TL4379
North Pickenham	No. 220(SM) Sqn	22 Jul 1959	10 Jul 1963	TF8506
Airhead:	LAKENHEATH			
NORTH LUFFENHAM	No. 144(SM) Sqn	1 Dec 1959	23 Aug 1963	SK9404
Harrington	No. 218(SM) Sqn	1 Dec 1959	23 Aug 1963	SP7777
Polebrook	No. 130(SM) Sqn	1 Dec 1959	23 Aug 1963	TL0986
Melton Mowbray	No. 254(SM) Sqn	1 Dec 1959	23 Aug 1963	SK4715
Folkingham	No. 223(SM) Sqn	1 Dec 1959	23 Aug 1963	TF0430

N.B. Airhead: Cottesmore.

No. 1 GROUP	BAWTRY HALL			
HEMSWELL	No. 97(SM) Sqn	1 Dec 1958	24 May 1963	SK9490
Bardney	No. 106(SM) Sqn	22 Jul 1959	24 May 1963	TF1471
Caistor	No. 269(SM) Sqn	22 Jul 1959	24 May 1963	TF0802
Coleby Grange	No. 142(SM) Sqn	22 Jul 1959	24 May 1963	TF0060
Ludford Magna	No. 104(SM) Sqn	22 Jul 1959	24 May 1963	TF1471
DRIFFIELD	No. 98(SM) Sqn	1 Aug 1959	18 Apr 1963	SE9956
Catfoss	No. 226(SM) Sqn	1 Aug 1959	9 Mar 1963	TA1348
Carnaby	No. 150(SM) Sqn	1 Aug 1959	9 Apr 1963	TA1464
Breighton	No. 240(SM) Sqn	1 Aug 1959	8 Jan 1963	SE7134
Full Sutton	No. 102(SM) Sqn	1 Aug 1959	27 Apr 1963	SE7454

N.B. Hemswell Airhead: Scampton. Driffield Airhead: Leconfield.

Appendix 5
Markings

The RAF Thors carried few markings other than the RAF roundel and a serial number. The missiles were painted overall in white, which coincidentally echoed the V-force white anti-flash paintwork. Initial consideration was given to applying yellow 'trainer bands' for the first missiles to arrive to emphasise their training role, but this was never carried out. Serial numbers were applied which were clearly designed to match the missile to its launch emplacement number, and while this may initially have been carried out, as missiles were recovered for servicing it was inevitable that a mismatch of numbers should occur. Later missiles appeared to bear the Douglas serial number, e.g. '214' rather than an LE identifier, but when this started is not clear. Some squadrons placed their squadron badge or the badge of the wing squadron on the nose.

Appendix 6
Thor Programme Major Contractors

Accessory Products Company
AC Spark Plug Div. of General Motors
Altec Lancing Corporation
Amelco Inc.
American Brass Company
Anderson Greenwood Valve Company
Annin Company
Associated Piping Company
Bendix Aviation Corporation
Brooks Rotameter Company
Cambridge Corporation
Columbus McKinnon Chain Corporation
Clark Brothers Company
Crescent Valves, Barkdale Valves Inc.
Cummins Engine Company
Douglas Aircraft Co. Inc.
Electric Auto-Like Company
Food Machinery & Chemical Corporation
Fruehauf Trailer Company
General Electric Company

Grove Valve & Regulator Company
C. G. Hokason Company
Manning, Maxwell & Moore Inc.
Marrison Company
North Electric Company
Pacific Valves Inc.
Packard-Bell Electronics Corporation
Permanent Filter Company
Powell Valve Company
Republic manufacturing Company
Rocketdyne Division, NAA Inc.
A. O. Smith Corporation
Southwestern Valve Corporation
Stellar Hydraulics Company
United Control Corporation
Vickers Inc. Div., Sperry Rand Corporation
(TEL)
Viking Pump Company
Westinghouse Electric Corporation
Williams Pine Company

Appendix 7

AZIMUTH COVERAGE OF THOR SITES ORIGINAL ALIGNMENT OVERLAID WITH RE-ALIGNMENT

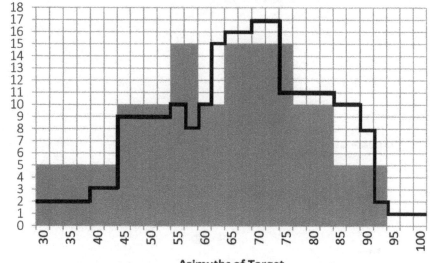

Appendix 8

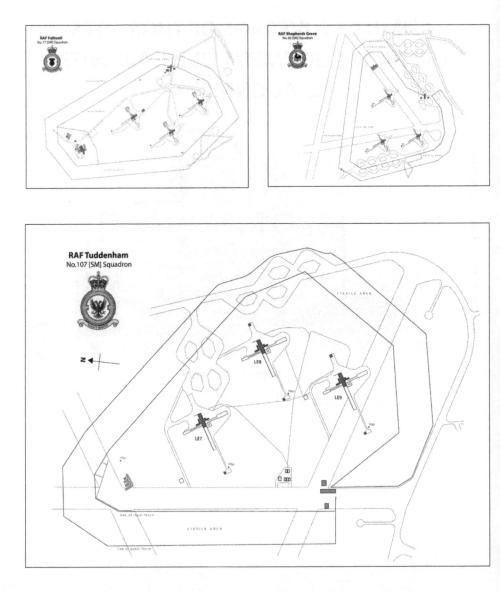

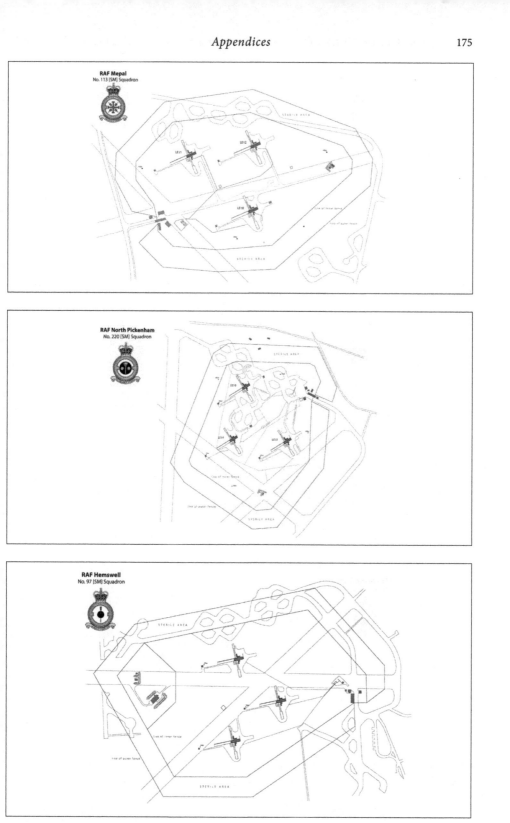

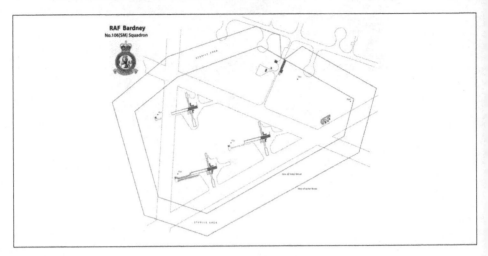

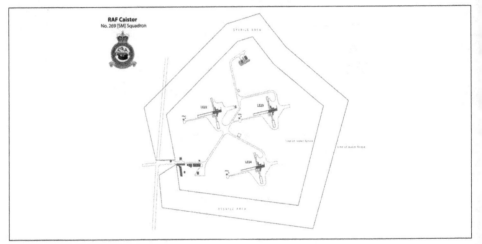

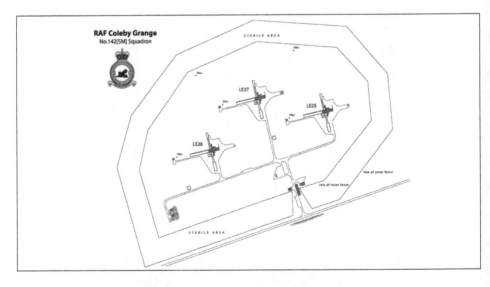

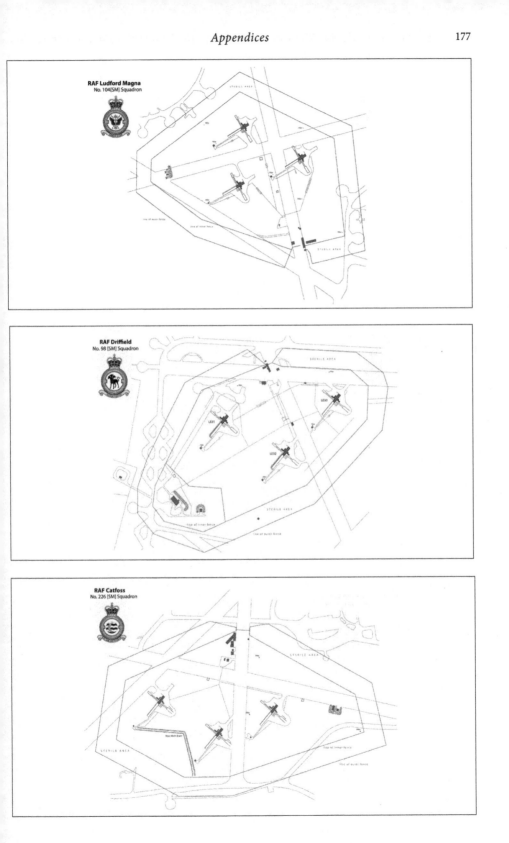

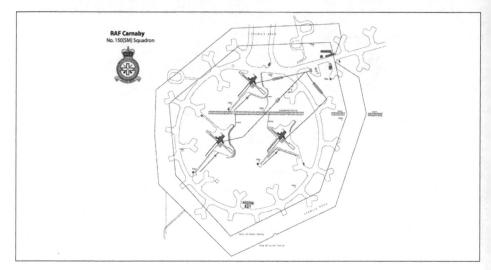

RAF Carnaby
No. 150[SM] Squadron

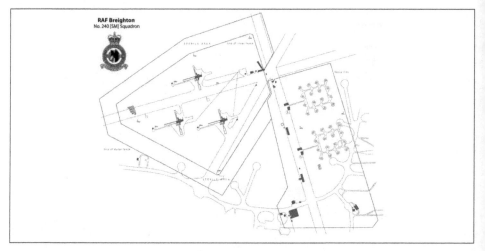

RAF Breighton
No. 240 [SM] Squadron

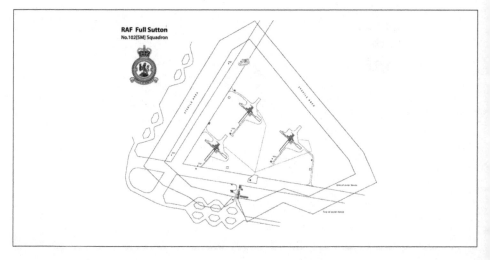

RAF Full Sutton
No.102[SM] Squadron

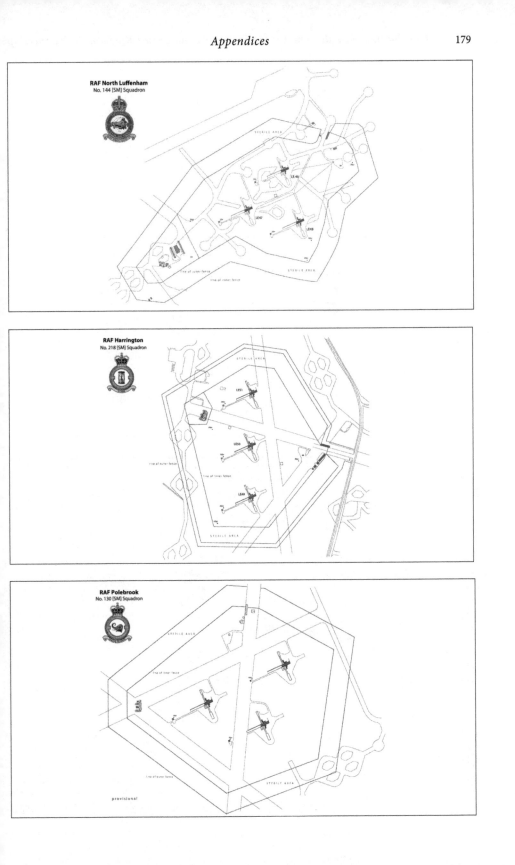

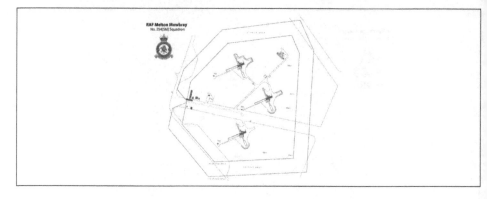

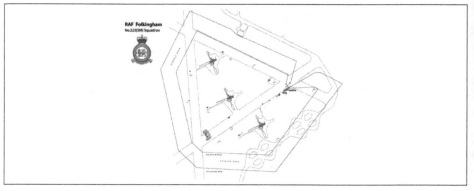

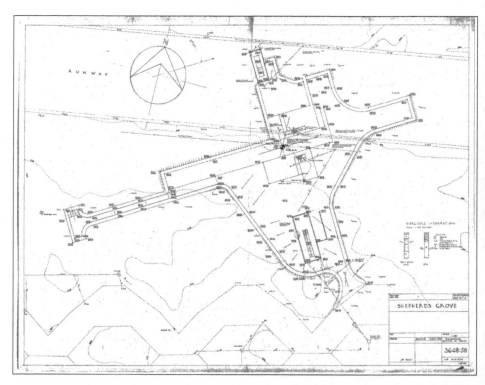

Based on LE7 at RAF Tuddenham with generic detail from other sites.

1 Long-range theodolite building
2 Theodolite pillar
3 Shelter causeway
4 Shelter rails
5 Launcher erector mounting
6 Blast wall
7 Short-range theodolite platform
8 Shelter door runners
9 Fuel catch pit
10 F6 Tanker parking
11 Liquid oxygen dump pit
12 Emergency shower
13 Liquid oxygen tank catch pit

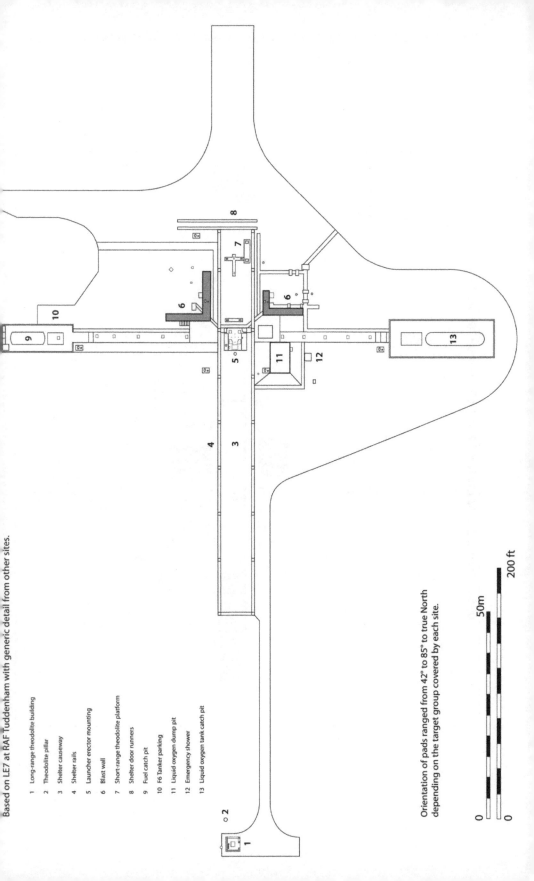

Orientation of pads ranged from 42° to 85° to true North
depending on the target group covered by each site.

50m

200 ft

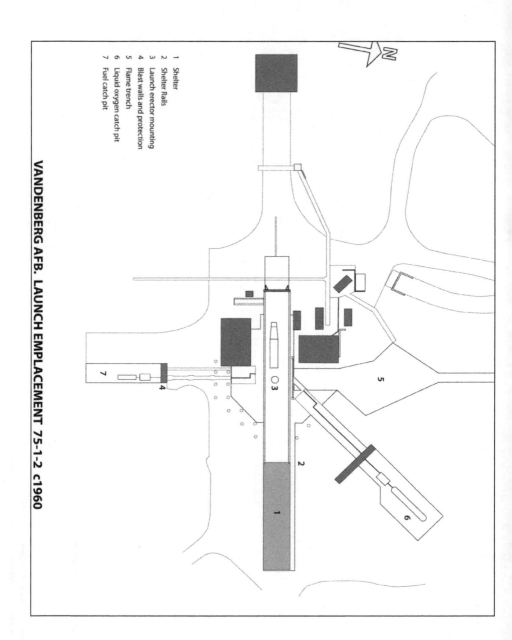

1   Shelter
2   Shelter Rails
3   Launch erector mounting
4   Blast walls and protection
5   Flame trench
6   Liquid oxygen catch pit
7   Fuel catch pit

VANDENBERG AFB. LAUNCH EMPLACEMENT 75-1-2 c1960

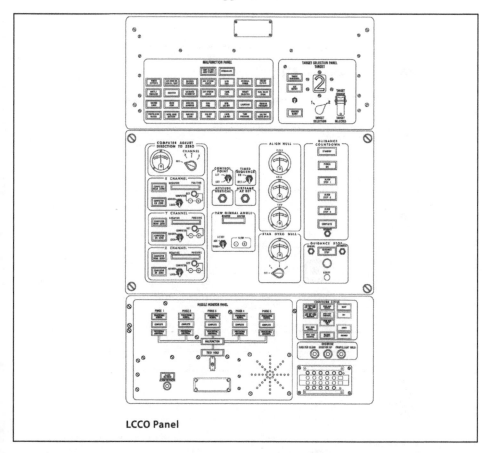

LCCO Panel

'anel

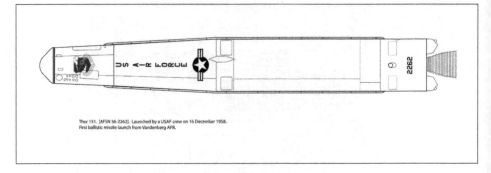

Thor 151. [AFSN 56-2262]. Launched by a USAF crew on 16 December 1958.
First ballistic missile launch from Vandenberg AFB.

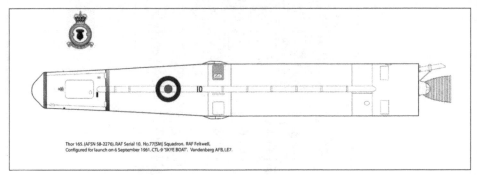

Thor 165. [AFSN 58-2276]. RAF Serial 10. No.77[SM] Squadron. RAF Feltwell.
Configured for launch on 6 September 1961. CTL-9 'SKYE BOAT'. Vandenberg AFB, LE7.

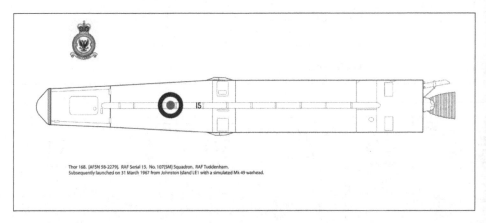

Thor 168. [AFSN 58-2279]. RAF Serial 15. No.107[SM] Squadron. RAF Tuddenham.
Subsequently launched on 31 March 1967 from Johnston Island LE1 with a simulated Mk 49 warhead.

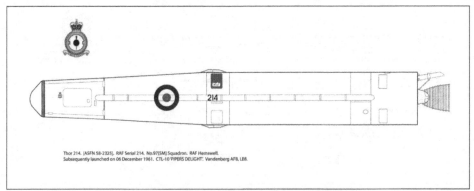

Thor 214. [ASFN 58-2325]. RAF Serial 214. No.97[SM] Squadron. RAF Hemswell.
Subsequently launched on 06 December 1961. CTL-10 'PIPERS DELIGHT'. Vandenberg AFB, LE8.

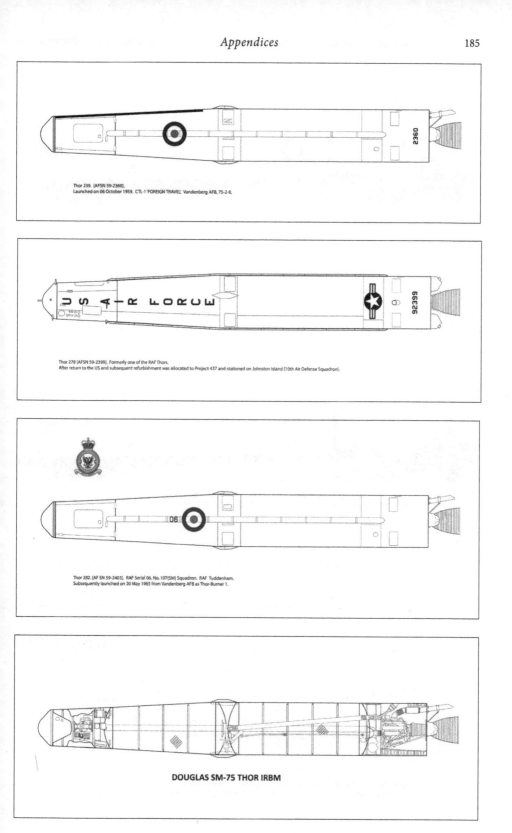

Thor 239. [AFSN 59-2360].
Launched on 06 October 1959. CTL-1 'FOREIGN TRAVEL'. Vandenberg AFB, 75-2-8.

Thor 278 [AFSN 59-2399]. Formerly one of the RAF Thors.
After return to the US and subsequent refurbishment was allocated to Project 437 and stationed on Johnston Island [10th Air Defense Squadron].

Thor 282. [AF SN 59-2403]. RAF Serial 06. No. 107(SM) Squadron. RAF Tuddenham.
Subsequently launched on 20 May 1965 from Vandenberg AFB as Thor-Burner 1.

DOUGLAS SM-75 THOR IRBM

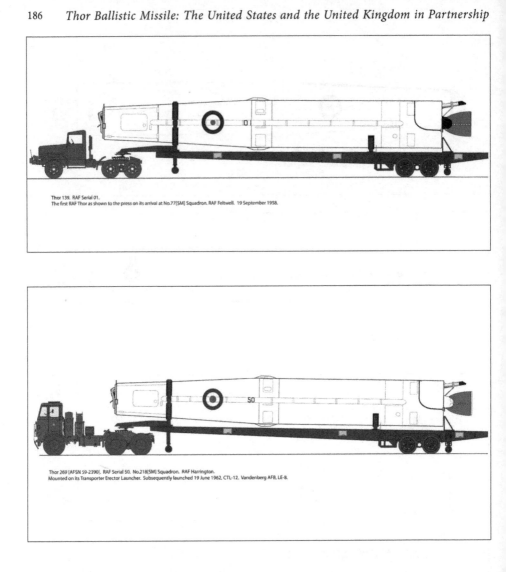

Thor 139. RAF Serial 01.
The first RAF Thor as shown to the press on its arrival at No.77[SM] Squadron. RAF Feltwell. 19 September 1958.

Thor 269 [AFSN 59-2390]. RAF Serial 50. No.218[SM] Squadron. RAF Harrington.
Mounted on its Transporter Erector Launcher. Subsequently launched 19 June 1962, CTL-12. Vandenberg AFB, LE-8.

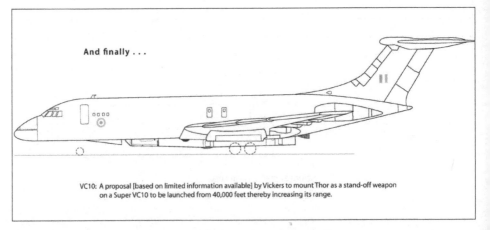

And finally . . .

VC10: A proposal [based on limited information available] by Vickers to mount Thor as a stand-off weapon
on a Super VC10 to be launched from 40,000 feet thereby increasing its range.

Endnotes

Introduction

1 The Glenn L. Martin Company and Convair were excluded as they were already committed to the ICBM programme.
2 Thor had various designations during its operational career. The original USAF designation was B-75, a bomber classification. This was done to strengthen the Air Force's case in its rivalry with the Army over who would operate medium-range missiles. This became SM-75 (Strategic Missile) and ultimately, in 1963, PGM-17A ('P' Soft Pad, 'G' Ground Attack, 'M' Missile.)
3 The WDD was re-named the Ballistic Missile Division (BMD) in June 1957.
4 The name also followed the US pattern of adopting mythological names for the early strategic missiles.

Chapter 1. From Second World War to Cold War

1 In part, the betrayal in 1946 by a Soviet defector of the British scientist Alan Nunn May gave credence to those who thought foreign involvement was a risk to American security.
2 The flights took off from Misawa AFB in Japan and landed at Eielson AFB in Alaska. Operated by the weather service, they were conducted on behalf of the USAF Office of Atomic Energy-1 (AFOAT-1). Misawa had been used by the Japanese Navy to rehearse the attack on Pearl Harbor. The sample in question showed a count of 85 per minute, which was 35 counts above the identified threshold.
3 A Halifax and a number of Mosquitos were deployed to gather samples. The US was keen for the UK to assist in its monitoring of atomic debris but was thwarted by the McMahon Act. Agreement was eventually reached with the exchange of US information for supplies of UK uranium.
4 The first Soviet atomic bomb, RDS-1, was exploded on 29 August 1949 at a test site at Semipalatinsk.
5 *Time*, 5 December 1949.
6 It is worth considering that at its height the Manhattan Engineer District was almost equal in size in terms of employees and capital resource to the entire US automobile industry.
7 This lack of funding was to be turned on Kurchatov when the US atomic bomb became a reality. In defending his position when asked by Stalin to explain why he had not demanded extra funds, the Soviet leader replied, 'if the baby doesn't cry, its mother doesn't know it's hungry.'
8 The RAND Corporation had confirmed in 1950 that the design of an ICBM was technically a possibility. The Air Force still preferred to concentrate on manned bombers but initiated a theoretical ICBM study with Convair. This became the Atlas ICBM—so named after Convair's parent company, the Atlas Corporation.
9 A new military aircraft would, at that time, typically take seven years to develop from contract agreement.
10 'Operation Paperclip' was supposedly so called because the scientists that had been selected for transfer to America had a paperclip attached to their file.

11 The first operational Redstone Unit was 40th Artillery Group based at Bad Kreuznach and Wackernheim in West Germany in 1958.

12 Medaris had served in the US Marine Corps in France during the First World War. During the Second World War he served with the Army Ordnance Corps. Attached to the US First Army in Normandy he identified the first V-2 fired against the First Army.

13 ABMA was established at Redstone Arsenal on 1 February 1956 under the Chief of Ordnance, with the responsibility to develop the Army's IRBM. ABMA also took on responsibility for the Army's satellite programme, but this was assigned to the Agency under special orders and not as a core responsibility.

14 *Flight*, 7 December 1956, p. 906.

15 By coincidence, Jupiter was the Roman king of the gods and the god of sky and thunder. Thor was the Norse god of thunder.

16 This designation was originally a bomber designation, the missile being seen as a 'pilotless bomber'. It was changed to TM-61A in 1955, in recognition of its tactical missile status.

17 LeMay's biographer, Coffey, described Power as 'a man so cold, hard and demanding that several of his colleagues and subordinates have flatly described him as sadistic.'

18 'National Security Policy, Document 9', *Foreign Relations of the United States, 1955–1957, Volume XIX* (US Department of State, Office of the Historian).

19 Killian, *Sputnik, Scientists and Eisenhower: A Memoir of the First Special Assistant to the President for Science and Technology* (Cambridge, Massachusetts: MIT Press, 1977), p. 77.

Chapter 2. Thor—The Early Days

1 Email correspondence with Colonel Bon Tempo, July 2010.

2 *Flight*, 22 May 1959, p. 713.

3 IOC: Initial Operational Configuration. The US Department of Defense defined it as: 'The first attainment of the capability to employ effectively a weapon, item of equipment, or system of approved specific characteristics, and which is manned or operated by an adequately trained, equipped, and supported military unit or force.'

4 Arms, *Thor—The Workhorse of Space* (Huntington Beach, California: McDonnel Douglas Astronautics Company, 1972).

5 This requirement has led to an inaccurate assumption that Thor had the capability to be deployed to mobile sites. The mere weight of the necessary components precluded this. Like the Army's Jupiter design, which was too big to be accommodated in a Globemaster—although it could be in the later Cargomaster—the two missiles were transportable only.

6 The early drawings of the UK's Blue Streak MRBM appear to incorporate a similar blunt nose design.

7 The Jupiter warhead adopted an ablative covering whereby the heat was absorbed on the outer layers of the RV. This allowed higher re-entry velocities which reduced the effects of wind drift on the RV and theoretically would lead to greater accuracy over the target.

8 The Mk-28 nuclear bomb was the second most numerous US nuclear weapon and was produced in twenty differing modifications and variants.

9 Hansen, *Bulletin of the Atomic Scientists*, Vol. 57, No. 2 (March/April 2001), p. 55.

10 Dr Blasingame left the Air Force in 1959 to join AC Spark Plug, where he would eventually become the division's manager. His further work involved the guidance and navigation systems for both the Apollo Command and Lunar Modules.

11 Docherty, No. 269 Squadron OCA Newsletter.

12 RP-1 was an RAF term. The Americans tended to call the fuel 'kerosene'.

13 Correspondence with Brian Robertson, December 2011.

14 *Air Power History*, Vol. 56, No.3, p. 30.

15 Rocketdyne had been established as a separate division of NAA in 1955.

16 Production testing involves subjecting the engines to a pre-determined number of starts and other checks that are sufficient to identify problems without adversely affecting the service life of the engine.

17 Modifications were not as difficult as some people feared. One major change was the decision to use a higher specific impulse kerosene/ LOX combination instead of the Navaho's alcohol/LOX mix.

18 Specific Impulse: the ratio of thrust produced to the weight flow of the propellants.

19 The power of these pyrotechnics was described to the maintenance staff as being capable of propelling a 240-kg man at twice the speed of sound in 30 seconds.

Chapter 3. Failures and Successes

1 It may be noted that the serial numbers started at 101 in part to confuse Soviet intelligence about the actual numbers of missiles in production.

2 This was first demonstrated in May 1947, when an errant missile flying south instead of north flew over El Paso, Texas, before finally crashing—albeit harmlessly—in Mexico, leaving a 50-foot crater.

3 After Major-General Mason M. Patrick, Chief of the Air Service from 1921–1927.

4 It is interesting to consider that such problems would never have been allowed to hinder the Soviet missile programme!

5 Colonel Hall (1914–2006) was generally regarded as the 'father' of the Minuteman ICBM. He was appointed Director of WS-315A in February 1956 and directed the Thor programme until mid-1957.

6 'Activity Report, Deputy Commander Technical Operations', 7 December 1956.

7 Parker Temple III and Portanova, 'Project Emily and Thor IRBM Readiness in the United Kingdom. 1955–1960', *Air Power History*, Vol. 56, No. 3.

8 During the first 24 seconds of flight, the missile was within the range area. However, from 24 to 109 seconds into the flight, destruction would be ordered if the primary instrumentation signalled red or if the condition of the missile was unknown. After 110 seconds the missile was clear of any danger and would be declared 'safe', even if it subsequently suffered a malfunction.

9 Doppler velocity and position.

10 The results of a launch were based on the Army classification which had been adopted by all the services: Success, all primary objectives met; Partial Success, most primary objectives met; Failure, less than 50 per cent of primary objectives met.

11 Memorandum from the SecDef to the SecAF, 'IRBM Program'.

12 'Report of Special Assistant to the Secretary of Defense for Guided Missiles on Thor-Jupiter Studies', 8 October 1957.

13 *Baltimore Sun*, 5 June 1958.

14 The nomenclature IOC was changed sometime during 1960 to CTC, 'Combat Training Capability'.

15 *The New York Times*, 29 January 1959.

Chapter 4. A British IRBM

1 Truman-Attlee meeting, 7 December 1950.

2 Truman-Churchill communiqué, 9 January 1952.

3 'Use of United Kingdom Bases and Consultation with the United Kingdom on the Use of Atomic Weapons', Memorandum of Conversation, 6 March 1953 (Department of State).

4 The AIA, originally called the Aeronautical Chamber of Commerce of America, had co-ordinated the production of US aircraft during the Second World War. Afterwards it became the industry's trade association. It was therefore well placed to assess the state of the UK aircraft industry.

5 Originally the warhead was to be a 1-megaton thermonuclear device, but this was later modified as a result of the UK nuclear trials in the Pacific.

6 Cleaver was once described by the science fiction writer Arthur C. Clarke as the man who should have been the 'British von Braun'.

7 Rolls-Royce had built a copy of the S-3D, called RZ-1. From this design evolved the RZ-2.

8 TNA. AIR 2/13373. F.36A.

9 For a detailed study of the proposed Underground Launchers, see *RAF Historical Society Journal*, No. 58 (May 2014).

10 Hill, *A Vertical Empire*, second edition (London: Imperial College Press, 2012), p. 77.

11 LOC Twining Papers, Box 92.

12 *Ibid.*
13 *Ibid.*
14 British Joint Services Mission (Air Force Section).
15 TNA. DEFE 13/216.
16 TNA. AIR 2/13373.
17 TNA. DEFE 13/216.
18 *Ibid.*
19 Macmillan, *The Macmillan Diaries: The Cabinet Years, 1950–1957* (London: Macmillan, 2003).
20 TNA. DEFE 7/1756.
21 Memorandum from the Acting Secretary of State and the Secretary of Defense (Wilson) to the President.
22 Bermuda had been used on three previous occasions as a location for meetings between the US and the UK.
23 TNA. DEFE 13/216.
24 Operation GRAPPLE was a series of tests of early British H-bomb designs.
25 TNA. DEFE 13/189. Memo from Sir Frederick Brundrett.
26 *Ibid.*
27 This appointment was re-designated 'Chief of the Defence Staff' on 1 January 1959.
28 The first nuclear-tipped Atlas ICBM went on alert at Vandenberg AFB on 31 October 1959.
29 For a summary of the Joint Statement, see: www.presidency.ucsb.edu/ws/index.php?pid=11002.
30 'Memorandum of Discussion at the 339th Meeting of the National Security Council, Washington, October 10, 1957', Eisenhower Library, Whitman File, NSC Records.
31 TNA. CAB 129/86.
32 *Ibid.*
33 *Ibid.*
34 The name Baikonur—a mining town 400 km north-east of the Cosmodrome—was given as 'disinformation' on to the actual site of the launch facility, which was at Tyuratam, 40 km north of Leninsk. In 1995 Leninsk was officially renamed Baikonur by Boris Yelstin. The Cosmodrome, officially TyNIPP-5 or Tyuratam Scientific Research Test Range-5, was instituted by order on 12 February 1955.   Only when high-flying U-2 reconnaissance flights penetrated Soviet airspace was the actual location identified in August 1957.
35 The actual official designation of the satellite was PS-1 (Elementary Satellite-1).
36 Rockefeller, Alfred Jr, *History of Thor 1955–1959* (Air Force Ballistic Missile Division, Air Research and Development Command, 1960).
37 Others criticised him for being a part-time President more interested in golf.
38 'Memo, Asst SAF (R&D), R. E. Homer, to SOD, 12 Nov 57, subj: Outer Space Vehicle'.
39 'Memorandum of Discussion at the 339th Meeting of the National Security Council, Washington, October 10, 1957'.
40 TNA. DEFE 7/1756.
41 *Ibid.*
42 Killian, p. 145.
43 *Ibid*, p, 146.
45 Pincher was the pre-eminent investigative journalist of the period. He had served in the Rocket Division of the Ministry of Supply during the war and joined the *Daily Express* in 1946 as its science and defence correspondent. Hated by many for his revelations, he was nonetheless a valuable ally and contributed much to the public's understanding of Thor during this period.
46 TNA. DEFE 13/189.
47 Killian, p. 145.
48 *The New York Times*, 5 May 1958.
49 *Ibid.*
50 TNA. DEFE 13/189.
51 *Ibid.*
52 Killian, p. 113.

Chapter 5. The Thor Agreement—Substance and Interpretation

1 TNA. AIR 2/13373.f.1A. Telegram from BAFS Washington to Air Ministry, 10 July 1956.

2 TNA. DEFE 13/593. fE35.

3 TNA. AIR 2/133373.

4 TNA. DEFE 13/394.

5 *Ibid.* Memo from DCOS to Air Minister.

6 *Foreign Relations of the United States, 1955–1957*, Vol. 19, National Security Policy, Document 158.

7 In parallel, the report recommended an increased IOC capability of ICBMs (Atlas and Titan) from 80 to 600.

8 TNA. AIR 2/14718.

9 IWST [Integrated Weapons System Training] History (Douglas Aircraft Company, undated).

10 TNA. AIR 2/13337.

11 TNA. AIR 19/962.

12 Randolph W. Burgess, Chief of the Mission to NATO and European Regional Organisations in Paris.

13 TNA. AIR 2/14718.

14 TNA. AIR 19/942. Note by Boyle 28 January 1958.

15 Probert, *High Commanders of the Royal Air Force* (London: HMSO, 1991), p. 54.

16 TNA. AIR 19/962.

17 TNA. DEFE 13/594.

18 TNA. DEFE 5/81.

19 TNA. AIR 2/14718.

20 The Firestone Tire and Rubber Company MGM-5 Corporal SSM was the first US missile to be approved, in December 1950, to carry an atomic warhead. It was developed as an offshoot of the US Army White Sands V-2 programme. Douglas Aircraft Company was design partner. First issued to the US Army in July 1954, it was operationally deployed in Germany from February 1955. It had a 90-mile range but was notoriously inaccurate and was phased out in mid-1964. A memorandum of the conversation between Eisenhower and Macmillan dated 22 March 1957 confirmed that the Corporals would be assigned to SACEUR and that $30.5 million, the equivalent cost of the missiles, would be used to finance projects to modernise the RAF.

21 *Baltimore Sun*, 25 February 1958.

22 Typical was a letter from Mr D. A. Sutherland of Wick, who wrote in December 1957 to his MP, Sir David Robertson: 'On behalf of my wife and myself I wish to protest against the proposal to place four rocket bases in Scotland. Surely the people of Scotland should have been consulted first before such a decision was taken.' TNA. AIR 19/942.

23 TNA. DEFE 13/120.

24 *Baltimore Sun*, 25 February 1958.

25 *Hansard*, 5 March 1958.

26 *Ibid.*

27 A combat veteran of the Second World War when he commanded the 509th Bombardment Wing, General Blanchard later became VCOS but died suddenly at the Pentagon on 31 May 1966 at the early age of fifty. The fiercely sought after Blanchard Award for the best SAC Missile crew was named after him.

28 Searby had been the Master Bomber on the RAF's Operation Hydra, the bombing of the German experimental rocket facility at Peenemunde on 17/18 August 1943.

29 TNA. MS 2055/58.

30 TNA. AIR 20/10555.

31 TNA. DEFE 13/120. E.11.

32 An interesting, though purely coincidental comparison may be made with the Luftwaffe's deployment of V-1 firing units in Northern France: six squadrons of sixteen sites each (a total of ninety-six sites). USAF, RAF, and Luftwaffe methods of deployment essentially reflect the natural way in which Air Force units were organised

33 TNA. AIR 2/14947.

34 TNA. AIR 19/942.

35 'Secret Thor Sites Revealed', *Daily Express*, 12 June 1959, p. 2.

36 TNA. AIR 14/2409.

37 Conversation with Rowland Hall, November 2012.

38 *Ibid* and letter from Hall to Jim Wilson copied to the author.

39 Hall believed it to be the celebrated Pirelli Calendar, but sadly this publication did not start until 1964.

40 The Type-C hangars are characteristic of the 1930s Expansion Phase. Sometimes referred to as 'austerity hangars', they were the largest hangars constructed by the RAF.

41 Conversation with Rowland Hall, and detail extracted from Air Ministry Drawing No. 8261-58.

42 Extract from the Station Commander's foreword to the station's information booklet.

43 North Luffenham was listed Grade II by English Heritage in 2011.
    The 'Reasons for Designation' were: architecture, for the Thor structures at North Luffenham fluently express the functionality and distinctive arrangement of a Thor missile main base; intactness, for the components and infrastructure of the Thor base survive remarkably well and include a Surveillance and Inspection Building unique to this country (at no other British site does the missile base remain within its contemporary military context); and historic interest. Its outstanding level of survival provides a vivid reminder of the Cuban Missile Crisis of 1962.

44 TNA. WO 402/277.

45 TNA. WO 402/278.

46 The correct title is 'Royal Air Force Station Lakenheath'. Though many RAF stations were used exclusively by USAF or SAC units, they all retained their RAF status and were nominally commanded by an RAF station commander.

47 See TNA. AIR 2/14947.

48 RAF Burtonwood, also known as Base Air Depot 1 (BAD 1), was the largest airfield in Europe during the Second World War and a major servicing centre for USAAF aircraft.

49 Lynford Hall is now a hotel and Brandon Park Great House is a residential nursing home, while little remains of North Court Guest House.

50 Email correspondence with Harvey Mathis, November 2009.

51 Comments noted at the 50th Project Emily Reunion, Costa Mesa, California, October 2008.

52 Correspondence with Vernita Laws, September 2009.

53 *Ibid.*

54 Email correspondence with Ronald Muggleton, February 2010. Muggleton also commented on the names of some of the personnel: 'Whether or not those responsible for selecting personnel to be posted to RAF North Luffenham were doing so deliberately or whether it was entirely coincidental I cannot know, but we had men stationed there whose surnames were MARRS, VENUS, LE MOON and ROCKET!'

55 Email correspondence with Robert Hallbauer, March 2011.

56 *Ibid.*

57 Temple and Portanova. p. 11.

58 BCMC was formed in 1954 at RAF Lindholme, moved to Hemswell in August 1956 and disbanded there on 15 October 1962. The unit had been set up with the aim of reducing a backlog of modification programmes, primarily concerning Canberras. Some aircraft were flown in to be worked on; in other cases, and increasingly later on, working parties were detached to operational stations. Among other things, BCMC built the 'Sim Start' trolleys (essentially a bomb trolley with a load of accumulator batteries) that permitted the Mk 1 V-bombers to start all four engines at once and get airborne within a matter of minutes—a capability that was first demonstrated publicly at the 1960 SBAC Show.

59 Email correspondence with Neil Trotter, November 2010.

60 *Ibid.*

61 *Ibid.*

62 *Ibid.*

63 *Ibid.*

64 *Ibid.*

65 The designation of the training squadron had caused a security problem. The original designation, 672nd Strategic Missile (Training) Squadron, had led to administrative difficulties in de-classifying

their base of assignment, RAF Feltwell, or even acknowledging unit's existence in the UK. This was caused by the inclusion of the word 'Missile' in the unit's title. On an instruction from ACAS(Ops) AVM Ronald Lees, Colonel Doan, Director of Personnel for 7AD, discussed the various implications with Wing Commander Knight and it was agreed that the unit would drop the 'Missile' nomenclature and be re-designated '672 TTS'. This would allow its existence in the UK to be acknowledged.

66 Correspondence with Lee Wise, July 2010.
67 *Ibid.*
68 Memo from Major Woirol to W. F. Shaver, undated.
69 *Daily Mail* and *The San Mateo Times*, 10 January 1959.
70 *The Salt Lake Tribune*, 11 January 1959.
71 TNA. DEFE 13/120.
72 TNA. AIR 20/10325.
73 50th Project Emily Reunion, Costa Mesa, California, October 1959.
74 TNA. AIR 14/4297.

Chapter 6. Opening for Business

1 Conversation with John Moles, January 2013.
2 *Daily Express*, 7 August 1958, p. 2.
3 *Ibid.*
4 The date of actual arrival varies. A contemporary project chronology gives the date as 6 September—Temple and Portanova, p. 12. The August arrival date is based on RAF records.
5 *Daily Express*, 9 September 1958, p. 2.
6 *Ibid.*
7 *Daily Express*, 25 August 1958, p. 4.
8 *Daily Express*, 20 September 1958, p. 2
9 At this stage it was clearly still a Wing responsibility, as the F540 for the Feltwell Squadron, No. 77(SM) Squadron, gives the following key dates. 'Construction of emplacements, June 1958, Completion, August 1958. First missile brought to the Sqn, November 1958. Functional demonstration by DAC engineers, January 1959. Hand over to RAF, March 1959.'
10 Temple and Portanova.
11 *Flight*, 5 December 1958.
12 The normal missile convoy consisted of: Police motor cycle, RAF Land Rover (Convoy Commander), Missile Transporter, Land Rover (Technical Specialist), 2 x Police motorcycles.
13 Email correspondence with Neil Trotter, November 2010.
14 Routes were given codenames. Polebrook: PLUM and BLACKBERRY. Folkingham: CHERRY and APPLE. Harrington: GREENGAGE. Melton Mowbray: ORANGE and LEMON. Numeric codes were transmitted back to the Wing HQ to confirm that certain waypoints had been reached or that problems had been encountered. North Luffenham Operation Order No. 2/60.
15 Correspondence with Robert Hallbauer, March 2011.
16 Later British warheads, too, were to be sealed.
17 Taken from notes by John Moles in 'The Nickel', May/June 2012.
18 TNA: AIR 2/13782.
19 *Flight*, 19 September 1958.
20 Project 'E'—not to be confused with 'Project Emily'—provided for US nuclear weapons to be made available to be carried on RAF bombers in the event of war.
21 TNA: AIR 2/13782.
22 *Ibid.*
23 Schlosser, *Command and Control* (London: Allen Lane, 2013).
24 TNA. DEFE 13/394.
25 TNA. AIR 20/10325. Foreign Office to Washington.
26 TNA. AIR 27/2794.
27 *US News and World Report*, 29 February 1960.

28 *The New York Times*, 12 February 1960.
29 *Ibid.*
30 *Ibid.*
31 USAF nuclear forces were those stationed as part of the REFLEX programme of bomber dispersal.
32 *Missiles and Rockets*, 27 July 1959.
33 TNA. AIR 14/4293. Memo No. 208.
34 As an Air Bomber in 1944, Flight Sergeant Haines had survived a crash at the Lancaster Finishing School (LFS) at Syerston and had returned safely when his aircraft collided with a Ju 88 over Germany, knocking out two engines. He also survived a car accident when Ops BM.
35 Conversation with Sqn Ldr Broad, July 2015.
36 Both brick and concrete versions of these mountings can be found.

Chapter 7. Vandenberg Air Force Base—The Western Test Range

1 Training covered armoured, infantry, anti-aircraft artillery, ordnance, and combat engineer units.
2 Memorandum for Record of the meeting taken by Lieutenant-Colonel Vernon L. Hastings, Assistant for IOC, Director of Installations. A handwritten note by Hastings on the first page stated, 'OKed by Ritland—this was a Top Secret meeting. I fudged on this so I could pass it to the briefing team.'
3 The Air Force allocated in excess of $178 million to cover the construction of launch pads ($120 million), base infrastructure, buildings, an airfield ($32 million), and housing ($25 million), according to the 'Historic American Engineering Record of Space Launch Complex 10'.
4 *Ibid*: 'On 5 October 5, 1958, the formal dedication ceremonies were held with over 1,400 individuals attending. The distinguished guest list included the Governor of California, California Senators and Representatives from Congress, and several important personages from the US Air Force, including the Commander of the Ballistic Missile Division, Major-General Bernard Schriever. The President and Vice President were extended invitations to the event while the Secretary of the Air Force and the Chairman of the Joint Chiefs of Staff sent messages to be read at the dedication ceremony. The late General's wife, son and grandson also attended the ceremony with Mrs. Vandenberg presenting a portrait of her husband to the installation newly named in his honor. A Thor and an Atlas missile were placed next to the reviewing stand to reinforce the fact that the ceremony marked the dedication of SAC's first missile base. A performance by an acrobatic team in F-100 fighters and a flyover by a formation of B-52 bombers were intended to be part of the ceremony but heavy cloud cover forced the cancellation of the aerial aspects of the day.'
5 Most of the construction was undertaken by the Corps of Engineers, but some elements were sub-contracted and Air Force personnel installed launch instrumentation.
6 *Santa Maria Times*, 30 October 1958.
7 *Ibid.*
8 TNA. AIR 2/13675
9 *Ibid.*
10 Prebish, David, *My Years at Vandenberg Air Force Base* (unpublished memoir, undated).
11 Parker, *Recollections of the Thor-Delta Program at Vandenberg 1958–1970* (unpublished memoir, February 2013).
12 *Ibid.* Even for these the sand presented problems. On arrival at CC-2 one morning, the launch crew found that during the night the sand had built up all the way to the front entrance door knob.
13 IWST History.
14 Prebish, *Ibid.*
15 This blockhouse was subsequently known as the East Blockhouse after a second, West Blockhouse was added in 1964 to support later Thor-Agena satellite launches.
16 When the author visited the site in October 2008, the building had been renovated to its original white-washed finish with blue paintwork.
17 Conversation with Maurice Botley, October 2008.
18 Correspondence with Larry H. Kasulka, November 2012.
19 Parker.
20 The film canisters were ejected from the satellite and were caught in mid-air on their return to earth

by specially adapted aircraft. The program was declassified in 1992.

21 Correspondence with J. Atkison, April 2006.

22 *The Victoria Advocate* (Texas), 8 March 1958.

23 *Lubbock Evening Journal*, 27 February 1958.

24 Appropriately, Plumley had served with the US 9th Air Force's 513th 'Rocket' Squadron. Equipped with P-47 aircraft fitted with 5-inch unguided rockets, the squadron operated in support of the Allied armies after D-Day.

25 File X003-9909, RAF Museum.

26 Correspondence with Colonel Nick Gaynos USAF, April 2005.

27 *Santa Maria Times*, 16 December 1958.

28 Colonel Bon Tempo was a seasoned combat pilot, having flown twenty-two missions with the 15th USAAF in Italy during the Second World War. He had worked with atomic weapons at Albuquerque in 1952–53, and had later seen service in Japan and Germany.

29 Correspondence with Colonel Bon Tempo, April 2005.

30 *The Toledo Blade*, 17 December 1958.

31 Quoted from the Citation to Accompany the Award, curtesy of Colonel Bon Tempo and related correspondence, August 2010.

32 *Los Angeles Times*, 17 December 1958.

33 *Santa Maria Times*, 18 December 1958.

34 *Ibid*. In one respect, however, the editorial was to be proved wrong. It had predicted that, 'in all likelihood the first attempt to place a man in orbit around the earth will be made from a launching pad in Santa Barbara county.'

35 *The Toledo Blade*, 17 December 1958.

36 Chronology of the 392d Missile Training Squadron (Thor).

37 Parker.

Chapter 8. RAF Training Units

1 Correspondence with Colonel J. C. Bon Tempo. Note that *Flight* on 5 February 1960 gave as figures 270 officers and 1,520 airmen. The Recommendation for Air Force Outstanding Unit Award cites 1,154.

2 Contract AF 22(603)-7. The contract was to run until 19 July 1957, although provision was made to extend this due to the indefinite dates defined for training.

3 IWST History.

4 In the end, only 672d SMS was ever to exist, and this only for a short initial period at RAF Feltwell at the start of the UK deployment.

5 IWST defined as: The training which trains individuals to be proficient in the performance of simultaneous and sequential duties involved in the checkout, preparation for launch, and launch of missiles.

6 IWST History.

7 *Ibid*.

8 *Ibid*.

9 TNA. AIR 8/2239. Letter from AOCinC Bomber Command to AMSO. 23 February 1961.

10 See Boyes, *Project Emily: Thor IRBM and the RAF* (Stroud: Tempus Publishing, 2008), pp. 120-21.

11 Wing Commander Finlayson's third child, a son, was born auspiciously on the eve of the Cuban Missile Crisis.

12 From Nos. 77(SM) and 97(SM) Squadron.

13 Correspondence with Doug Browne, January 2009.

14 Conversation with Dave Humphrey, May 2010.

15 Email correspondence with Maurice Botley, January 2010.

16 *Ibid*.

17 Davis-Monthan was home to three Boeing B-47 Stratojet squadrons. An unexpected visitor one day was an Avro Vulcan on deployment to March AFB for a bombing/navigation exercise. It had a minor fault and landed at Davis-Monthan to effect repairs. A number of the Thor trainees had

V-bomber experience and quickly rectified the problem. As this was the first time most of the US staff had seen a Vulcan, its thunderous leap into the air on departure was something they would never forget. Their resident B-47s [of the 36 Air Division] struggled to get airborne. There were free beers in the messes that weekend, and a newfound respect for the RAF. Correspondence with Brian Robertson, December 2011.

18 *Tucson Daily Citizen*, 27 May 1958.
19 Conversation with Richard Pratt, August 2008.
20 Correspondence with Brian Robertson.
21 Conversation with John Thorndyke, March 2013.
22 Excerpt from No. 269 Squadron OCA Newsletter.
23 Correspondence with Brian Robertson.
24 Email correspondence with Maurice Botley.
25 Introductory Notes prepared by BJSM, Washington.
26 Correspondence with Brian Robertson.
27 Conversation with Group Captain Peter Finlayson, November 2014.
28 Classified as 173 maintenance men, 30 maintenance supervisors, and 30 staff officers.
29 Conversation with Dave Humphrey.
30 Conversation with Mrs Jean de Young, October 2010.
31 *Ibid.*
32 *Rocket Review*, Feltwell, Vol. 2, No. 3, April 1960.
33 Correspondence with Brian Robertson.
34 Email correspondence with Maurice Botley.
35 Correspondence with Brian Robertson.
36 Email correspondence with Maurice Botley and conversation with Richard Pratt.
37 Correspondence with Brian Robertson.
38 Correspondence with Lee Wise, July 2010.
39 Email correspondence with Maurice Botley.
40 Telephone conversation with Harry Hitchcock, June 2012.
41 Supporting documentation to the Air Force Outstanding Unit Award, 15 July 1963.

Chapter 9. The RAF Launches

1 IWST History. IWST was the designated term for the training, as the original 'Crew Training' was not considered definitive enough.
2 Operations Launch Order 300-75-59, 1MD, 1 March 1959.
3 The major British newspapers were represented by Chapman Pincher (*Daily Express*), John Madox (*The Manchester Guardian*), Vincent Rider (*The Daily Telegraph*), Kenneth Hord (*Daily Mirror*), Kenneth Owens (*Flight*), and David Devine (*The Sunday Times*).
4 TNA. AIR 20/10325. Major-General E. Moore to G. R. Ward.
5 Almost certainly not revealed to the journalists was the fact that the DISCOVERER program was a cover story for the CIA/Lockheed CORONA program of spy satellites. In this case no camera was aboard, and after the faulty separation it was believed that the re-entry capsule landed near Spitzbergen.
6 *Santa Maria Times*, 16 April 1959.
7 Extract from an article in the No. 269 Squadron OCA Newsletter by Jack Docherty.
8 *Flight*, 24 April 1959, p. 580.
9 *Long Beach Independent* (California), 17 April 1959.
10 *Ibid.*
11 Walker had been attending the World Congress of Flight at Las Vegas, where it was announced that Captain George A. Edwards Jr in a McDonnell Voodoo set up a new record of 816.28 mph over a 500-km closed course.
12 *Flight*, 24 April 1959, p. 580.
13 *The Gazette and Daily* (York, Pennsylvania), 18 April 1959.
14 *Santa Maria Times*, 16 April 1959.

15 TNA. DEFE 13/394.

16 Chronology of the 392d Missile Training Squadron (Thor).

17 TNS. AIR 20/9475.

18 Colonel Barton came from No. 576 Strategic Missile Squadron which was responsible for evaluating the Atlas missile system.

19 *Salt Lake Tribune*, 17 June 1959.

20 *Ibid.*

21 *Ibid.*

22 *Ibid*, 3 August 1959.

23 Sound Fixing And Ranging bomb. A long-range position-fixing system that uses explosive sounds in the deep sound channel of the ocean.

24 Correspondence with Brian Robertson, December 2011.

25 TNA. AIR 20/9474.

26 *Ibid.*

27 Lieutenant-General Wade's assignment to Vandenberg AFB included the unique distinction of being the commanding officer of the USAF's first operational missile unit.

28 Chronology of the 392 MTS.

29 *Flight*, 5 February 1960, p. 169. Also Message AM London to BJSM Washington, 5710/SofS, 20 January 1960.

30 Supporting documentation to the Air Force Outstanding Unit Award, July 1963.

Chapter 10. Combat Training Launches

1 Official documentation sometimes erroneously refers to these as Continuous Training Launches.

2 Chronology of the 392 MTS.

3 Email correspondence with Maurice Botley, January 2010.

4 *Anderson Daily Bulletin* (Louisiana), 23 October 1961.

5 Somewhat strangely perhaps, despite being the first Thor wing to be set up, this was the first time a Feltwell Wing crew had launched a Thor.

6 Correspondence with Brian Robertson, December 2011.

7 *Ibid.*

8 Whether or not the Mountbattens would have appreciated the headline in *The Progress-Index*. Va (7 October 1959), in which they were described as 'Lord and Lady Monty' is perhaps debatable.

9 *The Progress-Index. Va* (7 October 1959).

10 TNA. AIR 14/4303. *A Review of the Results of the First Four Combat Training Launches of Thor.*

11 Cowling had been on the first Thor Training Course, crossing the Atlantic on the *Île de France* in April 1958.

12 TNA. AIR 27/2794.

13 *The Register-Guard* (Oregon), 7 October 1959.

14 *The Miami News* (Florida), 7 October 1959.

15 *Ibid.*

16 Ziegler, *Mountbatten: The Official Biography* (London: Collins, 1985), p. 590.

17 One British representative arrived in the heat of the Californian summer wearing an overcoat and carrying a brief case, both of which had seen better days. On being driven to his accommodation he flicked his cigarette butt out of the window, whereupon the driver executed an immediate stop and rapidly retrieved the smouldering butt. It was a swift lesson in the dangers of inadvertently ignited LOX. Related by Group Captain Peter Finlayson, who was nearly precipitated from the back seat to the front seat during the sudden stop, November 2014.

18 The house is still used as a guest house and is adjacent to the Marshallia Ranch Golf Course.

19 TNA. AIR 14/4303.

20 TNA. AIR 20/9477.

21 *Ibid.*

22 *Fairbanks Daily News* (Alaska), 16 December 1959.

23 Conversation with Colonel Watters, November 2014.

24 This codename had been used before. CENTERBOARD I and II were the codenames for the atomic bomb missions against Japan.

25 TNA. AIR 20/9479.

26 The report was the idea of Colonel Watters, but initially he found it hard to 'sell' the idea. In the end it proved an invaluable document. Correspondence with Colonel Watters, December 2014.

27 Supporting documentation to the Air Force Outstanding Unit Award for No. 392d Missile Training Squadron, 15 July 1963.

28 Naile was later to command the Categorisation Flight within the Training Squadron.

29 'Simpson's Daily Leader', *The Times*, 23 June 1960

30 TNA, AIR 14/4303, p. 6.

31 *Ibid*, p. 8.

32 *Ibid*, p. 2.

33 Temple III and Portanova.

34 TNA, AIR 14/4303, p. 8.

35 Correspondence with Sir Brian Burnett, April 2007. Burnett was later to become AOC 3 Group, where thirty of the missiles were under his command.

36 *Redland Daily Facts*, 13 December 1960.

37 With a certain dry sense of humour the RAFLO at Vandenberg, on advising HQ Bomber Command of the codename for the launch, added: 'With a 20-missile programme we might reach PICCADILLY CIRCUS, but if we have 40 we might get as far as NORTH WEALD.' Telex RAFLO to HQBC, 23 March 1961.

38 TNA. AIR 20/9480.

39 *Ibid*.

40 Moles had been transferred to Thor on the cancellation of the Blue Streak program, where he was based at the de Havilland facility at Stevenage.

41 When Hemswell missile T214 was flown back to Vandenberg for CTL-10, the flight crew decided they had sufficient fuel to delete the Bermuda stop.

42 TNA. AIR 28/1502.

43 Conversation with John Thorndyke, March 2013.

44 It was believed that the Wing Commander in charge was determined to achieve 'something unplanned'. Conversation with John Moles, January 2013.

45 Conversation with John Moles, March 2010.

46 *MESA Missileer*, 8 September 1961.

47 For an 'alternative' view of the launch, see Appendix 2.

48 *Wisconsin State Journal*, 5 November 1961.

49 *Redlands Daily Facts*, 6 December 1961.

50 *Combat Crew, Strategic Air Command*, August 1962.

51 T226 was launched from Johnston Island on 1 November 1962 as part of the Operation FISHBOWL series of high-altitude nuclear tests.

52 Dunn had a distinguished career and was awarded the DFC when OC of No. 274 Squadron, the first Hurricane-equipped squadron to go to the Middle East in August 1940. He had previously come across missiles when responsible for anti V-2 operations with 12 Group.

53 Temple and Portanova.

54 TNA. AIR 8/2339.

55 *Ibid*.

56 Conversation with Sqn Ldr Broad, July 2015.

57 As a Group Captain, Menaul had flown aboard Valiant WZ366 on 11 October 1956, when it dropped Britain's first atomic bomb.

58 Favourable communication from HQ SAC General McConnell to Colonel Watters, 26 April 1962.

59 Letter from General Preston to Colonel Watters, 1 May 1962.

60 Letter from General Harris to HQ SAC, 10 September 1963.

61 *Combat Crew, Strategic Air Command*, August 1962.

Chapter 11. UK Bases

1 For a fuller description of squadron operations, see Boyes, *Project Emily: Thor IRBM and the RAF.*
2 Correspondence with Geoff Byrne, May 2010.
3 For a fuller description of the part played by Thor in the Crisis, see *Royal Air Force Historical Society Journal*, Vol. 42.
4 Correspondence with Ronald Muggleton, February 2010.
5 *Ibid.*
6 *Flight*, 11 March 1960.
7 TNA. AIR 2/13657.
8 The Soviet R-5 (NATO Reporting Name SS-3 Shyster) was the final Soviet ballistic missile design that was in essence a derivative of the V-2. Somewhat more basic than Thor, the missile took 2.5 hours to prepare for launch and could only be held in a launch-ready state for one hour
9 TNA. AIR 20/10555. AOCinC Bomber Command to DCAS. 27 February 1958.
10 TNA. DEFE 13/594, 30 January 1958.
11 TNA. DEFE 5/81.
12 *The New York Times*, 1 May 1959.
13 *Daily Express*, 29 April 1959, p. 2.
14 *Ibid.*
15 *Daily Express*, 5 March 1960.
16 TNA. AIR 20/10807.
17 *A Study on Evaluation of Warhead Safing Devices.* HQ Field Command, Armed Forces Special Weapons Project, March 1958.
18 TNA. AIR 20/10807.
19 *Ibid.*
20 *Ibid.*
21 *House of Commons Debates*, Vol. 589, 11 June 1958, pp. 195-96.
22 In the aftermath of this accident, Squadron Leader Bryant Bourne surely qualified for the shortest recorded Thor posting. He had completed a Launch Controller's course at RAF Hemswell and was due to be posted to take over command of No. 269(SM) Squadron from Squadron Leader Terry Dicks, and was attached supernumerary for about ten days. Following the accident his attachment to No. 269 Squadron was cancelled and his posting changed to the command of No. 104(SM) Squadron.
23 Conversation with Sqn Ldr Broad, July 2015.
24 *Hansard*, 17 July 2001, column 141W: 'Since this event pre-dates current reporting system it is unclear whether, in today's terms, it would be categorised as an accident.'
25 House of Commons Library, Dep 8203.
26 DULL SWORD is the term that describes reports of minor incidents involving nuclear weapons, components or systems, or which could impair their deployment.
27 No. 107(SM) Squadron History and conversation with Colonel Watters, November 2014.

Chapter 12. Logistics

1 The system was run on two IBM 705s and one Burroughs 220 high-speed computers.
2 Correspondence Chris Webb, October 2009.
3 *Ibid.*
4 *Ibid.*
5 *Ibid.*
6 Correspondence with Ronald Muggleton, February 2010.
7 *Ibid.*
8 Correspondence with Chris Webb, December 2013.
9 This system was later adopted by NATO for its stock control.
10 Correspondence with Chris Webb, December 2013.
11 E.g. the stock number for a digital voltmeter was MBAD (Mutual British and American Defence) 4935-650-2379. The first four numbers identified the type of item.
12 Correspondence with Chris Webb, December 2013.

13 Correspondence with Ronald Muggleton, February 2010.

14 Trip Report (UK Visit 22, 31 May 1960), SBAMA, dated 16 June 1960.

15 *Ibid*, p. 3.

16 *The San Bernadino County Sun*, 13 December 1960.

17 *Redlands Daily Facts* (California), 8 October 1962.

18 *Redland Daily Facts*, 5 October 1962.

19 *San Bernadino County Sun*, 6 June 1963

Chapter 13. What Happened to the RAF's Thors?

`1 *Daily Express*, 28 November 1963, p. 15.

2 Airfield Information Exchange and correspondence with William Burgess. May 2008.

3 Correspondence with Geoff Byrne, May 2010.

4 *Los Angles Times*, 12 December 1963.

5 Arms, pp. 4-1.

6 *San Bernadino County Sun*, 6 June 1963.

7 Prebish, *Johnston Island Memories*.

8 DNA 6040F, *Operation Dominic 1—1962*, Defense Nuclear Agency, February 1983.

9 Minutes of the Advisory Committee on Human Radiation Experiments, 8 May 1995.

10 Submegaton is defined as less than 1 megaton but more than 200 kilotons.

11 Program 437 Technical Manual, T.O.21M-437-1-1-1.

12 'Waste Not—The Use of ex-RAF Thor Vehicles', *Journal of the British Interplanetary Society*, Vol. 50 (1977), pp. 189-200.

Epilogue

1 The National Security Archive, *Secret Understandings on the use of Nuclear Weapons 1950–1974*, Document 18.

2 Bob Johnson, notes made at the 50th Project Emily Reunion.

3 Memorandum on the Substance of Discussion at a Department of State-Joint Chiefs of Staff Meeting, 23 March 1962.

4 *Redlands Daily Facts* (California), 8 October 1962.

5 *San Bernadino County Sun*, 9 October 1962.

Appendix 1.

1 The US Atomic Energy Commission (AEC) had an office in Albuquerque.

2 Major-General Dodd Starbird was one of the US Army's most prestigious engineers. He had been Director of Military Application at the AEC in Washington until, in 1961, he was appointed to command the Army North Pacific Division. He was, however, recalled to once again handle nuclear matters as commander of Joint Task Force Eight.

Bibliography

Archives

RAF Museum (Hendon)
The Airfield Information Exchange
The National Archives, Kew (TNA)

Press

Anderson Daily Bulletin, The
Baltimore Sun, The
Daily Express, The
Daily Mail, The
Daily Telegraph, The
Fairbanks Daily News, The
Flight
Gazette and Daily (Pennsylvania)
Long Beach Independent (California), The
Lubbock Evening Journal
Miami News, The
New York Times, The
Redlands daily Fact, The
Salt Lake Tribune, The
Santa Maria Times, The
San Mateo Times, The
The Progress and Index
Time
Toledo Blade, The
Tucson Daily Citizen, The
US News and World Report
Wisconsin State Journal, The

Periodicals, Reports, and Miscellaneous Papers

'392d Missile Training Squadron, Annual Maintenance Plan' (Vandenberg AFB, 1960)
A History of 107 Squadron, (privately published, 1963)
Air Power History, Vol. 56, No. 3
Atomic Energy. A General Account of the Development of Methods of Using Atomic Energy for Military Purposes under the Auspices of the United States Government (USGPO; reprinted by HMSO, 1945)
Bulletin of the Atomic Scientists, Vol. 57, No. 2 (March/April 2001)

Combat Crew (August 1962)

Cross, Air Marshal Sir Kenneth, 'Bomber Command's Thor Missile Force', *Journal of the Royal United Service Institution*, Vol. 108, No. 630 (May 1963)

'Historic American Engineering Record of Space Launch Complex 10', US Army Engineer Research and Development Center Construction (Engineering Research Laboratory, January 2002)

Foreign Relations of the United States, 1955–1957, Vol. 19, Document 158

Haines, Wg Cdr E. R. G., *Miscellaneous Papers in the RAF Museum*

Hunter, Peter, *Thor-Delta: Launches 1957–2004* (private compilation, Sydney, Australia, undated)

'Information about the Station and its neighbourhood for the newcomer', Royal Air Force North Luffenham, 1959

IWST [Integrated Weapons System Training] *History* (Douglas Aircraft Company, undated)

Journal of the British Interplanetary Society, Vol. 50 (1977)

Journal of the Royal Air Force Historical Society, Nos. 26 and 42

MESA Missileer

Melissen, Jan, 'The Thor Saga: Anglo-American nuclear relations, US IRBM development and deployment in Britain, 1955–1959', *Journal of Strategic Studies*, Vol. 15, No. 2

Missiles and Rockets, 27 July 1959

Parker Temple III, L., and Portanova, Peter L., *Preparing for the Space Age: The Story of Project Emily*, Proceedings of the 57th International Astronautical Congress, Valencia, Spain (2–6 October 2006)

—'Project Emily and Thor Readiness in the United Kingdom, 1955–1960', *Air Power History*, Vol. 56, No. 3

Report to the Committee on Appropriations, US House of Representatives on *Reliability Reports in Ballistic Missile Program. Part II* (December 1958)

Richards, G. R., and Powell, J. R., 'Waste Not—The Use of Ex-RAF Thor Vehicles', *Journal of the British Interplanetary Society*, Vol. 50 (1997)

Rockefeller, Alfred Jr, *History of Thor 1955–1959* (Air Force Ballistic Missile Division, Air Research and Development Command, 1960)

Rocket Review, Vol 1, No. 1; Vol 2, No. 3; Vol 3, No. 10

Thor Booster Systems (Missiles And Space Division, Douglas Aircraft Company Inc.)

Vandenberg 1958–2008 (30th Space Wing History Office, 2008)

Western Aviation Magazine (December 1958)

Unpublished Memoirs

Parker, Dick, *Recollections of the Early Thor-Delta Program at Vandenberg 1958–1970* (February 2013)

Kasulka, Larry H., *Various Vandenberg and Johnston Island Papers* (2012)

Prebish, David W., *Johnston Island Memories* (undated)

—*My Years at Vandenberg Air Force Base* (undated)

Robertson, Brian, *Thor Memories* (2011)

Books

Arms, W. M., *Thor, The Workhorse of Space—A Narrative History* (Huntington Beach, California: McDonnell Douglas Astronautics Company, 1972)

Boyes, John, *Project Emily: Thor IRBM and the RAF* (Stroud: Tempus Publishing, 2008)

Chun, Clayton K. S., *Shooting Down a Star* (CADRE Papers, Maxwell AFB, 2000)

Clark, Ian, *Nuclear Diplomacy and the Special Relationship* (Oxford: Clarendon, 1994)

Cocroft, Wayne D., and Thomas, Roger J. C., *Cold War* (English Heritage, 2003)

Gantz, Lieutenant-Colonel Kenneth F., ed., *The United States Air Force Report on the Ballistic Missile* (New York: Doubleday & Co. 1958)

Hansen, Chuck, *U.S. Nuclear Weapons: The Secret History* (Aerofax Inc. 1988)

Hartt, Julian, *The Mighty Thor* (New York: Duell, Sloan and Pearce, 1961)

Hennessy, Peter, *The Secret State* (London: Penguin, 2010)

Hill, C. N., *A Vertical Empire*, second edition (London: Imperial College Press, 2012)

Killian, James R. Jr, *Sputnik, Scientists and Eisenhower: A Memoir of the First Special Assistant to the President for Science and Technology* (Cambridge, Massachusetts: MIT Press, 1977)

Menaul, Stewart, Countdown: Britain's Strategic Nuclear Forces (London: Robert Hale, 1980)

Moore, Richard, *Nuclear Illusion, Nuclear Reality* (Palgrave Macmillan, 2010)

Navias, Martin S., *Nuclear Weapons and British Strategic Planning 1955-1958* (Oxford: Clarendon Press, 1991)

Neufeld, Jacob, *Ballistic Missiles in the United States Air Force 1945-1960* (Washington DC: USAF, 1990)

Page, Joseph T., *Vandenberg Air Force Base* (Charleston, South Carolina: Arcadia Publishing, 2014)

Probert, Henry, *High Commanders of the Royal Air Force* (London: HMSO, 1991)

Schlosser, Eric, *Command and Control* (London: Allen Lane, 2013)

Schwiebert, Ernest G., *A History of the US Air Force Ballistic Missiles* (New York: Frederick A. Praeger, 1964)

Sheehan, Neil, *A Fiery Peace in a Cold War* (New York: Random House, 2009)

Simmons, Geoff, and Abraham, Barry, *Strong Foundations—Driffield's Aerodrome from 1917 to 2000* (Cherry Burton, East Yorkshire: Hutton Press, 2001)

Spires, David N., *On Alert. An Operational History of the United States Air Force Intercontinental Ballistic Missile Program* (Colorado: Air Force Space Command, 2014)

Wilson, Jim, *Launch Pad UK* (Barnsley, South Yorkshire: Pen and Sword, 2008)

Wynn, Humphrey, *RAF Nuclear Deterrent Forces* (London: HM Stationery Office, 1994)

Yates, Raymond F., and Russell, M. E., *Space Rockets and Missiles* (New York: Harper and Brothers, 1960)

Index

ABMA 17, 30, 31, 190

Aircraft
  Avro Vulcan 8, 9, 52, 195, 196
  Boeing B-29 15, 101
  Curtis Wright C-46 Commando 100
  De Havilland Comet CMk2 100, 119
  English Electric Canberra 67, 194
  Douglas C-118 69
  Douglas C-124 Globemaster 21, 23, 24, 28, 68, 125, 128, 152, Photo 4
  Douglas C-133 Cargomaster 21, 165
  Douglas DC-7C 100
  English Electric Lightning 52
  Gloster Javelin 42
  Handley Page Victor 52
  Lockheed U-2 45, 190
  Vickers Valiant 52, 198
  X-20 Dyna-Soar 156

Attlee, Clement, MP 13, 33, 189
AWRE 77, 141

Beria, Lavrenti 15
Bourgès-Maunoury M. 41
Brooke, Sir Norman 43
Brundrett, Sir Frederick 35, 38, 190
Butler, R. A. 39

Caccia, Sir Harold 46, 53
Camp Cooke (US Army) 84, 85, 89, 104

Churchill, Sir Winston 13, 33, 34, 39, 40, 52
Cleaver, Val 35, 189
CND 41, 80

Code Names
  BLUEGILL Series 154, 155, 157
  STARFISH PRIME 154, 155, 158
  TIGERFISH 153, 155

CTL-1 87, 118, 119, 121, 123, 124, 130, 158, 167
CTL-2 86, 121, 124, 158, 168
CTL-3 87, 122, 123, 124, 159, 168
CTL-4 86, 118, 123, 131, 158, 168
CTL-5 87, 157, 168
CTL-6 87, 124, 158, 168
CTL-7 86, 124, 125, 126, 158, 168
CTL-8 86, 159, 168, Photo 41
CTL-9 86, 127, 157, 168
CTL-10 87, 129, 158, 169, 198
CTL-11 86, 129, 131, 144, 158, 169, Photo 44
CTL-12 87, 159, 169, Photo 42
CTL-13 131, 158
Cuban Missile Crisis 47, 134, 160, 161, 162, 192, 195

DAC/GE Personnel
  Anchordoguy, Arnold 29
  Bromberg, Jack L. 21
  Carter, Leo A. 21, 70, Photo 8
  Clawson, B. W. 99
  Cowell, S. E. 95
  Douglas, Donald Jr 12, 21, 32, 73, 161, Photos 2, 10, 50
  Ewing, F. D. 95

Hale, E. R. 95
Hallbauer, Robert 66, 67, 76, 192, 193
Hawkins, J. L. 95
Howard, Warren 66
Kasulka, Larry 7, 88, 89, 194, 202
Kurth, Fred 66
Laws, Vernita 7, 65, 192
Mathis, Harvey Photo 8
Mettler, Dr Ruben 29, 30
Neff, Errol M. 70
Ordahl, Charles 67
Portanova, Peter 67, 189, 192, 193, 198, 202, Photo 10
Posey, Jack A. 149
Raz, Dennis 67
Rehder, Tom 75
Roman, Andy Photo 10
Schmid, Jack E. 149
Shaver, W. F. 70, 193
Thomas, Fran 7
Thomas, Hal M. 21
Wheaton, E. A. 26
Yanez, Tony 65

Daily Express 48, 58, 73 ,74, 139, 190, 192, 193, 196, 199, 200, 201
Daily Mail 70, 71, 193, 201
Dean, Patrick 43
Douglas-Home, Sir Alec 160
Douglas Aircraft Corporation 8, 12, 20, 21, 23, 25, 29, 30, 31, 32, 45, 60, 63, 64, 65, 66, 67, 68, 69, 70, 71, 80, 86, 89, 94, 95, 99, 103, 112, 117, 125, 130, 152, 161, 165, 169, 171, 172, 191
Douglas, James 78, 131

Dulles, John Foster 33, 34, 36, 40, 46, 47

Eden, Sir Anthony 33, 34, 39
Eisenhower, Pres. Dwight D. 78, 138, 191
Exercise, MICKY FINN 134

Fairbanks Daily News (Alaska) 121, 197
Flight 20, 75, 135, 188, 193, 195, 196, 197, 199
Fuchs, Klaus 14, 16, 37

Glushko, Valentin 26
Greenglass, David 16

Hall, Rowland 7, 60, 61
Hiroshima 13
Hobbs, Brig Godfrey 47, 106, 108
Holaday, William M. 31, 32, 44, 45, 46
Horner, Richard E. 38, 46

ICBM 12, 14, 16-19, 23, 26, 31-33, 36, 38, 45, 47, 50, 77, 84, 112, 161, 187, 189-191
IRBM 8, 12, 17-19, 21, 23, 26, 28, 31, 33-40, 42-50, 52, 54, 59, 60, 77, 84, 87, 91, 104, 133, 138, 161, 163, 188, 189, 195, 199, 202
IWST 86, 96, 103, 104, 106, 111-113, 121, 127, 157, 167, 168, Photo 37, 38
IWST-3 112
IWST-6 113, 128, Photo 39
IWST-8 122, Photo 40
IWST-9 122

Johnson, Sen. Edwin C. 15
Johnson, Lyndon B. 160, Photo 2
Johnston Island 152-154, 156

KATHLEEN GUIDE 124
Kennedy, Pres. John F. 120, 125
Killian, Dr James R. Jr 18, 47, 48, 160
Khrushchev, Nikita 119, 188, 161
Kurchatov, Igor 15, 187

Larkin, Gen. T. (US Army) 75
Lindsay, Maj.-Gen. Richard

C. 37
Los Angeles Times 93

Macmillan, Sir Harold 39, 40, 42, 43, 46, 161, 191
Makins, Sir Roger 37
Manhattan Project/Engineer District 15, 16, 187
McElroy, Neil H. 45, 48-50, 139
McLeod, Lt-Gen. Roderick W. 137
McMahon Act 37, 46
Medaris, Maj.-Gen. John B. (US Army) 17, 31, 90
MESA Missileer 129, 198
Miami News 120, 197

Missiles
Atlas 16, 18-20, 22, 23, 25, 28, 29, 31, 35, 37, 43, 45, 85, 93, 112, 119, 120, 161, 187, 190, 191, 194, 197
Black Knight 36
Bloodhound 136
Blue Streak 34-36, 38, 40-44, 54, 56, 60, 99, 136, 161, 162, 188, 198
Corporal 55, 191
SS-3 Shyster 136
Thor: Agreement 35, 45, 55, 131, 138; arrival in UK 73, 74, 75, 77; basing proposals 51, 55, 56, 58; concurrency concept 20, 30; contract with Douglas 12, 21; deployment 8; engine 21, 25, 26, 29, 30, 96, 103, 110, 119, 152; first launch 28, 29; first launch at Vandenberg 91-94; logistic plan 145; in the press 47, 70, 74, 79, 106, 110, 151; opening of Thor Missile School 99; operational capability 79, 80, 106, 108, 109, 118, 125, 138, 139, 140; reconnaissance satellite program 32, 43, 46, 89, 94, 106, 112, 130; safety incidents 142-144; site layout 7, 81; warhead 22, 23, 27, 35, 40, 53, 66, 77, 137, 139, 140, 141; photo 22, 23; withdrawal from service 117, 131, 151
T110 75, 159

T114 32, 46
T115 32
T116 46
T118 46
T138 32
T139 73
T142 87
T146 94
T151 91, 94
T156 154
T161 107, Photo 37
T163 94
T165 127
T170 106
T177 153
T178 106
T180 154
T184 110
T185 121, 122, Photo 40
T191 109-111
T195 154
T211 131
T214 129, 200
T215 113
T220 113, Photo 39
T226 129, 200
T228 112, Photo 38
T229 129, 130
T233 123
T243 125, 126
T267 124, Photo 18
T269 130, Photo 42
T272 113, 122
T276 Photo, 41
Arrival in UK
Contract 21
Warhead
Jupiter 31, 31, 35, 40, 43, 45-48, 60, 90, 138, 142, 155
Matador 17
Navaho 26, 189
Polaris 20, 53, 162
Redstone 17, 29, 30, 33, 90, 188
V-2 7, 14, 16, 17, 25, 28, 34, 188, 191, 198, 199

Missiles and Rockets 78, 194
Monroe, Rear Adm. Jack P. 91
Montgomery, FM Bernard 54, 138
Moscow 59
Mountbatten, Lord Louis and Lady 55, 119-121, 131, 197

MRBM 18, 34, 37, 42, 188
MV *Britannic* 98

Nagasaki 13, 15, 101
Nasser, Gamal Abdel 39
NATO 34, 39, 43, 53, 54, 59, 75, 138
The New York Times 48, 79, 189
No. 13 Field Survey Sqn, Royal Engineers 62

Operation DOMINIC 153
Operation GRAPPLE (nuclear Test) 41, 190
Operation MUSKATEER 39
Operation TUNE UP 93, Photo 30, 31
Oregon Register-Guard 120

Pincher, Chapman 47, 74, 190, 196
Potsdam Conference 13
Powell, Sir Richard 42, 43, 46, 50, 54, 78, 109
Prebish, David 86, 153, 194, 200
Profumo, John 39
Program 437 156, 165
Project ASSET 156
Project 'E' 77, 193
Project Emily 7, 8, 61, 65, 124, 152, 153, 161, 164, 165
Project FISHBOWL 153, 155, 156, 164, 165, 198

Quarles, Donald A. 38, 50, 78, 84, 85, 109

RAF Personnel
Anderson, M/Plt J. 107
Baldock, Sqn Ldr Stanley 73
Baldwin, Sr Tech R. 113
Beresford, Chf Tech E. M. 128
Berthiaume, Cpl Tech. R. J. L. 130, Photo 44
Botley, Chf Tech. M. 7, 88, 101, 104, 194-197, Photo 32
Bowers, Cpl E. 146
Boyle, ACM Sir Dermot 38, 52-54
Broad, Sqn Ldr R. N. 7, 80, 121, 131, 194-197
Broadhurst, ACM Sir Harry 57, 73, 77, 136, 137

Burch, Wg Cdr Colin 130
Burnett, AVM Brian 124, 150, 198
Carpenter, Chf Tech. R. M. 107, Photo 36
Chivers, Chf Tech. Frederick A. E. 107
Clark, Cpl Tech. D. A. 114
Coles, Air Cdr William 73
Cook, Sgt V. 121
Cooper, Chf Tech. R. 128
Cooper, Sgt T. W. 111
Copelah, WO J. L. 111
Coulson, Sqn Ldr Peter G. 107, 108, 123, Photo 36
Cover, M/Plt A. E. 107
Cowling, Flt Lt Richard 79, 97, 98, 118, 120
Cross, AM Sir Kenneth B. B. 73-75, 79, 97, 98, 124, 125, 150, 151, 160, 162
Davis, AVM John G. 80
Daws, Cpl Tech. E. L. 114
Dickson, MRAF Sir William 42
Dixon, W. M. Gp Capt. Photo 46
Docherty, Flt Lt J. 107, 111, 188
Downs, Sqn Ldr David 125, 127, 129
Dunn, AVM Patrick 130, Photo 43
Dwyer, AVM Michael 79, 114, Photo 46
Finlayson, Wg Cdr Peter J. F. S. 7, 98, 102, 113, 14, 195-197
Flood, Sqn Ldr R. P. 118
Ford, Flt Lt E. V. 107
Forstad, Chf Tech. B. 111
Freeman, Sgt G. 113
Frogley, Gp Capt. Robert T. 107, 108
Goldsmith, Mst Sig. C. L. 111
Grandy, AVM John 141
Gudgion, Chf Tech. R. H. 114
Haines, Wg Cdr E. R. G. 80, 194
Harman, Gp Capt. Rod 110
Hart, Sqn Ldr P. I. 130, Photo 44
Heath, Chf Tech. J. 113
Hitchcock, Cpl Tech H. 105, 134, 196

Hodson, Sgt M. 111
Hubery, Sgt D. 111
Hughes, F/O W. O. 113
Humphrey, Cpl D. 98, 102
Hunter, Flt Lt Kenneth 139
Keen, Cpl I. 121
Lynch, Cpl M. 121
McIntyre, Chf Tech. J. D. 128
McMillan, Gp Capt. E. L. 110, 114
Menaul, AVM Stewart 132, 198
Milburn, Chf Tech. 118, 120
Mills, Fg Off. R. S. 99
Milne, Cpl Tech. G. J. N. 114
Moles, Plt Off. John 127, 193
Morris, Sqn Ldr E. R. 109
Mortimer, Flt Lt Denis A. H. 111
Muggleton, Jnr Tech. R. 146, 149, 192
Naile, Flt Lt F. S. 123, 198
Parkinson, Chf Tech. J. E. 130, Photo 44
Perkins, AVM Maxwell 150
Pratt, Chf Tech. R. 7, 99, Photo 32
Purnell, Chf Tech. G. A. 111
Pye, Flt Sgt J. 111
Quinton, Fg Off. Cyril D. 91
Rankin, Sgt J. D. 111
Robertson, Cpl B. 100, 101, 103, 118, 119, 196
Reeve, Flt Lt Colin 113, 128
Roseveare, Flt Lt Leon A. 111
Salmond, MRAF Sir John 73, Photo 46
Scott, Flt Lt David 113
Searby, Air Cdr John H. 56, 71, 191
Sheen, AVM W. C. 75, 103, 108, 114
Stenee, Snr Tech. W. H. 111
Sloan, M/Plt Maurice H. 107
Snow, Cpl R. 111
Stapley, Cpl Tech. I. F. 130, Photo 44
Strawn, Sgt A. E. 111
Thompson, Flt Sgt G. H. 130, Photo 44
Thorndyke, Jnr Tech. J. 100, 198
Tinton, Cpl Tech. J. M. 130, Photo 44

Trotter, Cpl N. 67, 68, 75, 194

Tuttle, AVM Geoffrey 34, 55, 57, 73, 77, 78, 131, 136, 140, 141

Waiting, Flt Lt John 121

Walker, AVM Gus 79, 108, 196

Ware, Chf Tech. K. S. 128

Webb, LAC C. 146-149, 201

Weston, Wg Cdr George 150

Whitley, Sir John 75

Whitcher, Flt Lt R. A. 130, Photo 44

Willan, Gp Capt. Frank 74, 75, 79

Willis, M/Sig. M. W. 128

Wilson, Sqn Ldr John 150

RAF Stations

Bardney 57, 72, 83, 170

Bircham Newton 146

Burtonwood 63, 69, 73, 192

Caistor 57, 62, 72, 81, 170

Cottam 152

Dishforth 57, 59

Driffield 57, 58-63, 72, 76, 79, 123, 125, 127, 129, 130, 148, 149, 152, 170, Photo 5, 19

East Kirby 51

Feltwell 51, 57, 59, 60, 62, 63, 69-76, 78-81, 102, 104, 118, 127, 128, 134-141, 146-150, 152, 170, 193, 195, Photo 13

Folkingham 59, 60, 72, 75, 170

Full Sutton 57, 60, 71, 72, 171

Halton 98

Harrington 7, 59, 60, 71, 72, 75, 83, 130, 150, 170

Hemswell 51, 57, 59, 60, 62, 63, 67, 68, 70-72, 102, 118, 129, 141, 144, 148, 149, 152, 170, 192, 199

Holme-on-Spalding-Moor 57

Honington 57

Kirton-in-Lindsey 67, 68

Lakenheath 62-65, 67, 69, 74, 141, 170

Leconfield 57, 129, 171

Leeming 57

Ludford Magna 8, 57, 72, 98, 142, 144, 170

Lyneham 100

Manby 98

Marham 57

Marston Moor 57

Melton Mowbray 59. 60, 72, 170

Mepal 57, 72, 170

Methwold 51

Mildenhall 63, 73, 125, 128, 129, 146, 148, 149, 170

North Luffenham 56, 59-63, 66, 71, 72, 108, 113, 124, 130, 134, 135, 146-150, 152, 161, 177, 192, Photo 17, 27

North Pickenham, 71, 73, Photo 12, 46

Polebrook 8, 59, 60, 72, 170

Riccall 57

Scampton 68, 76, 141, 144, 171

Scorton 52

Sherburn-in-Elmet 57

Sturgate 51, 65

Waddington 57

Watton 57, 100

Witchford 57

Yatesbury 98

RAF Units

77(SM) Sqn 73, 74, 120, 127, 195

98(SM) Sqn 110, 111

102 (SM) Sqn 123

104(SM) Sqn 144

107(SM) Sqn 118, 201, Photo 26

113(SM) Sqn 162

144(SM) Sqn 113, 121, 124

150(SM) Sqn 80, 144

218(SM) Sqn 130

220(SM) Sqn 73

226(SM) Sqn 130

542 Sqn 67

BCMC 67, 194

RMS *Queen Elizabeth* 98

RMS *Sylvania* 100

Roberts, Sir Frank 53

Rocketdyne 21, 25, 29, 35, 64, 68, 103, 152, 190

Rusk, Dean 160

SACEUR 36, 43, 50, 53, 54, 73, 138, 191

Sandys, Duncan 34-36, 40-42, 44-46, 49, 54-56, 73, 103, 109, 137, 141

Sandys 1957 Defence White Paper 36

Santa Maria Times 85, 92, 93. 110, 111, 129, 194-196

SBAMA 79, 80, 145, 147-149, 151-153

Simmons, Jay 7, 25, 164

Space Launch Complex 10 84, 89

Sputnik 1 45, 46, 161

SS Île *de France* 98, 197

SS *Nieuw Amsterdam* 100

Stalin, Josef 13, 14, 16, 19, 187

Strategic Air Command (SAC) 14, 19, 49, 54, 62, 78, 79, 85, 90, 92-94, 114, 132, 138, 140, 142, 146, 194

Symington, Sen. W. Stuart 14, 138, 139

Toledo Blade 92

Truman, Pres. Harry S 13, 15, 28, 33, 189

USAF Personnel

Addison, MSgt Thomas F. 92

Auer, MSgt Michael J. 93

Arnold, Gen. Henry H. 14

Barton, Col. Richard E. 110, 197

Bish, Sgt E. 146

Blanchard, Maj.-Gen. William H. (Butch) 56, 73-75, 131, 140, 191

Bon Tempo, Col. J. C. 20, 92, 94, 195, Photo 35

Bruck, Maj. Charles E. 91

Christy, Col. Robert W. 91, 109

Cloyd, Col. Virgil M. 112

Crowder, Maj. N. F. 99

Davis, Maj.-Gen. W. Austin 152

Delahay, Col. William A. 73-75

Erlenbusch, Col. William C. 90

Gifford, SMSgt Charles E. Sr 92

Greene, Lt-Col. Sid 165, Photo 3

Hahn, Col. C. W. 149

Hall, Lt-Col. Edward N. 29

Harris, Lt-Gen. Hunter Jr 133

Harvan, Capt. Fran I. 113

Hastings, Lt-Col. Vernon L. 84, 194

Hellenbreck, Capt. Emanuel 121

Hodges, MSgt William L. 93

Hollis, Capt. Sammy J. 111

Le Maire, TSgt Otis J. 93

LeMay, Maj.-Gen. Curtis E. 14, 19, 162

Maddox, Brig.-Gen. Sam Jr 99

Mathison, Lt-Col. Charles 28, 29

Mazik, 1Lt Robert 139

McConnell, Maj.-Gen. John P. 49, 132, 133, 198

Meyer, SSgt Max L. 93

Mitchell, Maj.-Gen. Clyde H. 153

Myers, Col. Mike 165

Norstad, Gen. Lauris 50, 54, 73

Ostrander, Gen. Don R. 85

Owens, Maj. Robert C. 91

Plumley, Maj. Richard A. 91, 195

Power, Lt-Gen. Thomas S. 18, 85, 94, 188

Preston, Maj.-Gen. Joseph J. 132, 133, 198

Putt, Lt-Gen. Donald L. 18

Reaver, Capt. W. P. 149

Riepe, Col. Quentin B. 156

Ritland, Col. Osmand J. 84, 194

Schriever, Gen. Bernard 19, 23, 30-32, 84, 156, 194, Photo 2

Smith, Lt-Col. W. D. 12

Sifford, Col. Lynn DeWitt Jr 151

Sullivan, Lt-Col. Woodruff T. 61

Tharp, Capt. G. M. 114

Twining, General Nathan F. 36, 131, 138

Wade, Lt-Gen. David 90-92, 94, 114, 197, Photo 45

Wells, Maj.-Gen. Selmon W. 133

Werstbert, Col. Leslie J. 99

White, Gen. Thomas D. 37

Westover, Gen. Charles B. 150

Wilson, Brig.-Gen. Delmar E. 99

Wilson, Lt-Col. Sam 165

Wise, Sgt Buck 104

Wise, Sgt Lee 69

Woirol, Maj. Warren S. 70

Zink, Col. Harry 74, 90

USAF Air Force Bases

Bakersfield 128

Chanute 99

Cooke 84, 85, 89, 104

Davis Monthan 98, 99, 101, 104, 195

Donaldson 128

Edwards 26

Hickham Field 164

McGuire 69, 128

Norton 125, 145, 150, 151, 162

Patrick (AFETR) 28, 29, 32, 43, 69, 104, 106

San Bernadino 150, 151

Sheppard 91, 99

Tucson 95-99, 100, 102-104

Vandenberg (AFWTR) 7, 8, 20, 63, 84-87, 91-96, 98, 102-106, 108, 110, 112-114, 117-119, 121, 122, 124, 126-133, 137, 144, 148, 153, 154, 156, 160, 161, 165, 190, 198

USAF Units

1 Strategic Aerospace Division 122

7 AD 56, 70, 71, 73, 142, 150, 163

375 Weather Reconnaissance Squadron 15

3750th Technical Training Wing 99

392d Strategic Missile Squadron (Training) 91, 92, 105, 109, 110, 113, 117, 121, 122, 125, 127, 129, 133, 144

4315th Combat Crew Training Squadron 87

6540th Missile Test Wing 85

672d–675th SMS 51

672d Technical Training Squadron 69, 192, 193

704th Strategic Missile

Wing 91, 104

7510 Hospital 70

864th SMS 90

Von Braun, Wernher 17-19, 28, 31, 33, 90, 155,

Waggoner, Walter H. 79

Ward, George 40, 49, 56, 114

Watkinson, Harold 131

Wilson, Charles E. 19, 31, 34, 36, 49, 85

Woomera, Long-Range Weapons Establishment 38

Zilliacus, Konni MP 141

Zuckert, Eugene B. 156